The Tragedy of Vietnam

HarperCollins
Historical Interpretations Series
Editor Mark A. Kishlansky

Patrick J. Hearden,
The Tragedy of Vietnam

Titles in Preparation:
Peter Hays,
Nazism in Theory and Practice

Jack R. Censer,
The French Revolution

Matthew Dennis,
Discovery of North America

David T. Konig,
Origins of American Law

HISTORICAL
INTERPRETATIONS

The Tragedy of Vietnam

Patrick J. Hearden
Purdue University

HarperCollins*Publishers*

SPONSORING EDITOR:	Bruce Borland
PROJECT EDITOR:	Ellen MacElree
ART DIRECTION:	Jaye Zimet
TEXT DESIGN:	Richard Oriolo
COVER COORDINATOR:	Jaye Zimet
COVER DESIGN:	Richard Oriolo
COVER PHOTO:	Sal Lopes
PRODUCTION:	Willie Lane/Sunaina Sehwani
COMPOSITOR:	Ruttle Graphics, Inc.
PRINTER AND BINDER:	R. R. Donnelley & Sons Company
COVER PRINTER:	New England Book Components, Inc.

The Tragedy of Vietnam

Copyright ©1991 by HarperCollins Publishers Inc.

Library of Congress Cataloging-in-Publication Data

Hearden, Patrick J., 1942–
    The tragedy of Vietnam/by Patrick J. Hearden.   p.   cm.
    Includes bibliographical references and index.
    ISBN 0-673-52126-5
    1. Vietnamese Conflict, 1961–1975—United States. 2. United States—Foreign relations—Indochina. 3. Indochina—Foreign relations—United States. 4. United States—Foreign relations—1945– I. Title.
DS558.H42 1991
959.704'3373—dc20   90-46128
                                                  CIP

90 91 92 93 9 8 7 6 5 4 3 2 1

In Memory of
My Father

One day, in another faraway place, other teenage Americans may fight and die for a reason as criminal as our mere reluctance to discuss Vietnam. For if we do not speak of it, others will surely rewrite the script.

—An American Veteran of the Vietnam War, 1984

C O N T E N T S

PREFACE

Since the fall of Saigon to communist forces in 1975, Americans have exhibited a continuing interest in the Vietnam War. Many have been disturbed because the conflict was not only the longest military struggle in American history but also the first war that the United States ever lost. And the consequent blow to the American ego has given birth to a large body of polemical literature that focuses on the issue of what went wrong. Some writers have blamed American military leaders for failing to devise an effective strategy to defeat the enemy on the battlefield. Others have criticized politicians in Washington for imposing restrictions on American commanders who were responsible for achieving victory in Vietnam. Still others have argued that the news media eroded public support on the home front for the American war effort. In addition to the numerous books and articles that attempt to find a scapegoat for the failure of Americans to accomplish their objectives in Southeast Asia, library shelves abound with volumes that center their attention on the question of how the United States fought the Vietnam War.

But while many works offer excellent descriptions of the American military experience in Vietnam, few accounts address the two vital questions concerning the role that the United States played in the conflict: Why did the United States become entangled in Vietnam in the first place? And why did Americans sustain their involvement in Vietnam for a quarter of a century? American writers ignore these twin issues only at the peril of their country. For unless the American people receive adequate answers to these crucial questions, the United States may well be condemned to repeat in another part of the world the disaster that befell it in Southeast Asia.

This study examines the key decisions that resulted in the tragic American entanglement in Vietnam. In the process, it grapples with the following pivotal queries: Why did President Franklin D. Roosevelt abandon his commitment to liquidate the French empire in Southeast Asia? Why did President Harry S Truman bankroll the French expeditionary force in Indochina? Why did President Dwight D. Eisenhower block general elections to determine the future of Vietnam? Why did President John F. Kennedy rapidly expand the number of American military advisers in Vietnam? Why did President Lyndon B. Johnson dispatch U.S. combat troops to Vietnam? And why did President Richard

M. Nixon extend the American military campaign into Cambodia and Laos?

This investigation uncovers the fundamental causes of the escalating American involvement in Indochina. While the personality traits and party affiliations of those wielding power in Washington changed, the evidence shows that the broad U.S. policy to prevent the spread of communism in Southeast Asia remained the same. Yet the documents reveal that American leaders were not primarily concerned about extending the blessings of political liberty to the Vietnamese people. Rather the records demonstrate that the basic reasons for the tragedy that unfolded in Vietnam were rooted in a bipartisan commitment to maintain an international order that American policymakers deemed essential to the survival of free enterprise in the United States.

Acknowledgments

My students at Purdue University deserve special thanks for listening attentively and asking thoughtful questions while my ideas on the deepening American entanglement in Vietnam were developed in the classroom.

Several historians gave me the benefit of their critical judgment and friendly encouragement. Thomas J. McCormick of the University of Wisconsin helped me gain a better understanding of the economic factors underlying the American intervention in Vietnam. Gunther E. Rothenberg of Purdue University shared with me his keen insights into the strategic problems that the United States encountered in Southeast Asia. Walter LaFeber of Cornell University and Mark A. Kishlansky of the University of Chicago read a draft of the entire manuscript and made many valuable suggestions for revising the content.

Gaylord Nelson kindly provided me with a candid explanation of the pressure that was exerted on him and other members of the United States Senate in August 1964 to vote for the Gulf of Tonkin Resolution.

Useful stylistic comments offered by James M. Hall, John L. Larson, William C. Lloyd, and J. Michael Thorn helped make my work more readable.

Patrick J. Hearden

ABBREVIATIONS

ARVN	Army of the Republic of Vietnam
CIA	Central Intelligence Agency
DMZ	Demilitarized Zone
EDC	European Defense Community
ERP	European Recovery Program
JCS	Joint Chiefs of Staff
MAAG	Military Assistance Advisory Group
MACV	Military Assistance Command, Vietnam
NLF	National Liberation Front
NSC	National Security Council
NVA	North Vietnamese Army
OSS	Office of Strategic Services
POW	Prisoner of War
SEATO	Southeast Asia Treaty Organization
SVN	South Vietnam
VC	Vietcong

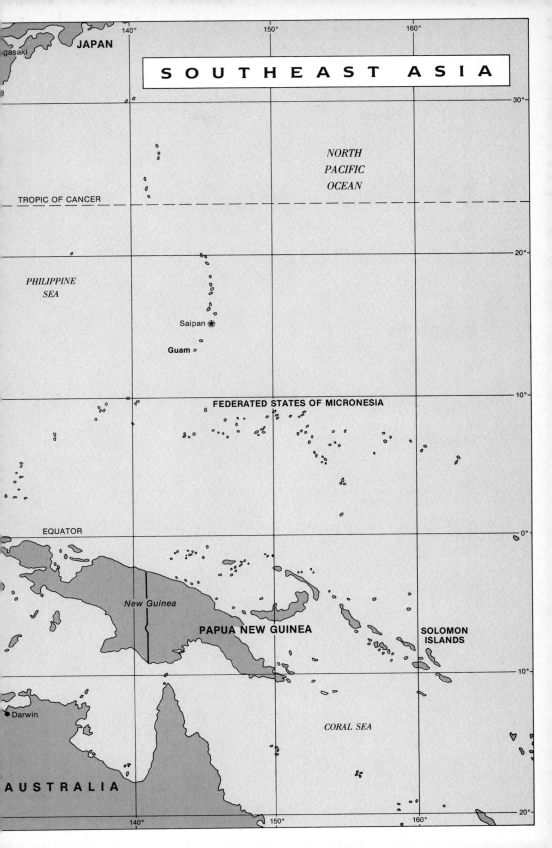

ONE

The French Indochina Empire

Social stability in this industrial age clearly depends on outlets for industrial goods. . . . The European consumer-goods market is saturated; unless we declare modern society bankrupt and prepare, at the dawn of the twentieth century, for its liquidation by revolution (the consequences of which we can scarcely foresee), new consumer markets will have to be created in other parts of the world.

Jules Ferry, French statesman, 1890

The Emergence of Vietnam

More than 2,000 years ago, the Vietnamese people emerged as a distinct ethnic group possessing a common language and a resilient culture. Their long historical journey began with the establishment of flourishing agricultural settlements on the fertile alluvial soil deposited by the Red River flowing down from the mountains to the sea. The cultivation of rice on the triangular plain at the mouth of the river provided the economic basis for the development of a social structure composed of a small number of prominent landlords and a large mass of ordinary peasants. But while agriculture served as the foundation of their feudal society, the Vietnamese did not limit themselves to harvesting the resources of the land. Since the vast majority of inhabitants of the Red River valley lived within fifty miles of the coast, they were able to supplement their basic diet of rice with fish and salt gathered from the ocean. And these three staples—rice, fish, and salt—continued to be the principal sources of food for the Vietnamese people throughout their tumultuous history.

In 111 B.C., the Chinese invaded the region inhabited by the Vietnamese, and during the next 1,000 years Vietnam remained a Chinese colony. After defeating the indigenous Vietnamese population, the conquerors from China introduced new agricultural methods into the rich Red River delta. The Chinese brought plows and draft animals to work in the rice paddies. They also brought sophisticated systems of irrigation and flood control. These agricultural innovations resulted in the intensification of rice cultivation, and the consequent increase in food production led to a population boom. As their agricultural base widened and their numbers swelled, the Vietnamese found that their very survival depended upon their ability to harness the vital water of the Red River. Thus they banded together to build the dams, dikes, and canals needed to obtain greater rice yields to satisfy their expanding nutritional requirements.

In addition to introducing efficient agricultural techniques into the Red River basin, the imperial authorities from China established a mandarin system to administer the Vietnamese territory under their rule. The Chinese proconsuls governing Vietnam appointed a few native landlords to hold minor bureaucratic posts in the new regime. Acting as public officials and civil servants, the local mandarins helped run their country in the interest of China. These indigenous functionaries also began to speak the language and ape the life style of their foreign taskmasters. But while these servants of power readily absorbed the manners and morals emanating from China, the great bulk of the Vietnamese people continued to toil in the rice fields where they clung to their traditional customs and values. As a result, a fundamental division developed between the mandarins residing in the provincial towns and the peasants living in the surrounding countryside.

The upper-class members of Vietnamese society, though quick to embrace the trappings of Chinese culture, slowly began to harbor a strong desire for political autonomy. While they continued to enjoy their social and economic privileges, the mandarins gradually came to resent their political subservience to outside authorities. As their discontent steadily mounted, they began to regard the heavily taxed peasants as indispensable allies if they were ever to throw off the yoke of Chinese oppression. These urban Vietnamese leaders eventually reverted to speaking their native language and to honoring ancient practices in an effort to restore their ties with their rural neighbors. After mobilizing the masses into a powerful resistance force, the mandarins launched a determined struggle to achieve national independence. A long series of violent and bloody confrontations ensued. Finally, in A.D. 939, the

Vietnamese rebels defeated the Chinese imperialists and drove them out of their homeland. Henceforth the smaller Vietnamese dragon would no longer pay tribute to the Chinese colossus to the north.

The great victory against China marked the beginning of 900 years of growth and development for Vietnam as an independent country. Shortly after winning their emancipation from foreign domination, the triumphant Vietnamese established a stable and effective government. The new Vietnamese regime revolved around a strong monarch who exercised sovereign authority over his subjects. A long line of emperors lived in the city of Hanoi, which sat strategically along the banks of the Red River, and upon the death of each ruler the royal prerogative was passed on to his eldest son. Yet while Vietnam evolved as a unified nation with a central government based upon a hereditary monarchy, the country nevertheless suffered from considerable political turmoil due to the haughtiness of the large landlords and native mandarins. These two troublesome groups did not always passively submit to the mandate of the monarchs, and they frequently rebelled when an emperor interfered with their exploitation of the peasants. As a result, Vietnam was constantly plagued by feudal dissension that sometimes erupted into full-scale civil war.

Besides suffering from these domestic disturbances, Vietnam also fell victim to foreign encroachments. The Chinese invaded Vietnam once again in 1406, and after rapidly conquering the country they ruthlessly exploited the Vietnamese people. The Chinese intruders immediately imposed a heavy tax burden as well as a system of forced labor on the vanquished population. But the Vietnamese soon revolted against the despotic Chinese. Le Loi, the youthful leader of the uprising, became a pioneer in the art of guerrilla warfare. Realizing that he lacked the manpower to engage the Chinese in large battles, Le Loi directed his forces to employ hit-and-run tactics in order to wear down their gargantuan enemy. Small rebel units under his command made sudden thrusts against Chinese troops, and then they would quickly dissolve into the jungle to prepare for yet another surprise attack. These guerrilla tactics ultimately proved successful, and in 1428 the Chinese were pushed out of Vietnam. It was a proud moment for the Vietnamese, who celebrated their tremendous victory with the following poem:

Henceforth our country is safe.
Our mountains and rivers begin life afresh.
Peace follows war as day follows night.
We have purged our shame for a thousand centuries.
We have regained tranquility for ten thousand generations.

After winning their independence from their northern neighbor, the energetic Vietnamese embarked upon their own program of empire building. They gradually began expanding beyond the Red River area, and during the next 400 years they moved southward step by step along the seacoast until they reached all the way down to the Gulf of Siam. This Great March to the South was propelled by an economic imperative. The Vietnamese needed more land in order to raise more rice to feed their growing population. Rice could be cultivated in abundance in only two accessible places: along the narrow strip of coastal lowlands stretching from one end of the Indochina peninsula to the other and along the floodplains of the rivers flowing from the mountains down to the ocean. Driven by their land hunger, the Vietnamese advanced down the coast in spurts jumping from one river valley to the next. After each move, these vigorous pioneers established new settlements and harvested more rice until they outgrew their food supply and the time came to make yet another bound to the south.

Armies of ravenous Vietnamese peasants spearheaded these recurrent imperial thrusts. Whenever an increase in their numbers created a need for additional rice fields, the pastoral Vietnamese became aggressive soldiers who pushed back weaker peoples from their expanding southern frontier. And after conquering sufficient living space, the peasants exchanged their swords for plows and settled down to farming once again. This intermittent pattern of territorial aggrandizement, repeated over and over, came at the expense of two adjoining dominions. The militant Vietnamese first attacked the kingdom of Champa, and within a few hundred years this once flourishing state ceased to exist. The Vietnamese then pressed farther south against the sprawling empire of Cambodia, and by 1800 they succeeded in expelling the Khmers from the coveted Mekong River basin. Thus the Vietnamese had gained control of the second of the two great rice-producing regions of Indochina.

After the Great March to the South had run its course, Vietnam was shaped like an elongated S extending for more than 1,200 miles between the ninth and twenty-sixth parallels. The country has often been pictured as two baskets of rice at the opposite ends of a bamboo pole carried on the back of a peasant. The baskets of rice are the two rich alluvial deltas formed by the Red and Mekong rivers, and the bamboo pole is the long chain of mountains with peaks ranging from about 10,000 feet in the north to around 4,000 feet in the south. The mountains form a vast watershed that serves as a boundary separating Vietnam from Laos and Cambodia. Eighty percent of the geographical area of Vietnam is covered by bush, forest, or heavy jungle, and these highlands are sparsely populated by different ethnic tribes that were forced out of the fertile valleys below by the Khmers and Vietnamese. The vast majority of Vietnamese live at an altitude of less than 900 feet in the coastal lowlands and floodplains which together constitute the remaining 20 percent of the country.

The great leapfrogging movement southward, while providing the Vietnamese with essential farmland, intensified their political difficulties. For many centuries, Vietnamese monarchs had sat on their throne in Hanoi and ruled over the people of the Red River valley. As the Vietnamese population extended farther and farther to the south, however, the emperors exercised less and less control over their migrating subjects. Settlements established at great distances from the seat of empire in Hanoi came to enjoy a considerable amount of political autonomy. Ultimately rival factions rebelled against dynastic authority, and as a consequence Vietnam was divided into two parts. The separate governments that emerged in the northern and southern halves of the country depended upon the support of the great landlords and provincial mandarins, and these two groups were therefore allowed to line their pockets by collecting high land rents and excessive taxes from the peasants. But this economic exploitation provoked a series of peasant uprisings.

More and more the forces of revolt in Vietnam were expressions of peasant discontent rather than articulations of elite ambition. While the peasants took up arms against their oppressors with increasing frequency, however, their sporadic outbursts remained unsuccessful for a long time because they lacked adequate leadership. But finally, in 1772, a local insurrection assumed the dimensions of a national revolution. The rebellion, led by three brothers from the village of Tay Son in the Mekong River valley, drew support from the upstart merchants in the nearby villages and the distressed peasants in the surrounding rice paddies. The ranks of the rebels continued to swell until in 1786 their leaders succeeded in bringing the northern and southern parts of the country back together once more. Although the Tay Son rulers were overthrown in 1802, the country remained united under a single government, and the Vietnamese people maintained their strong sense of national identity.

The Establishment of French Rule

Despite their long history of militant nationalism, however, the Vietnamese had already become a target of Western imperialism. The European economic penetration began during the sixteenth century when Portuguese ships brought enterprising traders to Vietnamese ports, and following closely in their wake were commercial adventurers disembarking from Dutch and British vessels. After establishing several trading posts in Vietnam, these agents of empire gradually turned their attention to more lucrative areas of exploitation elsewhere in Southeast Asia. But the French exhibited a more persistent determination to harvest the wealth of Vietnam when they entered the scramble for Oriental riches during the seventeenth century. The French were driven by a potent mixture of economic ambition and religious enthusiasm. Gallic merchants, spurred by a desire for profit, and Catholic missionaries, stirred by a sense of piety, joined forces, and in 1664 they organized both the French East India Company and the Society of Foreign Missions. Hoping that trade would follow the cross, the merchants offered to pay the cost of transporting men of the cloth to Vietnam. The transaction proved to be mutually satisfying. Besides introducing French commodities throughout Vietnam, the missionaries preached their Christian gospel wherever they could find an audience.

But the Vietnamese often responded with suspicion and hostility toward the proselytizing endeavors of the missionaries from France. Their negative reaction was rooted in the fundamental tension that exists between the Christian commitment to individual sanctity and the Confucian concern for social stability. While the teachings of the Christian church stress personal salvation and devotion to biblical precepts, the philosophy of Confucius places greater emphasis on communal welfare and respect for parental authority. Vietnamese leaders feared that it would be difficult to maintain control over peasants who fell under the spell of Catholicism. Convinced that the spread of Christianity would disrupt their community, government officials in Vietnam frequently jailed Catholic converts and deported French missionaries. These measures of religious repression had a dampening effect, and as a consequence in 1800 there were less than 30,000 Christians living in Vietnam.

During the first half of the nineteenth century, Catholics in France began urging their government to take military action to prevent religious persecution in Vietnam. Their propaganda campaign drew support from an aggressive group of naval officers who were more interested in extending the reach of French sea power than in expanding the bounds of Christendom. But the government in Paris paid little attention to pleas for the deployment of military force in Vietnam until growing numbers of French merchants and manufacturers started to demand protection for their overseas commerce. Adding their voice to the mounting expansionist chorus were a new breed of nationalists who began promoting the idea that France had a mission to bring the blessings of civilization to backward areas around the world. But while these cultural chauvinists were moved by impulses of national pride, the influential business interests were motivated more by desires for personal enrichment. And their appetite for Asian trade intensified after the Opium Wars ended in 1842 and China was forced to open its doors to British and American exports.

Succumbing to the pressure exerted by the commercial imperialists, the French government decided to authorize a military assault on Vietnam. Fourteen warships and 2,500 soldiers left France in 1858 with orders to take the city of Tourane on the coast in the central part of Vietnam. The French forces encountered only limited native resistance, but when many of the invading troops died from the scourge of tropical diseases, policymakers in Paris quickly withdrew their beleaguered warriors. Yet the undaunted French attacked Vietnam three years later with even greater military strength. This time the French struck with seventy gunboats and 3,500 men against the city of Saigon and the surrounding area in the southern part of Vietnam. After breaking the local resistance in a succession of bloody battles, the French extracted a very favorable treaty in 1862 from the humiliated Vietnamese government. Emperor Tu Duc agreed not only to give the French possession of three Vietnamese provinces adjacent to Saigon but also to open three ports in Vietnam to French traders and to permit Catholic missionaries to propagate their faith throughout the country.

Emperor Tu Duc felt compelled to sue for peace and accept such harsh terms because his government lacked popular support. Many public officials and petty bureaucrats, after being appointed to administrative positions by Tu Duc, had became indifferent to the needs of the Vietnamese people. And while his army was fighting in southern Vietnam against the foreign invaders, peasants in northern Vietnam were rebelling against corrupt mandarins. Tu Duc did not have enough troops to repel the French and at the same time to suppress the peasant uprising. Thus he was confronted with a difficult dilemma. And when Tu Duc opted to make peace with his foreign enemies in order to wage war against his own subjects, he was forced to grant the French valuable concessions.

After obtaining possession of the area around Saigon, the French pressed ahead with their quest for empire on the Indochina peninsula. A series of successful military campaigns between 1863 and 1867 enabled the French to complete their conquest of the Mekong River delta and then to establish a protectorate over Cambodia. While digesting these distant acquisitions during the next decade and a half, the French rapidly developed their industrial base at home. The demands for overseas markets grew louder as business profits were plowed back into manufacturing plants, and in 1883 the French government sent another expeditionary force to Vietnam. After French troops penetrated the Red River valley and bombarded the capital at Hué in the central part of the country, the Vietnamese quickly capitulated and signed a treaty that virtually ended their independence. The French completed the creation of their Indochina empire ten years later when they took control of Laos.

The acquisition of these colonies in Indochina provoked a great debate over the issue of empire within France. On the one hand, socialists and humanitarians argued that an imperial policy would mean economic enslavement rather than cultural improvement for the colonial people. These critics also charged that imperialism would benefit only a few big businessmen and colonial administrators while the great majority of French citizens would have to pay the cost of empire with the blood and money needed to maintain metropolitan control over distant territories. On the other hand, special business interests provided strong backing for a program of imperialism. Bankers and manufacturers viewed colonial areas not only as sources of raw material for French industry but also as markets for French capital and commodities. Narrowly preoccupied with their economic self-interest, these business groups hoped that overseas colonies would provide immediate opportunities for profitable enterprise.

But the most influential proponents of imperialism exhibited a broad concern about the long-run functioning of the entire French political economy. These system-conscious leaders noted that domestic industries were turning out more goods than the home market could absorb, and they pointed out that French manufacturers would have to dismiss more and more workers unless they could obtain foreign markets for their surplus commodities. Fearing that the twin problems of overproduction and unemployment were creating the material conditions for a social revolution, these elite cosmopolitans concluded that the preservation of capitalism depended upon a policy of imperialism. Jules Ferry, who served as the French prime minister twice between 1880 and 1885, was a strong exponent of this argument. Ferry repeatedly advocated a program of overseas economic expansion in order to avoid the danger of a radical social upheaval. "Social stability in this industrial age," he declared, "clearly depends on outlets for industrial goods." Along with their allies in the business community, prominent politicians like Ferry convinced the government in Paris to make a concerted effort to consolidate French control of Indochina.

Having won the heated controversy over the colonial question, the French imperialists realized the need to rationalize their Indochina empire. Vietnam, Cambodia, and Laos did not generate enough revenue to pay for their own domination when they first became colonies. Since the empire remained in the red for many years, the citizens of metropolitan France had to bear a heavy tax burden to provide salaries for the civil servants and armed forces sent to rule the colonial population. The members of the French National Assembly soon came to understand that administering the far-flung empire was not a money-making operation. But on the assumption that the colonies would pay off in the future, the legislators continued year after year appropriating funds to run them. The French government finally gave Paul Doumer the challenging job of transforming the Southeast Asian colonies from financial liabilities into profitable possessions. As the governor-general of French Indochina between 1896 and 1902, Doumer strove to put the empire in the black by transferring the cost of imperial administration from the French taxpayers to the colonial subjects. He also began building a modern transportation network to pave the way for the economic exploitation of the colonies.

Doumer ruthlessly imposed a new tax system to accomplish his two basic objectives in Indochina. First, to meet the expenses of administering Vietnam, Cambodia, and Laos, the governor general created three distinct local budgets that depended exclusively upon the direct taxation of the people living in each respective colony. Second, Doumer established a general budget to defray the costs of developing the whole Indochina empire. He generated revenue for the general budget by placing a high tariff on goods imported into the colonies and by organizing state-controlled monopolies that sold licenses for the production and distribution of opium, alcohol, and salt. Most of the money raised through the indirect tax on these three items and through the customs duties went for the construction of roads, bridges, railroads, and harbors. Hence Doumer began establishing an infrastructure in Indochina to facilitate the extraction of raw materials from the Southeast Asian colonies and the importation of manufactured products from the mother country back in Europe.

The French also established a new land policy to promote the economic exploitation of the southern portion of Vietnam. Most of the arable land seized during the conquest of the Mekong delta and most of the additional tracts opened to tillage by the construction of canals and the drainage of marshes were sold to rich French colonists and wealthy Vietnamese natives. This pattern of land distribution created two distinct social classes in southern Vietnam: a powerful group of large landlords and a great mass of landless tenants. If the Vietnamese peasants owned their own land, the French authorities reasoned, they would eat almost all of the rice they produced and therefore there would be very little left to sell abroad at a profit. The French wanted large quantities of rice made available for shipment to the huge rice-consuming populations in China and Japan. And they got what they wanted. Between 1880 and 1930, the amount of rice land under cultivation in the Mekong delta more than quadrupled. Rice exports simultaneously soared, and by the start of World War II Vietnam was the third largest rice-exporting country in the world.

Besides accounting for this spectacular rise in rice exports, the French land policy generated a vast pool of cheap labor in Vietnam. Hordes of landless peasants did much of the dirty and dangerous work required to expand the exchange of products between the colony and the metropolis. The French used large numbers of Vietnamese natives to build railroads, work in mines, and toil on rubber plantations. During the 1930s, big French corporations invested heavily in the development of rubber plantations in the area around Saigon. The huge Michelin firm alone was responsible for almost 45 percent of all the rubber produced in Indochina. The landless peasants endured terrible working conditions on the rubber plantations where disease ran rampant. In fact, the death rate for the native rubber workers was four times higher than for the rest of the Vietnamese population. Because most peasants would rather go hungry than submit themselves to such horrendous working conditions, the French imposed a system of forced labor to obtain large gangs of Vietnamese workers needed for gathering latex from rubber trees.

Despite the rapid growth in rubber production in Vietnam, however, no local rubber industry developed in the colony. Large quantities of raw latex were sent to France to be converted into rubber tires and other articles. These finished products were shipped back to Vietnam and elsewhere to be sold at a handsome profit. French authorities refused to allow a local rubber industry to take root in Vietnam because they wanted their rubber factories to remain in Europe and thereby provide employment and prosperity for their home population. Nor did they permit the development of any other industries in their Indochina empire. The French subscribed to the traditional imperial theory that held that industrial countries have a built-in advantage when trading with agrarian regions because the process of manufacturing adds labor costs to the value of the final product. Believing that colonies should ship low-priced raw materials to their mother country and buy back high-priced factory goods, policymakers in Paris kept their Indochinese possessions on the agricultural half of an imperial relationship with industrial France. In other words, they were determined that their Indochina empire should continue serving as a farm vis-à-vis the French city.

In addition to prohibiting the development of colonial industry, French policymakers tried to prevent foreign competitors from exporting manufactured articles to Vietnam, Cambodia, and Laos. The French sought to establish sheltered markets in their Southeast Asian possessions by placing discriminatory import duties and transit charges on goods coming into them from the United States and other foreign countries. American consular officials reported from Saigon that the United States was having great difficulty selling merchandise in Vietnam. They explained that compared with their French rivals, American exporters had to pay higher tariffs to land their wares in Vietnam and higher railroad freight rates to transport them to the interior of the colony. In 1939, the last year of normal trade before World War II disrupted the colonial regime, more than 55 percent of all Vietnamese imports came from France while less than 5 percent of the total came from the United States. As these figures indicate, the French had succeeded in closing the doors of their Indochina empire against foreign competition and in monopolizing the markets of their Southeast Asian colonies.

The Bank of Indochina, the real master of French colonial policy, achieved its economic objectives. Jointly owned by finance capitalists in Paris and the French government, the Bank of Indochina became the key institution where businessmen and statesmen worked hand in hand in arranging colonial affairs for the economic benefit of metropolitan France. The colonies in Southeast Asia, operating under the dominion of this partly private and partly public institution, became both ready sources of raw materials for French manufacturers and protected markets for their surplus industrial goods. These colonies also produced revenue to pay the cost of imperial administration and thereby provide relief for French taxpayers. And because the bank succeeded in keeping the Indochina empire in the profit column, anticolonial sentiment in France subsided. But while fewer and fewer people in France raised their voice against the evils of imperialism, more and more of their subjects in Vietnam joined the ranks of a vigorous anticolonial movement.

The Roots of Nationalism and Communism

From the very outset, the Vietnamese fought against the French colonization of their country. Although Emperor Tu Duc had ceded the provinces around Saigon in 1862, local Vietnamese partisans continued to resist the French military intrusion. Rebel bands employed hit-and-run tactics to harass the French army, and these small guerrilla units were both elusive and resilient. Even after their country had become a formal French protectorate in 1883, many Vietnamese kept on fighting against the imposition of French authority in the name of their humiliated emperor. Tu Duc had died just before the treaty of surrender was signed in Hué, and in announcing his death the imperial court declared that he "was killed by sorrow over seeing foreigners invade and devastate his empire and he died cursing the invader." Vietnamese patriots were urged to "keep him in your hearts and avenge his memory." Since many answered this call to action, it took the French another ten years to subdue the native guerrillas and pacify their country.

During the last decade of the nineteenth century, the French set out to destroy the national identity of their Vietnamese subjects. The French referred to the Vietnamese people as Annamites, and the actual name of their country ceased to exist in French writings. Vietnam was divided into three separate entities. The northern portion of Vietnam, encompassing the Red River delta, became Tonkin. The central region of the country, containing the long strip of coastal lowlands, was called Annam. The southern part of Vietnam, embracing the Mekong River delta, became Cochinchina. Then after partitioning Vietnam, the French created the Indochinese Union, which was composed of these three distinct units along with Cambodia and Laos. Consequently the Vietnamese found themselves submerged in a grouping of states that were governed in the interest of their French masters.

The imperial rule imposed by the French sowed the seeds of peasant discontent deep in Vietnamese soil. By the 1930s, for example, 45 percent of the arable land in the Mekong delta was owned by only 2 percent of the population. The large and often absentee landlords forced the peasants to pay excessive rents for the right to cultivate their small plots in the rice fields. The peasants also suffered at the hands of the Vietnamese natives appointed by French governors to serve as bureaucrats in low-level administrative positions. Many such political collaborators, coming as they did from families that had previously converted to Catholicism, practiced the religion of their rulers. These functionaries not only collected taxes to support the French regime, but they also coerced the landless to work on the deadly French rubber plantations. Besides oppressing the peasants, corrupt mandarins often embezzled funds to supplement their regular salaries. "On our side," admitted a candid French official, "we have only Christians and crooks."

Besides angering the great mass of exploited peasants, French colonial policy also aroused the wrath of many upper-class members of

Vietnamese society. Whereas the British depended largely upon native inhabitants to maintain control over the entire subcontinent of India, the French refused to give the indigenous population a major role in administering their Indochina empire. So while only 5,000 civil servants from England ruled 325 million Indians in 1925, it took an equal number of civil servants from France to manage a mere 30 million Vietnamese. Not only did the French style of colonial administration make it difficult for ambitious Vietnamese natives to obtain attractive positions in the government bureaucracy, but the French policy of retarding the development of colonial industry meant that there were few employment opportunities for talented and educated Vietnamese in the business community. And even when aspiring natives did get jobs commensurate with their abilities, they usually received two or three times less pay than French colonists for doing the same work. More disturbing still was the situation at the University of Hanoi where a Vietnamese professor received lower wages than a French janitor.

Life in the French empire could be especially frustrating and humiliating for young Vietnamese men of wealthy origins. The sons of Vietnamese landlords and merchants frequently traveled to Paris to complete their formal education, and some earned advanced degrees in science, medicine, and law at the University of Paris and other French institutions of higher learning. They also enjoyed the liberal atmosphere of the Latin Quarter where they could openly debate political issues and read socialist literature criticizing French imperialism. But a very painful experience awaited these young Vietnamese scholars when they returned home. The colonial police force regarded them as potential subversives and confiscated any of their books that might be tainted by some kind of European radicalism. These returning Vietnamese students likewise discovered that they could not find jobs in either business or government that matched their educational achievement. And after they had been addressed in Paris with the formal "monsieur" used for normal adults, colonial bureaucrats addressed them with the familiar "tu" as if they were children or servants.

But more than anything else it was the question of colonial education that became the focal point in the conflict between the opposing forces of Vietnamese nationalism and French imperialism. Hoping to destroy the cultural identity of Vietnamese students, the French authorities prohibited the use of traditional Chinese characters in the schools of Tonkin, Annam, and Cochinchina. But many native teachers went on strike in protest against the French effort to undermine the coherence of Vietnamese culture. Occurring in the midst of this confrontation, the

Japanese victory over Russia in 1905 had a strong impact on Vietnamese nationalists. They learned that a yellow Asian people, if armed with Western scientific and technical knowledge, could defeat a white European power. Vietnamese nationalists quickly concluded that their students needed exposure to Western ideas, and in 1907 they established the Free School of Tonkin in Hanoi. But the French regarded their attempt to modernize Vietnamese thought as an act of political subversion. After only eight months, they closed the school and arrested the teachers.

Although the French crushed the Free School of Tonkin, they could not prevent Phan Boi Chau from keeping the Vietnamese national resistance movement alive during the first quarter of the twentieth century. Chau was the driving force among the Vietnamese scholars who believed that Eastern peoples needed Western knowledge to defend themselves against European imperialism. In 1905, he organized an underground service to send gifted Vietnamese students to Japan where they could study western science and technology. During the next three years, some 200 Vietnamese students participated in what they called "the exodus to the east." Chau also advocated the formation of a transnational alliance to put an end to white rule throughout the Orient, and in 1908 he helped create the East Asia League. Composed of nationalists representing several different Far Eastern countries, the organization began to lay the foundations for a Pan Asiatic movement against European domination.

Yet if Phan Boi Chau provided the campaign against imperialism with dynamic leadership, his brand of nationalism was doomed to fail. Chau did not go beyond the political demands of the wealthy landlords and middle-class intellectuals who were frustrated and humiliated by French policies. These two elite groups wanted freedom from French dominion, but they had no interest in making any sweeping changes in the Vietnamese social structure. Opposed to a radical redistribution of wealth, they never developed a program that addressed the fundamental economic needs of the peasant masses. Chau remained tied to the great landlords and urban intellectuals. Unable to transcend his middle-class orientation, he appealed to the privileged minority rather than the oppressed majority. Chau ultimately failed because his resistance movement could not free Vietnam from colonial bondage without the support of the lower class.

Among the Vietnamese nationalists, only the communists were able to rally the masses in a drive to expel the French from their homeland. The communists aimed to offset the technological superiority possessed by the French colonists with the numerical strength of the Vietnamese peasants. The Vietnamese communists had dual objectives. They were determined not only to burst the shackles of colonialism but also to solve the problem of landlordism. After achieving their immediate nationalist goal of home rule, the communists intended to implement their long-range program aimed at creating a more equitable social order. They planned to divide the large estates of the great landlords into small plots and to distribute them to the landless peasants. Thus the communists promised the peasants that they would have a better life after the French were thrown out of their country.

Ho Chi Minh emerged as the indisputable father of Vietnamese communism. Born in 1890 in a small village in central Vietnam, he grew up in a family of modest means. His father had studied hard to climb above his peasant origins and become a public official, but he lost his administrative job because of his sympathy for Phan Boi Chau and other Vietnamese nationalists. As a boy, Ho heard stories from his elders about how the arrogant French colonists had mistreated the Vietnamese people. Ho attended school in the old imperial capital of Hué, and his nationalist feelings grew stronger while he studied in this great center of Vietnamese culture. After teaching for a brief time, Ho decided to leave Vietnam, and in 1912, at the age of twenty-two, he got a job as a kitchen boy on a French freighter. Ho spent the next two years sailing around the globe, but when World War I began, he left the ship to find work in England. While living in London, he joined a group of Asian students and workers who were supporting the Irish struggle for national independence. Then, in 1917, Ho decided to move to France where he could deal with the problems of his own country.

Ho Chi Minh plunged into the vortex of world politics when he arrived in Paris. The United States had already entered the Great War, and American statesmen were planning to use their influence to shape the peace settlement. In his famous Fourteen Points speech delivered in 1918, President Woodrow Wilson announced that the United States stood for the democratic principle of national self-determination. Ho was excited about what Wilson had said. He hoped that the concept of home rule would be applied to the black, brown, and yellow people living in the colonial areas of the world and not just to the white people residing in Europe. Fast becoming the leading figure in the Vietnamese community in Paris, Ho drafted a petition calling for self-government for Vietnam. He intended to hand his petition to Wilson at the Versailles Peace Conference in 1919, but the president refused to see him. Ho was deeply disappointed when he discovered that there was a wide gap between Wilsonian rhetoric and American diplomacy.

After being rebuffed by Wilson and his European allies at Versailles, Ho became more deeply involved in radical politics in France. The shock waves of the Bolshevik Revolution in Russia were beginning to split the French Socialist Party into rival factions. Although Ho was not interested in many of the subtle points that were driving French socialists and communists apart, he was keenly concerned about their respective attitudes toward the issue of colonial independence. When the socialists refused to join with the communists in supporting Lenin's demand for the immediate emancipation of all colonial areas, Ho decided that he would be a communist rather than a socialist. Ho helped found the French Communist Party in 1920, and he quickly became its leading expert on the colonial question by repeatedly attacking every aspect of French imperialism in both public addresses and newspaper articles. As a delegate of the French Communist Party, Ho traveled to Moscow in 1924 to participate in the Comintern meeting and to speak for the liberation of the colonial masses around the world.

The leaders of the Comintern promptly dispatched Ho Chi Minh to China where Chiang Kai-shek and the nationalists were cooperating with Mao Tse-tung and the communists. Ho went directly to Canton, which was a major center for young Vietnamese political exiles. While living in Canton between 1925 and 1927, he helped organize an Eastern alliance against Western imperialism called the League of Oppressed Peoples of Asia. Ho also trained hundreds of Vietnamese students in Canton to become radical activists, and some were infiltrated back into Vietnam to form a hard-core political cadre. Pham Van Dong, eventually to become Ho's most trusted deputy, stood out among those who were sent home to recruit their compatriots and to agitate against the French. Ho had to leave Canton in 1927 because Chiang broke with Mao and began attacking communist enclaves in China. But Ho slipped into Hong Kong undercover in 1930, and together with his radical followers he established the Indochinese Communist Party.

By then, after receiving their training in either Russia or China, hundreds of young Vietnamese communists had returned to their native land to foment a revolution against the old colonial order. These communist agents advanced a radical program that addressed the basic economic grievances of the downtrodden Vietnamese peasants and workers. Their social reform program held out the promise of lower taxes and land distribution for the peasants along with the prospect of higher wages and better medical care for plantation workers. The communists decided to provoke a peasant rebellion in 1930, but the premature uprising failed miserably. The French brutally smashed the rebels in a great bloodbath that left an estimated 10,000 Vietnamese peasants dead. This year of White Terror taught the communists a bitter lesson. Realizing that they were not yet ready to challenge French military power, the communists decided to go underground to make preparations for a successful revolt from below. But their opportunity did not come until the winds of World War II swept across the Pacific and loosened the bonds of French colonialism in Indochina. Then, in 1941, after traveling abroad for more than a quarter of a century, Ho Chi Minh returned to Vietnam to lead the forces of revolution.

The Rise of the Vietminh

A few months later, the Japanese launched a surprise attack on Pearl Harbor as part of their drive to establish a new order in East Asia. Their quest for empire, which had begun ten years earlier, was based upon economic necessity. The narrow chain of Japanese islands did not provide an adequate natural resource base to support the dense urban population living on them. Thus it was essential for the Japanese to export manufactured goods in order to pay for the foodstuffs needed to feed their people and the raw materials required to sustain their industries. But after the onset of the Great Depression in 1929, the United States and the European countries began erecting high tariffs against Japanese products. Policymakers in Tokyo responded by looking for Oriental markets that Japan could monopolize, and in 1931 they invaded Manchuria and set up a puppet state called Manchukuo. Then the Japanese promptly turned Manchuria into an exclusive sphere of economic influence whose doors were closed against American and European commodities.

But the Japanese had visions of a vast empire that extended far beyond the borders of Manchuria. Their desire to monopolize the entire China market of more than 400 million consumers was disclosed after Japanese and Chinese troops exchanged shots in July 1937 at the Marco Polo Bridge. Japan seized upon the skirmish as an excuse for making further conquests on the Asian mainland, and her aggression provoked a determined Chinese resistance. As the invaders pushed deep into the Middle Kingdom, they quickly assumed control of every major seaport, railroad, and industry in northern China. The Japanese were eager to extend their authority over the rest of China, and in November 1938

Tokyo boldly announced plans for the creation of a Greater East Asia Co-Prosperity Sphere. With Japan serving as the industrial core and her Oriental satellites accepting their inferior role as producers of foodstuffs and raw materials in this new order, the Land of the Rising Sun would enjoy as much economic self-sufficiency as either the United States or the British Empire.

It soon became evident that the Japanese included French Indochina in their grandiose dreams of economic hegemony in the Far East. When Nazi Germany defeated metropolitan France in June 1940, the Japanese imperialists cast covetous eyes on the French possessions in Southeast Asia. They immediately grasped their golden opportunity to extort valuable economic and strategic concessions from the vanquished European nation. Shortly after surrendering to Hitler, the French government agreed to close the Tonkin border adjacent to China and to allow Japan to place inspectors along the French Indochina Railroad to make sure that trains did not carry supplies to the Chinese resistance forces. Three months later, in September 1940, the distressed French gave Japan permission to station 25,000 soldiers in Tonkin. Finally, in May 1941, the French agreed that all the rubber, rice, corn, and coal available for export from their Indochinese colonies would be either reserved for the Japanese occupational troops or shipped to the Japanese home islands.

This readiness to collaborate with the Japanese occurred even though the French had a large military force deployed in Indochina. After learning that the United States would not come to their aid, policymakers in France decided not to spill Gallic blood defending their Southeast Asian protectorates against Japan. And while their home government was capitulating to pressure exerted by Tokyo, the French colonists in Indochina were cooperating fully with the occupational authorities sent from Japan. Not wanting to be bothered with the problems of colonial administration, the Japanese asked the local French officials to continue running the affairs of Vietnam, Cambodia, and Laos. But the Japanese insisted that they must have access to the raw materials and foodstuffs produced in the French possessions and that none of these resources could be sent to the Chinese armies fighting against Japan. Yielding to these demands, the French willingly administered their Indochina empire for the economic and strategic benefit of Japan.

The Vietnamese communists, by contrast, were determined to resist the Japanese occupation of their country. In May 1941, Ho Chi Minh summoned the Central Committee of the Indochinese Communist Party to discuss the need for a broad national front to fight against both the old French enemy and the new Japanese foe. The historic meeting, held at

Ho's headquarters in a remote cave in the mountains near the Chinese border, gave birth to the Revolutionary League for the Independence of Vietnam (better known as the Vietminh—meaning Vietnamese nationalist). Although the leadership of the organization was firmly in communist hands, the Vietminh included all shades of nationalist opinion. Ho and his comrades downplayed their radicalism in order to attract conservatives to their nationalist cause. Their pragmatic agrarian program, for example, promised that patriotic landlords could keep their property and that only treasonous landowners would have their holdings confiscated and distributed to landless peasants. Rather than discussing their ultimate goal of building a communist utopia, the leaders of the Vietminh emphasized their immediate aim of ousting their foreign adversaries. After receiving support from members of every social class, Ho issued a call in September 1941 for his countrymen to take up arms in order to create an independent Vietnamese republic.

Following his decision to employ military force, Ho asked Vo Nguyen Giap to build an army for the Vietminh. Giap had a unique background. He was politically active during his youth, and in 1933 at the age of twenty-one he joined the Indochinese Communist Party. After earning a law degree from the University of Hanoi, he taught history in a Vietnamese school and studied the guerrilla tactics used by the Chinese communists. Giap promptly set about organizing and training guerrilla units in the jungles of northern Tonkin. In this remote mountainous region, far from the French and Japanese soldiers down in the Red River valley, he began the difficult task of recruiting mountain tribesmen. The Vietnamese had historically regarded the ethnic peoples living in the mountains as savages, but Giap demanded that his troops overcome their traditional ethnocentric attitudes. He realized that it was critical for the Vietminh to maintain friendly relations with the mountain tribes not only to get them to join his army but also to keep them from telling the French and Japanese the whereabouts of his training centers. Giap successfully wooed many tribesmen by promising that they would have autonomy in areas traditionally under their control after the foreigners were expelled from the country.

General Giap gradually expanded his base of operations deep in the mountains of northern Tonkin. After winning the support of numerous tribesmen, he began recruiting village chiefs and training Vietnamese peasants in the art of guerrilla warfare. Giap instructed his Vietminh forces to strike with superior numbers against tiny and isolated French outposts, to capture guns and supplies, and then to melt back into the jungle before making another surprise attack. But while the Vietminh guerrillas began to overrun small French garrisons in 1944, they avoided any major battles where the French could use their superior firepower to greater advantage. Giap spent most of his time during World War II recruiting troops and training them to capture weapons and ammunition. He concentrated on strengthening the Vietminh forces in the hope that when the war ended they would be able to emerge triumphant.

In the meantime, Ho Chi Minh crossed over the border into southern China to obtain support for his resistance movement. Ho wanted to get Vietnamese exiles to return to their homeland and join the ranks of the Vietminh. He also hoped to receive economic aid from the warlords who controlled southern China. When Ho arrived in China in August 1942, however, the warlords arrested him and put him in prison. Hoping that someday they could dominate Indochina, the warlords tried to organize their own Vietnamese independence movement. But the group backed by the Chinese lacked able leadership and popular support, and consequently it could not provide information about Japanese plans and operations in Indochina. Realizing that only the Vietminh could give them what they wanted, the warlords released Ho from prison and began supplying him with money in exchange for intelligence about the Japanese. The Chinese subsidy helped the Vietminh establish a strong underground network throughout Tonkin, where they continued preparing for their chance to seize power.

They did not have to wait long before what remained of French authority in Indochina came to an abrupt end. Most French colonists in Indochina had been actively collaborating with the Japanese ever since 1940 when their native country fell under the shadow of the swastika. But many Frenchmen underwent a change of heart at the end of 1944 when they heard that American forces under General Douglas MacArthur were in the process of reconquering the Philippines. As rumors spread that the Americans would soon liberate Indochina, General Charles de Gaulle decided that his Free French troops should prepare for military action. During the first two months of 1945, de Gaulle parachuted French agents and arms into Vietnam with orders to attack the Japanese as soon as American soldiers hit the beaches. But the French plans were a poorly kept secret, and on March 9 the Japanese moved suddenly to nip the uprising in the bud. Despite the presence of almost 100,000 French troops in Indochina, the Japanese met with little resistance. Most of the French soldiers were quickly disarmed and imprisoned while about 5,000 of them fled from the Japanese and straggled into China. The Japanese coup signaled the end of all pretense of French sovereignty in Indochina.

The American military and intelligence personnel stationed in south-western China had not until then showed much interest in the activities of the Vietminh. But almost immediately after the Japanese takeover of French Indochina in March 1945, American army officers made a deal with Ho Chi Minh. The Americans agreed to provide the Vietminh with communications equipment, medical supplies, and small arms, and in return Ho offered to give the United States information about Japanese troop movements and to help rescue downed American pilots. The Office of Strategic Services (OSS) also established a friendly relationship with the Vietminh. A small OSS team, headed by Archimedes Patti, parachuted into northern Tonkin on July 16 to make contact with General Giap at his mountain redoubt. After reporting to Washington that 85 percent of the people living in Tonkin supported the Vietminh, Patti and his fellow OSS officers began helping Giap train his forces for operations against the Japanese. But the principal effect of the brief American association with the Vietminh was political rather than military in nature. It looked as if Ho and Giap had an alliance with the United States, and so their prestige among the Vietnamese people was greatly enhanced.

The Vietminh also gained popularity because of their militant actions during a ghastly famine that engulfed northern Vietnam. To satisfy their military requirements, the Japanese had forced many Vietnamese peasants to raise jute, hemp, and castor beans rather than food crops. Adverse weather conditions and widespread flooding in the Red River delta during 1945 exacerbated the food shortage in Tonkin. Yet the Japanese continued requisitioning their rice quotas, which were stored in huge granaries in anticipation of an Allied invasion. During the ensuing famine, an estimated 2 million of the 10 million inhabitants of the northern half of Vietnam died. The massive starvation produced a deep hatred for the Japanese oppressors and provoked the Vietnamese peasants to fight for their very survival. When the famine became acute, Vietminh soldiers led hungry peasants who succeeded in breaking into some of the storage depots and distributing the rice to their starving countrymen. Their action in seizing the granaries marked the Vietminh as the patriotic champions of the Vietnamese peasants.

Then suddenly, along with the blast of atomic bombs over Hiroshima and Nagasaki, the great opportunity came for the Vietminh to lead a revolution in Vietnam. On August 16, two days after Japan surrendered to the United States, Ho Chi Minh called for a general uprising. Ho aimed to mobilize the masses throughout Vietnam and then welcome the Allied troops when they arrived to disarm the Japanese. On August 19, the Vietminh marched into Hanoi and occupied the government buildings without firing a shot. The Japanese offered no resistance, and there were no Vietnamese reprisals. While bright red Vietminh flags fluttered over Hanoi, throngs of happy people paraded down the streets proclaiming Vietnamese independence and chanting death to the French. The revolt spread with incredible speed. Revolutionary committees quickly took over provincial governments, and within just six days the Vietminh had gained control of the entire country. Red flags flapped in every part of Vietnam, and in a burst of exuberance Saigon was renamed the City of Ho Chi Minh.

The Vietminh thereupon decided to dispose of Emperor Bao Dai and set up their own government in Hanoi. Bao Dai had functioned as a puppet under the French, and in March 1945 he became a figurehead in the new client administration that the Japanese installed in Vietnam. His willingness to serve foreign rulers discredited him in the eyes of his countrymen. And when thousands of angry peasants stormed into the royal capital of Hué, the Vietminh pressured the besieged emperor to abdicate his throne. Bao Dai promptly yielded, and on August 30 he turned over the royal seal to a revolutionary committee. The Vietminh then established the Democratic Republic of Vietnam. The new regime received widespread and enthusiastic support, and the Vietnamese people were delighted when the charismatic Ho Chi Minh became their president. And it was with a show of warmth and affection that they referred to their frail and gentle leader as Uncle Ho.

The great revolution of August 1945 filled Ho with hope for the future of his country. On September 2, speaking before a crowd of 500,000 people assembled in Hanoi, Ho proclaimed Vietnamese independence. Wearing a faded khaki suit and rubber sandals, he began his address by quoting from the American Declaration of Independence. "We hold these truths to be self-evident," he told his cheering audience, "that all men are created equal." Ho concluded his speech by appealing to the United States to acknowledge the independence of Vietnam. Four years earlier, in August 1941, President Franklin D. Roosevelt and Prime Minister Winston Churchill had met off the coast of Newfoundland to discuss Anglo-American war aims, and in the highly publicized Atlantic Charter they pledged to restore self-government to all people who had been forcibly deprived of home rule. Although he had been bitterly disappointed at Versailles when Woodrow Wilson failed to make good on his rhetoric, Ho hoped that this time American leaders might abide by their promise to support the democratic principle of national self-determination. Because the French had collaborated with the Japanese and the Vietminh had worked with the Americans, Ho thought that perhaps the United States might prevent the French from recovering their Indochina empire.

The Dream of a Pax Americana

Continuing, or even maintaining, Japan's economic recovery depends upon keeping Communism out of Southeast Asia, promoting economic recovery there and in further developing those countries, together with Indonesia, the Philippines, Southern Korea and India as the principal trading areas for Japan.

Joint Report of the State and Defense Departments, 1950

Blueprints for a New World Order

Even before the United States formally entered World War II, American leaders began making plans for the creation of a peaceful and prosperous international order after hostilities ceased. President Franklin D. Roosevelt and his State Department advisers hoped to establish a liberal capitalist world system based upon the principle of equal commercial opportunity. Confident that the United States would emerge from the conflict with a preponderance of military and economic power, they aimed to promote an open door policy that would give all industrial countries equal access to raw materials and commodity markets around the globe. American leaders realized that Great Britain would no longer be able to rule the world in the interest of free trade, and they believed that the United States should be prepared to fill the power vacuum. They hoped that, just as the last century had belonged to England, an Allied victory over the Axis would mark the dawn of an American century. In short, they envisioned the establishment of a Pax Americana that would replace the Pax Britannica and thereby sustain the capitalist epoch.

But the nightmare of a depression haunted American leaders when they contemplated the nature of the postwar world. Following the stock market crash on Wall Street in 1929, the United States had plunged into a decade of depression. Businessmen shut down plants and laid off workers because of a lack of demand for consumer goods, and as unemployment increased and household spending declined, more companies closed their doors. President Roosevelt launched his New Deal program to counteract the vicious circle, but economic recovery did not come until the onset of World War II. When the shooting started in Europe in 1939, American factories began receiving orders for a vast array of weapons and munitions from both the United States government and the Allied nations. The stimulus of military spending continued turning the wheels of industry and creating jobs for those without work, and in 1942 Roosevelt boasted that "Dr. Win-the-War" had replaced "Dr. New Deal." Though pleased about the wartime prosperity, Roosevelt and his advisers realized that the New Deal had failed to overcome the Great Depression. Thus they feared that, when the demand for military hardware declined at the end of the war, the twin problems of overproduction and unemployment would return to plague the United States.

Top government officials and corporate executives who participated in the decision-making process understood that there were two different ways of avoiding a postwar depression in the United States. Either they could plan the American economy so that domestic production would match the requirements of the home market, or they could obtain foreign markets to absorb the surplus output of the farms and factories in the United States. American policymakers rejected the option of centralized economic planning to create an internal balance between supply and demand because they believed that excessive governmental controls would destroy the essentials of free enterprise. Fearing that an extension of New Deal regulations would undermine entrepreneurial freedom by taking management decisions out of private hands, American leaders chose the alternative of overseas commercial expansion to solve the problem of domestic overproduction. In other words, they looked to new frontiers in the markets of the world in hopes of preserving capitalism in the United States.

President Roosevelt and his State Department advisers also hoped to promote world peace by liberalizing international commerce. During the Great Depression, many manufacturing nations had erected high tariff walls around both their internal and colonial markets. The consequent decline in the volume of world trade had a particularly harmful impact on countries that did not have enough natural resources to sustain themselves in economic isolation. Germany and Japan, after being denied access to essential foodstuffs and raw materials, led a group of these "have-not nations" in an attempt to redivide the world in order to satisfy their material needs. Although American policymakers assumed that the Allies would defeat the Axis drive to partition the planet into exclusive spheres of influence, they feared that a resumption of economic nationalism in the postwar era would sow the seeds for yet another global conflict. They were therefore intent on establishing a liberal international trading system after the war so that "have-not nations" like Germany and Japan could achieve prosperity by engaging in peaceful commerce rather than military conquest.

During their postwar planning sessions between 1941 and 1945, State Department officials drafted blueprints for the creation of a peaceful and prosperous international capitalist utopia. They carefully advanced a multidimensional economic program embracing the following five key points: (1) the extension of American loans to underwrite the economic reconstruction of industrial countries that had been devastated by the long military ordeal; (2) the reintegration of Germany into the global economy; (3) the limitation of armaments to permit small countries to devote their sparse resources to economic rehabilitation rather than military preparation; (4) the reduction of American tariffs to allow foreign countries to increase their exports to the United States and thereby earn dollars that they could use to purchase American products; and (5) the modification of the European imperial preference systems to give all nations equal access to raw materials and commodity markets in colonial areas such as British Malaya, Dutch Indonesia, and French Indochina.

The architects of the new world order spent much of their time in the State Department discussing the dangers of colonialism. Adolf Berle, Leo Pasvolsky, and others pointed out that the continuation of colonial monopolies in the postwar period would not only undermine American economic interests but that imperial preferences might even provoke dynamic "have-not nations" into taking aggressive actions that would culminate in World War III. These State Department experts also noted that continued colonial exploitation might stimulate a wave of revolutionary upheavals throughout the Third World. They were particularly worried that the imperial policies of the British, Dutch, and French in the Far East would give rise to a strong anticolonial movement under the banner of Asia for the Asians. Many Oriental nationalists, noncommunist as well as communist, were talking about the need for a united Asian crusade to end European rule in the Far East. American diplomats feared that such a Pan Asiatic movement would threaten the economic interests of the United States along with the other industrial countries around the world.

Disturbed by such dismal prospects, the postwar planners in the Department of State sponsored an ambitious trusteeship scheme to solve the troublesome problem of colonialism. They proposed that all dependent areas should be administered by either a single trustee country or a group of trustees acting under the auspices of the United Nations. These trustees would be responsible for helping the colonial peoples under their guardianship attain political maturity. By progressively introducing measures of self-government in dependent regions, the trustees were to prepare their wards for eventual independence. The State Department plan also called upon the trustee nations to promote economic development in colonial areas for the benefit of both the native populations and the rest of the world. The trustees would therefore be required to open the territories under their tutelage to the trade and investments of all countries regardless of their size. Under Secretary Sumner Welles stressed this point when he told his subordinates in the State Department that the issue of equal access to natural resources and commodity markets was "the keystone of the whole structure of trusteeship for dependent areas."

President Roosevelt gave the trusteeship proposal strong support. He liked to point out that during the last four decades the United States had been preparing the Philippine Islands for self-government, and he frequently suggested that the American treatment of the Philippines should serve as a model for the European powers to emulate. Roosevelt believed that colonial peoples should go through an interim period of international guardianship until they were ready for independence. He thought that the training period might be as short as a decade or so for advanced areas like Indochina and as long as a century or more for backward regions like Borneo. Although he was a gradualist with regard to the decolonization question, Roosevelt emphasized the need for the European powers to fix definite timetables for granting independence to their wards. He insisted that dependent peoples should not be held in tutelage after they were able to stand on their own feet. In a nutshell, Roosevelt regarded the trusteeship interval as a transitional stage along the road from the colonialism of the past to the self-determinism of the future.

President Roosevelt and his counselors in the State Department also planned to establish an international security system based upon the Big

Four police powers. After disarming their Axis enemies at the end of the war, the United States, Great Britain, Soviet Russia, and China were to cooperate with each other in maintaining world peace. Although China was weak and divided, American leaders insisted that the disorganized Asian giant must be included in the Big Four. They hoped that China would eventually become an important trading partner and military ally of the United States. They also figured that China would be a valuable political associate that would support American positions in the United Nations. Their grand strategy called for Russia and Britain to shoulder most of the burden for keeping peace in Europe while the United States would assume primary responsibility for maintaining security in the Western Hemisphere and the Pacific Ocean. Realizing the need for distant naval and air bases, American policymakers decided that the United States would have to maintain complete control of the islands taken from Japan during the sweep across the Pacific.

At first State Department planners did not think that France would play a major strategic role in the postwar world. Although the French had a huge army on the European continent when World War II began, they surrendered to Germany within six weeks after Hitler launched his blitzkrieg against the western front. Then they quickly began collaborating with both the Germans in Europe and the Japanese in Indochina. As a result, American diplomats regarded France as a third-rate power. They not only viewed the French with contempt because of their anemic war record, but they also blamed them for having caused an arms race in Europe. The United States had tried to get France to enter into an arms limitation agreement after World War I, but the French wanted to maintain military superiority on the continent, and many smaller European countries followed the French in building up their military forces. Recalling that Hitler had used the French refusal to disarm as an excuse for rearming Germany, American policymakers reasoned that France should be disarmed when the current conflict ended.

In addition, neither President Roosevelt nor his State Department advisers thought that the French had any claim to regain their Indochina empire. It is true that in an effort to encourage the French to resist their Nazi oppressors, American officials made public pronouncements favoring the return of all French colonies in the postwar period. In their private conversations, however, they made it quite clear that French Indochina should be administered by an international trusteeship. Sumner Welles lectured his colleagues in August 1942 that France had no inherent right to exploit Indochina. "There is a great moral question involved here," he observed, "and it is a question that will shape and color the history of the world after this war is over." President Roosevelt agreed. He told Secretary of State Cordell Hull in January 1944 that Indochina should not go back to France after the war. "France has had the country—thirty million inhabitants—for nearly one hundred years, and the people are worse off than they were at the beginning," Roosevelt complained. "France has milked it for one hundred years. The people of Indochina are entitled to something better than that."

American leaders hoped that their Russian allies would support their plans for the postwar era. After crossing through Eastern Europe, the German Wehrmacht had penetrated deep into the Soviet Union. Millions of Russians were dying in defense of their homeland, and the Nazi armies were destroying thousands of Soviet factories. Seeking to reduce Russian fears about a future German invasion, American officials indicated that the United States would participate in policing the postwar world. They also thought that they might be able to win Soviet cooperation in Eastern Europe by offering American loans for Russian economic reconstruction. But the apprehension grew in Washington that the Russians would attempt to dominate the countries of Eastern Europe in order to satisfy their security needs. As they became increasingly concerned about the likelihood of Soviet expansion on the European continent if both Germany and France were disarmed, American leaders began thinking that France should resume her traditional position as a principal European power. By November 1944, they concluded that it would be necessary to rearm France with American weapons.

After reversing himself with regard to the issue of French militarism, President Roosevelt also began changing his mind about the question of French colonialism. Roosevelt wanted to postpone making a final decision concerning Indochina until the peace settlement following the war, but after the Yalta Conference in February 1945, there was growing evidence that the Soviet Union aimed to dominate Poland and other countries in Eastern Europe. In a discussion with the American ambassador in Paris on March 13, General Charles de Gaulle pointed to the Russian menace to Europe in an attempt to blackmail the United States into supporting the restoration of the French empire in Indochina. "The Russians are advancing apace," de Gaulle warned. "When Germany falls they will be upon us. If the public here comes to realize that you are against us in Indochina there will be terrific disappointment and nobody knows to what that will lead. We do not want to become Communist; we do not want to fall into the Russian orbit, but I hope that you do not push us into it." On the next day, Roosevelt told one of his close advisers that he would agree to let the French retain their colonies in Indochina with the proviso that independence would be the ultimate goal.

Although Roosevelt died a month later and Harry S. Truman entered the White House, there was no sharp break in American policy toward Indochina. The State Department assumed the difficult task of attempting to reconcile American objectives in Europe and Asia. On the one hand, American diplomats thought that the United States should allow the French to keep their Indochina empire in order to maintain France as a military ally in the event of future Russian aggression in Europe. On the other hand, they believed that the United States should urge the French to grant local autonomy in their Southeast Asian possessions in order to prevent bloodshed in Vietnam. The State Department adopted these views on April 30 in a key policy paper that held that the United States should not oppose the restoration of French authority in Vietnam, Laos, and Cambodia but that American officials should seek assurance of French intentions to establish self-government in Indochina. A few days later, at the first meeting in San Francisco to create the United Nations, Secretary of State Edward R. Stettinius told the French ambassador that the United States had never questioned the sovereignty of his country in Indochina.

The First Indochina War

The French were eager to reestablish control over their Indochina colonies. Although Germany had delivered a sharp blow to their national pride by defeating and occupying their country, the French did not simply want to reassert their imperial authority because of a psychological need to compensate for the humiliation they had suffered at the hands of Hitler. Cosmopolitan French leaders were prompted by rational calculations rather than emotional feelings. The influential directors of the Bank of Indochina, hoping to safeguard their huge investments, demanded protection for French economic interests in the Orient. Concerned about maintaining the cohesion of their overseas empire as a whole, policymakers in Paris subscribed to the "tenpin theory," which held that if one French colony won its independence nationalism would be encouraged elsewhere in the French empire. If the first tenpin tumbled, it would strike others, and they in turn could bring down the whole stand. More specifically, should Vietnam fall to the forces of nationalism, the French might lose not only their economically less important colonies in Southeast Asia (Cambodia and Laos) but also their more valuable possessions in North Africa (Morocco, Tunisia, and Algeria).

The French received quiet assistance from the United States when they decided to send an expeditionary force to Vietnam. Two weeks after Japan surrendered in August 1945, the State Department informed the American embassy in India that the United States had no thought of opposing the reestablishment of French control over Indochina. But the American government did not merely acquiesce in the French effort to reconquer Vietnam. Although the State Department published a statement declaring that the United States would not participate in the forceful imposition of French authority in Indochina, American policymakers acted in ways that ran counter to their public posture of neutrality. The United States permitted the French to keep without payment the Lend-Lease equipment that had been given to General de Gaulle before Japan capitulated and to use these military supplies in Indochina after removing all the American insignia. The United States also provided a large number of ships for the transportation of French troops and American weapons to Vietnam.

While the American government attempted to conceal these actions, Great Britain openly supported the French campaign to recolonize Indochina. The Allied powers had agreed, at the Potsdam Conference in July 1945, that after the war the responsibility for disarming and repatriating the Japanese troops in French Indochina would go to the British in the region south of the sixteenth parallel and to the Chinese in the area north of that parallel. The first British troops arrived in Saigon on September 12, and a small detachment of French soldiers accompanied them. General Douglas D. Gracey, the commander of the British forces, promptly ordered the Vietnamese inhabitants of Saigon to turn over their weapons. When the Vietminh called a general strike in protest on September 17, General Gracey responded by proclaiming martial law, suspending all Vietnamese newspapers, and banning demonstrations of any kind. Gracey also released from prison and armed 1,400 French soldiers who had been interned by the Japanese after their March coup. The French troops immediately took over the public buildings in Saigon and stormed down the streets looking for Vietnamese to beat.

The brutal French rampage set the stage in southern Vietnam for the outbreak of a war for national liberation. The Vietminh called a general strike on September 24, and it was soon difficult to get food and supplies into Saigon. With insufficient British and French troops to restore order and expand his control beyond Saigon, General Gracey decided to use the Japanese soldiers he had been sent to disarm. Gracey threatened to treat Japanese officers as war criminals if they refused to order their men to help subdue the Vietminh. When the first military units arrived from

France on October 5, they joined with the British and Japanese in cracking the blockade around Saigon and then in driving through the Mekong delta. The Vietminh retreated into the highlands and resorted to guerrilla tactics. The Japanese, after suffering heavy casualties in the intense fighting, were gradually disarmed and replaced by reinforcements from France. As their numbers grew, the French were able to administer the larger cities and provincial towns in southern Vietnam. But they could not prevent the Vietminh guerrillas from controlling the surrounding countryside.

In northern Vietnam, by contrast, the Vietminh exercised firm control of urban as well as rural areas. The government established by Ho Chi Minh in Hanoi following the revolution in August 1945 enjoyed widespread public support. Even Catholic priests backed the Vietminh regime after Ho initiated a reformist rather than a communist program. Besides allowing native landlords who had not collaborated with the foreign enemies to keep their large holdings, the Vietminh wiped out the salt monopoly, abolished the forced labor system, reduced land taxes, legalized unions, and instituted an eight-hour day. Gambling and prostitution were banned, the use of opium and alcohol was prohibited, and free classes were set up to teach the illiterate masses how to read and write. In addition to introducing these social and economic reforms, the Vietminh established a system of universal suffrage to bring more people into the political process. All men and women over eighteen years of age were given the right to vote on both the local and national level.

However, Vietminh efforts to implement this liberal program in northern Vietnam were suddenly disrupted on September 9 when the first Chinese forces arrived in Hanoi to disarm the Japanese. General Lu Han, a warlord from southern China, led between 125,000 and 150,000 troops into famine-stricken Tonkin. Swarming down from China like a ravenous horde of human locusts, these soldiers plundered and looted everything in their path. Their officers were even more destructive. Establishing a new exchange rate between the Chinese dollar and the Vietnamese piaster, General Lu Han made Chinese money worth three times more in Hanoi than at home. The Chinese then began using their overvalued currency to buy local businesses and property at little cost to themselves. Unlike the British in the south, Lu Han had no intention of helping the French regain control of northern Vietnam. Instead, he was willing to let the Vietminh govern Tonkin while his army gouged the whole region. Lu Han and his cohorts in southern China viewed the occupation of northern Vietnam as an opportunity to impose their own long-range program of economic exploitation in Indochina.

But the Nationalist government in China, headed by Generalissimo Chiang Kai-shek, had different ideas. Uninterested in controlling any part of Indochina on a permanent basis, Chiang viewed the Chinese occupation of northern Vietnam as a chance to extract political concessions from France. The Generalissimo succeeded in working out a deal with the French on the last day of February 1946. The French agreed to relinquish their old imperial right of extraterritoriality in China, and in return Chiang agreed to allow French troops to replace Chinese forces in Tonkin. A week later, on March 6, Ho Chi Minh signed an ambiguous treaty with the French. Ho agreed to permit 15,000 French soldiers to land peaceably in northern Vietnam but with the understanding that they would be gradually withdrawn during the next five years. The French agreed to recognize the Democratic Republic of Vietnam as a free state but only on the condition that it would remain part of the French Union. Finally, both parties agreed that there would be a referendum in Cochinchina to determine whether it would be reunited with the rest of Vietnam or remain a separate state in the French Union.

Ho Chi Minh signed this unpalatable treaty because he feared the Chinese more than the French. Chiang was determined to make his own agreement with France operative, and he therefore pressured Ho to allow the return of French troops into northern Vietnam. Not wanting to risk war with both France and China at the same time, Ho decided to compromise with the French in order to get the Chinese out of his country. Many of his colleagues charged him with making a bad deal, but Ho answered his critics with a lesson in geopolitics. "You fools!" he lectured. "Don't you realize what it means if the Chinese remain? Don't you remember your history? The last time the Chinese came, they stayed a thousand years. The French are foreigners. They are weak. Colonialism is dying. The white man is finished in Asia. But if the Chinese stay now, they will never go. As for me, I prefer to sniff French shit for five years than eat Chinese shit for the rest of my life."

But the French had no intention of abiding by the provisions of their treaty with Ho Chi Minh. The French refused to hold a plebiscite in Cochinchina because they realized that the vast majority of the peasants would vote for reunification with the rest of Vietnam. The French also rejected a Vietminh request for a cease-fire in southern Vietnam. In the spring of 1946, therefore, Ho traveled to France to try to work out a permanent settlement. But he could not find a middle ground. The French were not interested in making peace if it meant that they would lose any part of their Indochina empire, and Ho was not willing to make peace if it meant that he would have to sacrifice the independence of his country.

Ho left France empty-handed after months of fruitless negotiations, and when he arrived home in the autumn of 1946 he found both sides preparing for a military showdown. While the French were building up their troop strength in Vietnam, General Vo Nguyen Giap had increased the size of his regular army from 30,000 to 60,000 men. The clash soon came. Using heavy naval guns, the French shelled Vietminh forces in the port of Haiphong on November 23, and when the Vietminh attacked French troops in Hanoi on December 19, a general war erupted.

After he had ignored repeated pleas from Ho Chi Minh for American support for Vietnamese independence, President Truman decided to assist France as full-scale fighting commenced in Tonkin. He and his advisers in the State Department chose not to exert pressure on Paris to make concessions that might end the bloodletting in Indochina for fear that France would refuse to help check the spread of Russian influence in Europe. Their Europe-first mentality was reinforced by their increasing concern about the communist leadership of the Vietminh. But while American policymakers preferred French colonialism over Vietnamese communism, they did not want to be charged with sponsoring Western imperialism in the Far East. Thus they tried to camouflage American aid for the French military campaign in Vietnam by channeling most of it indirectly through metropolitan France. The United States sent France huge amounts of money and large quantities of weapons ostensibly for French economic reconstruction and European strategic protection. But American officials realized that the French were using a considerable portion of this military and financial assistance to sustain their war effort in Indochina.

Yet the French, even with the aid they were receiving from the United States, still could not defeat the Vietminh. Beginning in December 1946, General Giap launched a series of intense attacks against French positions in the principal towns in Tonkin. But his poorly armed troops were no match for the overwhelming French firepower, and they were quickly driven out of the urban areas. The Vietminh then turned to guerrilla warfare in the north just as they had done earlier in the south, fighting chiefly at night when it was hard for the French to bomb them from the air or batter them with heavy ground artillery. Their hit-and-run tactics frustrated the French who had difficulty separating the guerrilla forces from the general population. The Vietminh frequently infiltrated villages and fired at French troops, and often the French responded by destroying the villages and killing many innocent civilians. As a result, more and more enraged peasants either joined the guerrillas or at least gave them information about French movements. So although the French were able to exercise their authority in most of the cities and towns throughout Vietnam, the Vietminh controlled over half of the countryside and over half of the population.

But the French were determined to crush the Vietminh. In October 1947, they mounted a major offensive against the Vietminh base area in the mountains north of Hanoi. The French captured large stores of Vietminh food and ammunition, yet they could not destroy their elusive foe. The guerrillas easily disappeared into the jungle when they heard the distant roar of French tanks and trucks rumbling along the narrow roads. Not only were the gains minimal, but the costs were prohibitive. The Vietminh staged ambush after ambush as the overextended French soldiers retreated slowly down the roads winding through the jungle-covered mountains of northern Tonkin. The French suffered heavy casualties: over 1,000 killed and over 3,000 wounded. The Vietminh were encouraged by their success, and early in 1948 they increased their attacks on isolated French outposts and exposed French convoys.

Unable to win a decisive battlefield victory, the French soon began to search for a political solution for their troubles in Indochina. They ultimately decided to install a puppet government in Vietnam under former Emperor Bao Dai with the hope of uniting all noncommunist nationalists behind the new regime. Bao Dai had fled to Hong Kong after the establishment of the Democratic Republic of Vietnam, but the French succeeded in persuading him to return home and assume the appearance of power. In an agreement with Bao Dai in June 1948, the French declared their recognition of Vietnamese independence within the framework of the French Union. Yet the status of Cochinchina remained unsettled, and Vietnamese nationalists were skeptical about French intentions. In a second agreement with Bao Dai in March 1949, the French promised that Cochinchina would be reunited with Annam and Tonkin, but they stipulated that both the military affairs and foreign relations of Vietnam must remain in their hands. Because the French were not willing to grant Bao Dai real independence, most noncommunist nationalists refused to back his regime. And since many of these conservatives concluded that they had no alternative but to follow Ho Chi Minh, the Vietminh achieved complete control of the Vietnamese resistance movement.

Despite the fact that Bao Dai lacked popular support, however, the Truman administration decided to back him. Red China and Soviet Russia opened diplomatic relations with the Democratic Republic of Vietnam in late January 1950, and a week later the United States formally recognized the Bao Dai puppet government. Still not satisfied, the French asked the United States for more aid for their military operations in Indochina. Secretary of State Dean G. Acheson worried that every franc that the French spent in Vietnam was one less franc they could use for the defense of Europe. Besides their desire to provide financial relief for France, Acheson and his colleagues in the State Department hoped to use American aid as a lever to compel the French not only to agree to the rearmament of West Germany but also to grant independence to the Bao Dai regime. But the French responded to American pressure by warning that without more support from the United States they might have to withdraw from Vietnam. Although the French remained intransigent, President Truman approved a $15 million aid package on March 10 to underwrite the French war effort in Indochina. With that seemingly small step, taken just a few months before the outbreak of the Korean War, the United States significantly moved from affording indirect to direct support for French colonialism in Indochina.

The Crisis of World Capitalism

The American decision to cross that bridge grew out of concerns over a profound dislocation in the international economic system following World War II. The United States had enormously expanded its industrial capacity during the war, and American leaders realized the need for an enlarged export trade to avoid falling back into the depths of a depression. They also understood that the industrial countries of Europe needed to import capital goods from the United States to get their devastated factories running once again. But the European nations, victors and vanquished alike, did not have enough dollars to pay for the vital products that they needed to buy from the United States. American leaders referred to this global economic disequilibrium as the "dollar gap" in world trade. The United States was exporting far more than it was importing, and as the American export surplus grew the dollar gap widened. In fact, the trade imbalance ballooned from $7.8 billion in 1946 to $11.6 billion a year later.

European countries responded to their shortage of dollars by resorting to a wide range of controls over their international economic transactions. They aimed to conserve their dollars by using them only for essential capital goods and not on less important products. European nations not only limited the amount of their currency that could be converted into dollars for the purchase of American merchandise, but they also erected high tariffs to protect their domestic industries from American competition. Besides impeding the flow of trade across the Atlantic with monetary restrictions and customs barriers, Europeans entered into bilateral barter arrangements that closed more doors against American commerce. Government officials and business leaders in the United States feared that if the dollar gap problem remained unsolved, these measures of economic nationalism would become permanent and the European countries would turn toward either state capitalism or socialism. In other words, they worried that the European governments would manage their economies and isolate their countries from world markets and thereby shatter the American dream of a liberal capitalist international community.

The Marshall Plan, formally called the European Recovery Program (ERP), was the major American response to the crisis in world capitalism. Between 1948 and 1952, the United States provided $17 billion for European economic recovery. This huge sum was a gift rather than a loan to the nations of Western Europe. The United States government decided against lending the money because when the time arrived for the European countries to service their debts they would have fewer dollars available to buy surplus American commodities. By giving the money without demanding repayment, the United States government aimed to reduce the European dollar deficit and thereby sustain a high level of American exports. The basic goal of the Marshall Plan was to reconstruct the industries of Western Europe and make them competitive in the markets of the world. If the European countries became strong enough to sell abroad, they could earn foreign exchange needed to buy goods from the United States. American leaders hoped to make European manufacturers lean and mean by insisting that they cut wages and pay less in taxes. They also demanded that European governments reduce social welfare spending and deflate their currencies in order to lower the price of their industrial products.

The State Department assumed the difficult task of convincing Congress of the need for the Marshall Plan. American diplomats did not think that Congress would appropriate funds to support the postwar reconstruction of Europe for humanitarian reasons. Nor did they believe that Congress understood the serious nature of the international economic crisis. But they knew that Congress was concerned about military security. In soliciting financial aid for the European Recovery Program, therefore, State Department officials emphasized strategic factors rather than humanitarian or economic considerations. They not only pointed to the communist coup in Czechoslovakia as an example of Russian expansion into Eastern Europe, but they also warned that countries in Western Europe might become communist if they remained impoverished.

Besides exaggerating the Red menace in Europe, American diplomats assured Congress that the Marshall Plan was only a temporary measure required to meet an emergency situation. They likewise asserted that the program was a great success when the time came each year for Congress to appropriate money for European recovery.

But they knew that their claims were not completely true. While industrial production was increasing in the nations of Western Europe, these countries did not have adequate export markets where they could acquire foreign exchange needed to cover their trade deficit. Not only did the Soviet Union close the doors of Eastern Europe against the products of Western Europe, but the United States also maintained relatively high tariff rates on European goods. Although the State Department advocated a liberal commercial policy, Congress refused to lower customs duties and thereby incur the wrath of protectionist interests. Nor could Congress be convinced to extend the Marshall Plan, which was due to expire in 1952. After receiving repeated assurances about the success of the European Recovery Program, Congress was in no mood to appropriate another $17 billion for the next four years. Secretary of State Acheson explained the situation to President Truman in February 1950: "Put in its simplest terms the problem is this: as ERP is reduced, and after its termination in 1952, how can Europe and other areas of the world obtain the dollars necessary to pay for a high level of United States exports, which is essential both to their own basic needs and to the well-being of the United States economy? This is the problem of the 'dollar gap' in world trade."

Before the dollar gap had created a crisis in American diplomacy, many government officials and business leaders hoped that China would become a golden market for the United States. They were captivated by the vision of a New China, containing 400 million customers, emerging from the ashes of World War II as a modern nation under the conservative leadership of Chiang Kai-shek. El Dorado beckoned from across the Pacific. But to keep the potentially vast China market free from the danger of foreign domination, the United States needed to declaw the Japanese dragon. General Douglas MacArthur was therefore commissioned to occupy Japan as soon as the war came to a close. Between 1945 and 1947, the American occupational authorities disarmed Japan and purged the military caste to prevent the old warlords from ever again threatening the peace of the Far East. The American authorities also aimed during the first two years of the military occupation to destroy the zaibatsu system of family capitalism in Japan and thereby render the interlocking monopolies less capable of manufacturing the sinews of war.

But the United States quickly reversed the course of its occupational policy in Japan when it became evident that Mao Tse-tung and his communist followers would emerge triumphant in China. Beginning in 1947, American administrators in Japan shifted thier emphasis away from political reform and toward economic recovery. Policymakers in Washington decided that the Japanese industrial structure should be rebuilt so that Japan could replace China as a large market for American products. They wanted Japan to be part of the trilateral core in a new liberal capitalist world system: the United States would be the major workshop in the Western Hemisphere; Western Europe would be a regional workshop centered around West Germany; and Japan would be the industrial workshop in the Far East. American policymakers also decided that the Japanese should be rearmed so that Japan could replace China as an important military ally of the United States. They wanted Japan to serve as the sheet anchor in an island chain of American military bases around the Asian rim. In short, Japan was to play a key role as a junior economic and strategic partner in the evolving Pax Americana.

The United States implemented the so-called Dodge Plan in 1949 in an effort to promote the postwar reconstruction of Japan. Like the Marshall Plan for Western Europe, the basic goal of the Dodge Plan was to revive industrial production in Japan and to make Japanese goods competitive in world markets. The United States did not, however, funnel billions of dollars into Japan for industrial renovation. Unlike the Europeans, therefore, the Japanese were forced to finance their own economic rehabitation. The Dodge Plan required severe cuts in wages and social welfare services and the reinvestment of profits in plant modernization. In addition, it demanded a balanced budget as well as the suppression of labor strikes to keep inflation down and prices low. But the Dodge Plan failed for the very same reason that the Marshall Plan proved inadequate. Although their industrial output increased, the Japanese lacked export outlets where they could acquire foreign exchange needed to purchase American goods. Thus Japan, like the countries of Western Europe, continued to suffer from a large dollar deficit.

The State Department advocated a huge rearmament program as a short-run solution to the global dollar gap problem. American companies would be less dependent upon foreign markets for civilian commodities if they received large military orders from the armed forces of the United States. Massive military spending would compensate both for the lack of foreign demand for American products and for the tariff wall that prevented foreign countries from obtaining a sufficient outlet for civilian goods in the United States. European countries and Japan could earn dollars if the armed forces of the United States purchased military hardware from overseas sources. In short, the offshore procurement of military equipment would replace foreign economic aid as a way of getting dollars to Europe and Japan. The State Department succeeded in persuading Congress to appropriate funds for a vast military buildup by playing upon fears of an international communist conspiracy to dominate the whole world. But the Mutual Security Program, conceived prior to the Korean War, was intended more as an interim solvent for the international economic crisis than as a check against Soviet expansion.

The State Department simultaneously called for the reintegration of colonial areas into a liberal international trading system as the long-run solution to the dollar gap problem. Before World War II, an important triangular trade pattern had evolved: the United States used dollars to buy raw materials from colonial areas; they in turn used these dollars to purchase industrial goods from European countries; and then they used the same dollars to pay for American products. For example, the United States purchased large quantities of rubber and tin from British Malaya with dollars, and British Malaya bought manufactured articles from Great Britain with these dollars, and finally the United Kingdom paid for American commodities with the same dollars. State Department officials hoped to reestablish this kind of triangular trade flow in order to restore international economic equilibrium, and they succeeded in getting federal funds earmarked for increasing the production of foodstuffs and raw materials in colonial areas. The precedent for this form of economic assistance was set in February 1950 when the Export-Import Bank received authorization to lend Indonesia $100 million to buy American equipment needed for the development of natural resources.

American policymakers believed that the expansion of primary commodity production in Southeast Asia was particularly important for the restoration of Japanese prosperity. They hoped that Japan would be able not only to obtain foodstuffs and raw materials in Southeast Asia without paying dollars for these essential imports but also to earn dollars by exporting manufactured goods to Southeast Asia. American leaders thought that in some parts of Southeast Asia the introduction of more irrigation would allow for the cultivation of two rice crops per year instead of the prevailing single crop. If these areas doubled their rice yield, they might also double their purchases of industrial products from Japan. Aiming to stimulate mineral and agricultural production throughout Southeast Asia, American economic experts estimated that by 1955 the region could absorb more than 50 percent of Japan's total exports. China had been Japan's most important market in the Far East before World

War II, but after China fell to communism in 1949, American diplomats feared that Japan, if denied access to noncommunist markets in Southeast Asia, might become economically dependent upon Red China and be lured into making a political accommodation with the communist bloc. Thus they hoped that Southeast Asia would become Japan's major market in the Orient.

But Southeast Asia lacked political stability. Although the economic task of increasing the production of primary commodities in that part of the world would not require a large amount of American capital, the United States faced a difficult political problem there. Communist rebels and conservative nationalists were challenging colonial rule in French Indochina, British Malaya, and the Dutch East Indies. Regarding the military pacification of the region as a prerequisite for the economic revival of Japan, American policymakers concluded that the United States would have to help contain the rising tide of revolution in Southeast Asia. Before the Japanese or anyone else could walk the commercial streets of Southeast Asia, they repeatedly argued, those streets would have to be made safe from communism. A joint report, made by the Departments of State and Defense in January 1950, went to the heart of the matter: "Continuing, or even maintaining, Japan's economic recovery depends upon keeping Communism out of Southeast Asia, promoting economic recovery there and in further developing those countries, together with Indonesia, the Philippines, Southern Korea and India as the principal trading areas for Japan."

Concerned about Japan's need for noncommunist markets in Southeast Asia, officials in both the State Department and the Pentagon regarded French Indochina as vitally important to the political stability of the entire region. They realized that Vietnam, Cambodia, and Laos could absorb only a small amount of Japanese goods, but they perceived these French colonies as the linchpin in the long crescent that stretched from Japan all the way to India. French Indochina, while possessing little intrinsic commercial value for Japan, occupied a key strategic position between Red China to the north and the vast Malaya Archipelago to the south. Following the fall of China to communism in 1949, American policymakers subscribed to what came to be called the "domino theory," which held that if the Vietminh defeated the French in Indochina the cancer of communism would spread throughout the whole region. Guerrilla forces in other parts of Southeast Asia would not only be encouraged by the success of their neighbors in overcoming European colonialism, but they would also be able to obtain weapons from nearby communist countries. American leaders therefore feared that if the Vietnam domino fell to communism, it would tip over others until finally the whole row would be knocked down.

Such dire prospects generated a debate in the State Department over the wisdom of supplying direct American aid for the French military campaign in Indochina. A few State Department officials were pessimistic about the chances for a French victory because the Vietminh had widespread backing. Noting that the French were fighting against a large portion of the Vietnamese population, these skeptics concluded that the French would ultimately lose even if they received a massive dose of American financial and technical assistance. But Secretary of State Acheson and most of his top aides argued that the United States should back the French and Bao Dai even if the odds were heavily against them. While acknowledging that Bao Dai lacked popular support, they assumed that he was the only alternative to Ho Chi Minh. Acheson and his followers noted that Ho aimed to establish a communist government in Vietnam after he achieved his nationalist aspirations. They feared that if the French were driven out of Vietnam the rest of Southeast Asia would be in grave danger of succumbing to the forces of communism. They also worried that the French would object to American plans to include West Germany in a multilateral European military force if the United States refused to subsidize their war effort in Indochina.

Secretary Acheson and his colleagues in the State Department were determined to resist not only the expansion of Russian influence in Europe but also the spread of indigenous communism in Southeast Asia. They understood that communism was not monolithic and that all communist leaders did not take orders from Moscow. Marshal Tito, for example, had established an independent communist regime in Yugoslavia that remained free from Soviet domination. Acheson admitted in May 1949 that Vietnam might in fact develop as a "National Communist State on the pattern of Yugoslavia," but he thought that the United States should explore that possibility "only if every other avenue closed." While clearly preferring the puppet Bao Dai to a Titoist Ho Chi Minh, Acheson envisioned three different scenarios for the Indochina War: the Vietminh might defeat the French and become tools of the Kremlin; the Vietminh might win and establish an independent communist government in Vietnam that would remain free from Russian control; or the French might emerge victorious and stamp out the germ of communism before it infected the whole region. Given these choices, Acheson and his associates favored French colonialism rather than either international or indigenous communism.

The State Department believed that it was imperative for economic reasons to prevent any kind of communism from sweeping across Southeast Asia. American diplomats feared that even if Asian communists steered clear of Soviet political influence, they would follow the Russian model for economic growth. By emphasizing industrial development rather than the production of primary commodities, communist countries in Southeast Asia would become more self-sufficient and less dependent upon foreign commerce. Thus the spread of economic nationalism along with indigenous communism would restrict the opportunity for Japan and the capitalist countries of Western Europe to exchange manufactured goods for foodstuffs and raw materials produced in Southeast Asia. Prompted by such thoughts, the State Department decided in February 1950 to recommend direct American financial support for the French war effort in Indochina. Acheson and his colleagues urged that the United States should furnish money but not soldiers so that the war could be fought with American equipment and French troops. As already noted, President Truman gave his approval on March 10 to the proposal to provide the French with $15 million for their military operations in Indochina.

The Korean War, which began three months later, reinforced the American determination to draw the line against the advance of communism in Southeast Asia. Although the conflict in Korea took American policymakers by surprise, it actually helped them accomplish their basic objectives in the Far East. The hostilities in Korea made it easier for the Truman administration to get Congress to appropriate larger and larger sums of money to fund the French struggle against the Vietminh. They also provided the United States with the opportunity to purchase more and more military equipment from Japan. But while the Japanese were temporarily able to earn dollars by selling military supplies to the American army fighting in Korea, President Truman and his advisers continued to regard Japanese economic integration with Southeast Asia as the permanent solution to the dollar gap problem in Japan. They likewise continued to worry that the Japanese would be pulled into the communist political and economic orbit if they were denied access to noncommunist markets in Southeast Asia. "Communist control of all Southeast Asia," a State Department memorandum warned in March 1952, "would remove the chief potential area for Japanese commercial development, and would so add to the already powerful mainland pulls upon Japan as to make it dubious that Japan could refrain from reaching an accommodation with the Communist bloc."

The Bao Dai Regime

The United States government, while sponsoring military action to keep the doors of Southeast Asia open to Japan and other industrial countries, advocated a political solution to the conflict in Indochina. Realizing that French colonialism was fanning the flames of Vietnamese communism, American officials repeatedly urged the French to make political concessions to Bao Dai to help him broaden his base of support. They hoped that if Bao Dai had more autonomy he would be able to woo the noncommunist Vietnamese nationalists who were backing Ho Chi Minh. In August 1950, the Policy Planning Staff in the State Department concluded that the only hope for peace lay in getting the French to set a definite date for granting independence to Indochina. The Joint Strategic Survey Committee similarly reasoned in October 1950 that a French military victory would provide only a temporary solution to the hostilities in Indochina. Even if the French defeated the Vietminh, the committee warned, there would be renewed outbreaks of guerrilla warfare unless the French satisfied the Vietnamese demand for self-government. Thus the committee concluded that a permanent solution to the war in Indochina depended upon the ability of Bao Dai to win the hearts and minds of the Vietnamese people.

But the United States government was not able to persuade the French to relinquish their imperial rule in Indochina. American policymakers regarded a noncommunist Vietnam as essential to their objectives in Southeast Asia, yet they feared a French withdrawal from Indochina if the United States threatened to stop funding their war effort. They also worried that politicians in Paris would continue to oppose American plans for German rearmament if France lacked sufficient resources to maintain a strong army in Europe. Realizing their leverage in Washington, the French warned again and again that without American aid for their Indochina campaign they would be unable to shoulder the burden of helping to defend Europe. The French not only ignored American political advice, they also refused to permit the small American Military Assistance Advisory Group (MAAG) to participate in strategic planning in Indochina. But the United States never threatened the French with a cutoff in aid for their military operations in Vietnam if they did not comply with American wishes. As a result, France obtained increasingly large amounts of American military assistance with no strings attached.

The French had goals in Indochina that differed fundamentally from those of their American benefactors. Rather than safeguarding commercial opportunities for Japan throughout Southeast Asia, they wanted to maintain their monopoly over the markets of Vietnam, Cambodia, and Laos. The French were struggling to suppress communism in order to perpetuate colonialism. Determined to protect their overseas economic interests and not to promote the development of democracy in Indochina, they repeatedly rejected mild American suggestions that a promise of independence for their Indochina possessions would wean noncommunist Vietnamese nationalists away from the Vietminh. The French were fighting to keep their colonial empire intact. In line with their tenpin theory, they aimed to preserve their economic privileges in North Africa as well as in East Asia. But the French were trying to crush a popular movement for national liberation, and this hard political fact meant that they faced an uphill battle.

The fall of China to communism added to their troubles by altering the strategic situation in Vietnam. In late 1949, Red China began supplying the Vietminh rebels with automatic weapons, mortars, howitzers, and trucks. Chinese advisers joined Vietminh units to show them how to use the new equipment, and Vietminh detachments crossed over the border to receive special training at camps inside China. Determined to keep open the vital supply routes from China, General Giap initiated a campaign to oust the French from their positions near the northern frontier of Tonkin. His forces began attacking isolated French military posts along the Chinese border in September 1950, and one by one the French garrisons fell as many of the French defenders fled in panic. During the autumn fighting, the French lost some 6,000 men and abandoned enough arms to equip an entire Vietminh division. It was the greatest colonial defeat for the French since General Montcalm had died during the Battle of Quebec 200 years earlier.

The Truman administration was alarmed about the state of affairs in Vietnam. Responding to urgent requests from Paris for help, President Truman promptly agreed to provide an additional $33 million in military aid for the French forces in Indochina. Secretary of State Acheson thought that the French needed more than money, however, and in January 1951 he told his colleagues that the only daylight he could see lay in the possibility of building a strong and effective Vietnamese national army to help the French. Besides expressing concern about the deteriorating military situation, American leaders worried about political conditions in Vietnam. They knew that the Bao Dai regime, largely composed of wealthy landlords, did not represent the interests of the great mass of Vietnamese peasants. During the next two years, therefore, the Truman administration tried to buy popular support for Bao Dai by supplying more than $50 million in economic and technical assistance to help buttress his puppet government.

While American leaders were pessimistic about circumstances in Vietnam, General Giap responded with optimism to his impressive victories in northern Tonkin. He mistakenly concluded that his Vietminh forces were now strong enough to embark upon a war of movement to drive the French out of the Red River valley. In January 1951, Giap led his regular troops down from their mountain retreat and launched a large-scale attack against French positions around the town of Vinh Yen, located only about twenty-five miles from Hanoi. Giap ordered human wave assaults for the first time, but the French superiority in aviation and artillery proved decisive. The Vietminh lost more than 6,000 soldiers during the battle. Although the French succeeded in inflicting heavy casualties, they too suffered large losses, and their narrow victory would not have been possible without the use of American technology. The terrifying napalm bombs and the 105-millimeter howitzers that the French had obtained from the United States enabled them to avoid being overwhelmed by the Vietminh.

But Giap was not deterred by his close defeat. He had yet to learn that napalm flames made human wave assaults a deadly and futile undertaking. Still confident that the Vietminh could take Hanoi, Giap directed two major attacks in the spring of 1951 against French positions in the Red River delta. The results were similar to those in the battle around Vinh Yen. The French defenders used American firepower to repulse the Vietminh attackers, and both sides sustained high losses. But while the French enjoyed a brief emotional uplift after the smoke cleared, they were unable to follow up their narrow victories over the Vietminh. The bloody encounters convinced Giap that his troops were not yet ready for a general offensive against the French. Once again the Vietminh reverted to hit-and-run tactics, and the French once more found themselves blindly stabbing at empty spaces in the jungles of Vietnam.

General Jean de Lattre de Tassigny, the commander of the French Expeditionary Corps in Indochina, had already decided to construct a chain of defensive fortresses around the entire Red River valley. Completed in the late spring of 1951, the de Lattre Line was designed to cut off the Vietminh guerrillas from their sources of food, money, and manpower in the Tonkin delta. But the de Lattre Line leaked like a sieve. The Vietminh walked right past the dispersed French forts at night, and by the end of 1953 the rebels controlled more than half of the villages in the Red River valley. In the meantime, de Lattre organized troops that were not engaged in static defense into mobile groups to pursue the guerrillas into the highlands. But these motorized French units, dependent as they were on American tanks and trucks, became prisoners of the roads. The heavily equipped forces could not catch the lightly armed rebels before they disappeared into the dense jungles. Worse yet, the Vietminh coaxed the slow-moving French pursuers into one ambush after another.

The Vietminh guerrillas had one crucial advantage over the French: the great majority of the Vietnamese population sympathized with their struggle for national independence. Their evasions and ambushes succeeded because the peasants rarely informed the French about their movements. The communist leaders of the Vietminh were viewed as authentic nationalists whose ultimate aims could not be achieved until after they had fulfilled the immediate aspirations of the Vietnamese people. The strength of the Vietminh rebels rested upon their ability to mobilize the masses. At night, the Vietminh dominated the entire countryside including areas nominally under French control. The guerrillas were therefore able to collect taxes in the form of rice, recruit soldiers, gather information about French plans, and terrorize their opponents. In fact, the Vietminh succeeded in organizing the bulk of the Vietnamese population in their war for national liberation. While many young men joined the rebel ranks, their parents and children often made booby traps and other primitive weapons to help defeat the French.

Fighting to free their country, Ho Chi Minh and his comrades did not act at all like Bao Dai and his dishonest cohorts. Vietminh agents collected a rice tax to promote their cause rather than to enrich themselves. The top Vietminh leaders led spartan lives, and not even their worst enemies accused them of corruption. At the same time, the high officials in the Bao Dai regime lived in luxury at the expense of the Vietnamese people. Bao Dai himself was receiving a personal allowance in excess of $4 million a year from the United States government, and he was transferring large sums of money into French and Swiss banks so that he would still be wealthy if someday he were run out of Vietnam. The pathetic figurehead was little more than a playboy who especially enjoyed having illicit affairs with beautiful French women. Realizing his own position in Vietnam, he once defended one of his blonde playmates when reporters penetrated her façade. "That girl is really good in bed," Bao Dai insisted. "She is only plying her trade. I'm the real whore."

Since large amounts of American supplies as well as dollars continued to go down the drain in Vietnam, General de Lattre traveled to Washington in September 1951 to plead for more military assistance. The United States promptly began shipping the French army in Indochina over 130,000 tons of equipment, including 53 million rounds of ammunition, 200 aircraft, 650 combat vehicles, and 14,000 automatic weapons. But many of these arms and materials were either destroyed by besieged French units or captured by the Vietminh. Between December 1951 and February 1952, General Giap directed a series of vicious attacks against French strongholds around Hoa Binh, located in the highlands southwest of Hanoi. The Vietminh quickly cut off both the water and land routes to Hoa Binh, and the French lost many men and armaments attempting to reopen their lines of communication. While de Lattre lay dying from cancer in Paris, the decision was made in Indochina to abandon Hoa Binh. The French completed the evacuation with relatively light casualties, but they blew up 150 tons of supplies and ammunition because they lacked the means to transport these materials back to the Red River delta.

Despite their readiness to continue making major contributions to the French war chest, however, American leaders were not about to dispatch United States ground forces to Vietnam. The Joint Chiefs of Staff had their hands full in Korea, and they argued firmly against American involvement in a second war on the Asian mainland. Always mindful of their worldwide strategic responsibilities, these military authorities did not want the United States to endanger the security of Europe by becoming overextended in the Far East. Many American leaders thought that Indochina might even have to be abandoned if the Chinese decided to send soldiers to help the Vietminh fight the French. But President Truman and his top advisers refused to write off Indochina. In June 1952, Truman approved a National Security Council (NSC) plan calling for the bombardment of Chinese cities and the blockade of Chinese coasts if Chinese troops swarmed into Vietnam. It was thus decided that in the event of Chinese intervention in Indochina the American reaction should be limited to naval and aerial attacks against China and that the United States should avoid becoming bogged down in another Asian ground war.

A few months later, the French started making plans for a massive attack against the Vietminh. Their offensive, launched in October 1952, was the largest one that they had ever mounted in Indochina. The French deployed more than 30,000 troops along with a great many tanks and airplanes in an effort to entrap the Vietminh guerrillas in the jungles northwest of Hanoi. But the French soon came under heavy Vietminh attack, and within a few weeks they began retreating back into the Red River valley. After this French offensive went into reverse, it became obvious to American leaders that the war in Indochina had reached a stalemate. But Truman and Acheson would not be in office much longer to deal with the disturbing situation. Dwight D. Eisenhower won the presidential election in November 1952, and he promptly appointed John Foster Dulles to serve as his secretary of state. In a meeting with the president-elect two weeks later, Acheson warned that a strong body of opinion in France regarded Indochina as a lost cause. So it would be up to Eisenhower and Dulles to try to figure out a way to break the military deadlock in Indochina before the French lost their will to carry on the war.

T H R E E

America's Mandarin

If we don't assist Japan, gentlemen, Japan is going Communist. Then instead of the Pacific being an American lake, believe me it is going to be a Communist lake.

President Dwight D. Eisenhower, 1954

The Road to Dien Bien Phu

The Republican administration of Dwight D. Eisenhower accepted without modification the basic principles of the Indochina policy bequeathed by the Democrats. When they assumed control of American diplomacy in January 1953, President Eisenhower and Secretary of State John Foster Dulles agreed that the United States should make a concerted effort to prevent the fall of Indochina to communism. They subscribed to the prevailing belief that, if the Vietminh were to win in Vietnam, the cancer of communism might spread throughout the entire region. They feared that Japan, if denied access to noncommunist markets in Southeast Asia, might be pulled out of the international capitalist trading network. They also worried that French officials, if deprived of American support for their war effort in Indochina, would continue to balk at proposals for the establishment of a European Defense Community (EDC) that would include West German forces. Eisenhower and Dulles thought much like Truman and Acheson before them. Although reluctant to commit American combat forces in Vietnam, they were determined to continue the policy of providing American financial support to buttress the French military campaign in Indochina.

President Eisenhower and Secretary of States Dulles, however, were alarmed about growing signs of war weariness in France. By the end of 1952, the number of French soldiers killed, wounded, missing, and captured in Indochina totaled more than 90,000 since the conflict had begun. The French were losing young officers in the jungles and rice paddies of Vietnam faster than they could be replaced with graduates from the military academy at Saint-Cyr. As French casualties continued to climb, public support for what the French had come to call the "dirty war" rapidly waned. More and more French politicians and newspapers began advocating negotiations with the Vietminh to stop the loss of lives and francs in Indochina. And as the antiwar sentiment intensified in France, the apprehension grew in Washington that French public opinion might impel the government in Paris to seek a negotiated settlement rather than a military victory in Indochina.

Eisenhower and Dulles were eager to break the stalemate in Indochina before French leaders bowed to public pressure and sued for peace. In March 1953, Dulles informed the French government that the United States believed that it was essential for the French to prepare a plan that would lead to a victory in Indochina within two years. Dulles urged the French not only to develop an aggressive military strategy but also to expand the indigenous Vietnamese National Army into an effective fighting force. But Eisenhower and Dulles, like their predecessors, realized that without a French promise to restore home rule in Vietnam after the war the Vietnamese people would have no reason to help the French win. They likewise understood that a battlefield victory alone would not solve the fundamental political problem in Indochina. In May 1953, therefore, Eisenhower urged the French government to make a clear and unequivocal statement that Indochina would be granted complete independence as soon as the Vietminh were defeated.

The Korean War armistice, which was concluded in July 1953, gave Eisenhower and Dulles additional cause for concern. They feared that the Chinese communists might intervene in Vietnam since their soldiers were no longer engaged in Korea. Dulles tried to deter the Chinese in September 1953 by issuing a stern public statement implying that the United States would drop nuclear bombs on China if that country entered the Indochina conflict. But while the Chinese refrained from sending combat troops to Vietnam, they did begin supplying the Vietminh with large numbers of trucks, heavy artillery pieces, and antiaircraft guns. The cease-fire in Korea, besides generating apprehensions about the Chinese, gave rise to worries in Washington that the Japanese dollar gap would widen because of a decline in American orders for military equipment made in Japan. Determined to keep Southeast Asia open to Japanese trade and investment, Eisenhower and Dulles repeatedly articulated their commitment to preventing the forces of communism from toppling the Indochina dominoes.

But the Korean War armistice gave added strength to the antiwar movement in France. If the United States had negotiated a settlement in Korea after failing to achieve a military victory, many French political leaders asked, why should not their country do the same in Vietnam? Such reasoning prompted the French parliament in October 1953 to endorse a resolution that called upon the government to explore every possibility for negotiating an end to the fighting in Indochina. In response to this mounting pressure, Premier Joseph Laniel announced on November 12, that if an honorable solution became possible, his government, "like the United States in Korea, would be happy to welcome a diplomatic solution of the conflict." But Laniel did not want to undertake negotations with the Vietminh from a position of weakness. In an attempt to improve his bargaining position before entering into peace talks, therefore, he decided to lead France into one final military campaign in Indochina.

General Henri Navarre had already been appointed to command the French Expeditionary Corps in Indochina. At the urging of American military leaders in July 1953, General Navarre prepared a new strategic plan calling for a vast augmentation in the size of the Vietnamese National Army and the deployment of nine additional battalions of French troops in Indochina. Navarre proposed to consolidate his units that were spread out in static defensive positions, to combine them with new reinforcements into a mobile striking force, and to initiate a major offensive to drive the Vietminh out of the Red River delta. In a secret report to Paris, however, Navarre warned that the Indochina war could not be won in a strict military sense and that the best that could be expected was a draw. Navarre and his government hoped to be able to regain the initiative in Indochina during the next two years with the objective of strengthening their battlefield position prior to the beginning of peace negotiations. Yet the French did not dare to disclose their limited war aims when they asked for American financial aid.

American leaders seriously debated whether or not the United States should bankroll the Navarre Plan. Skeptical about French intentions and capabilities, the Joint Chiefs of Staff (JCS) warned that military success in Indochina depended upon the establishment of a political climate that would give the Vietnamese people an incentive to support the French and to supply them with intelligence about the Vietminh. But the State Department feared that, if Washington refused to finance the Navarre Plan, the French government would negotiate a settlement that would mean "the eventual loss to Communism not only of Indochina but of the whole of Southeast Asia." Finally, after extracting a promise from Paris to pursue the Navarre Plan with vigor, the United States agreed in September 1953 to provide France with an additional $385 million in military assistance. The United States continued to meet the escalating French requests for money and supplies, and as a result American aid made up 78 percent of the French military budget in Indochina during fiscal 1954. In fact, between 1950 and 1954, the United States contributed more than $2.6 billion in direct assistance for the French war effort in Indochina.

Despite this enormous support from the United States, however, General Navarre could not achieve his central objective of recovering the initiative in the Red River valley. Bao Dai had previously cautioned the French not to rely upon Vietnamese recruits to fight for them. "It would be dangerous to expand the Vietnamese Army," he warned, "because it might defect en masse and go to the Vietminh." Nevertheless, in response to American prodding, the French went ahead and organized a 300,000-man Vietnamese auxiliary army. But this large indigenous military force remained poorly trained, poorly led, and poorly motivated. Few middle-class natives would serve as officers in an army fighting against rather than for Vietnamese independence. Nor were many Vietnamese peasant soldiers willing to risk their lives to protect the puppet government in Saigon. Not surprising to Bao Dai, a major reason for the failure of the Navarre Plan lay in the inability of the Vietnamese National Army to hold areas that the French troops had cleared in the Red River delta.

General Giap and his Vietminh forces not only mauled the auxiliary Vietnamese units, they also outmaneuvered General Navarre and his French regulars. While Navarre was concentrating his troops in the Red River valley, Giap intensified guerrilla activities in the Tonkin delta and simultaneously directed a thrust into Laos. Navarre reacted by scattering the very forces he had just combined. In response to the Vietminh drive into Laos, he decided in November 1953 to parachute 3,000 elite

French soldiers onto a plateau just outside Dien Bien Phu, a village located in the northwest corner of Vietnam near the Laotian border. Navarre hoped to cut the supply lines to the Vietminh in Laos and to lure Giap into a large set-piece battle. Confident that his forces were now strong enough for a major confrontation with French regulars, Giap quickly accepted the challenge and ordered his Vietminh troops to encircle the remote French garrison.

The military situation in Vietnam provoked serious concerns in both the United States and France. Although the French had sent another 10,000 soldiers to reinforce their fortress at Dien Bien Phu, the commander of the American Military Assistance Advisory Group warned in January 1954 that the French were operating from an inferior defensive position. He estimated that the French forces at Dien Bien Phu had only a 50–50 chance of survival. Worried more about the overall military picture in Indochina, American army staff planners cautioned on February 7 that there was little evidence that the French had the ability to bring the war to a successful conclusion. The French defense minister and his service chiefs were equally apprehensive. After making an inspection tour of the battlefields in Vietnam, they reported that they could hope for nothing better than an improved military position that might strengthen the hand of French diplomats at a future peace conference.

Faced with a steadily deteriorating military situation in Vietnam and a rapidly growing war-weariness at home, the French government decided to negotiate with the Vietminh. Premier Laniel insisted in February 1954 that the Indochina issue should be discussed at the Geneva Conference scheduled to begin in April for the purpose of working out a political settlement in Korea. The United States government, however, still hoped that France could achieve a military victory in Vietnam. Afraid that the French would consent to peace terms favorable to the Vietminh, Secretary of State Dulles sought to prevent a negotiated settlement. But Laniel warned that his country would not participate in the European Defense Community designed to shield the continent from the Soviet menace if the United States tried to block peace talks between the French and the Vietminh at Geneva. Dulles then reluctantly agreed to have the Indochina question added to the agenda of the forthcoming Geneva Conference.

On March 12, the eve of the Battle of Dien Bien Phu, a Joint Chiefs of Staff memorandum summarized American military thinking in the following way: in the absence of a substantial improvement in the French military position in Vietnam, a negotiated settlement would probably be inconsistent with basic American objectives in Southeast

Asia; a settlement based upon free elections would almost certainly lead to communist control of Indochina; the conquest of the rest of Southeast Asia would inevitably follow the fall of Indochina to the communists unless the Western powers took immediate and effective counteraction; the loss of Southeast Asia to communism would drive Japan into an accommodation with the communist bloc; the United States should therefore urge the French government not to abandon the aggressive prosecution of the war in Vietman until a satisfactory settlement could be achieved; but if the French surrendered any part of Indochina in negotiations with the communists, the United States should not associate itself with such a settlement so that it would remain free to join with other countries in continuing the struggle against the Vietminh without French participation.

On the very next day, March 13, the Vietminh began a massive assault against the French positions at Dien Bien Phu. Giap hoped to hit Navarre with a crushing blow that would sap the will of the French people to continue supporting the costly struggle in Indochina. Navarre likewise aimed to inflict a substantial defeat against Giap at Dien Bien Phu. The French had concluded that the Vietminh would not be able to get heavy artillery up to the high hills surrounding their fortress in the valley below. But the Vietminh used thousands of porters to carry 105- and 75-millimeter howitzers piece by piece up the hills and to reassemble them in caves impervious to French artillery and strafing. The Vietminh immediately trained their big guns on the strongholds along the perimeter of the garrison and quickly drove the French out. Unable to silence the Viteminh batteries, the French artillery commander committed suicide on the second day of the attack. Then the Vietminh pulverized the French airstrip and made preparations for an infantry assault on the besieged French bastion.

The Geneva Peace Settlement

General Paul Ely, the French chief of staff, hurried to the United States while the Vietminh were pounding the French positions at Dien Bien Phu. Upon his arrival in Washington on March 20, General Ely stressed that the French needed more American aircraft if they were to succeed in defending their fortress at Dien Bien Phu. He also argued that, in the event of Chinese intervention in the Indochina conflict, the French would need direct American air support. Noting that the French chances of holding out at Dien Bien Phu were no better than 50 percent, Ely made it clear that the French wanted additional American military aid to help them bolster their battlefield position before the peace conference opened at Geneva. Ely indicated that he had abandoned hope for achieving a military victory in Indochina and that he thought France should seek a diplomatic solution at Geneva.

American policymakers were deeply dismayed by the Ely mission. Secretary of State Dulles informed Ely that he and President Eisenhower would not consider deploying American forces in Vietnam until the French not only granted real independence to the Associated States of Indochina but also demonstrated their resolve to achieve a military victory over the Vietminh. Admiral Arthur W. Radford, the chairman of the Joint Chiefs of Staff, had become increasingly impatient with the French failure to create a strong and effective indigenous army in Vietnam. In a conversation with Ely, Admiral Radford proposed that the Military Assistance Advisory Group should be expanded so that American personnel could help train the Vietnamese National Army. But Ely replied that French prestige would be undermined if the United States assumed the responsibility for training the native forces in Vietnam.

Despite his disappointment, however, Radford told Ely that the United States might be willing to make a massive air strike against the Vietminh forces surrounding Dien Bien Phu. The plan, dubbed Operation Vulture, called for the use of sixty B-29 bombers based in the Philippines, escorted by fighter aircraft from the Seventh Fleet. Radford viewed the proposal not simply as a one-time action to improve the French bargaining position at Geneva but rather as the first step in an escalating American campaign to help defeat the Vietminh. Although Radford made no commitments, Ely returned to France with a strong impression that the White House would approve Operation Vulture if his government requested it. But President Eisenhower informed the National Security Council on March 25 that he would agree to American military intervention in Indochina only under the following two conditions: (1) if other nations would join with the United States in the war effort and (2) if Congress would sanction the deployment of American forces in operations against the Vietminh.

Mindful of these stipulations, American military authorities immediately began debating whether or not the United States should drop atomic bombs to relieve the beleaguered French garrison at Dien Bien Phu. The Army War Plans Division argued on March 25 in favor of such an operation. But General Matthew B. Ridgway, the army chief of staff, opposed the idea. Ridgway promptly ordered another study of the probable consequences of American military intervention in Indochina. This time the Army War Plans Division concluded that, even with the use of tactical nuclear weapons, American air and naval forces alone could not defeat the Vietminh. The army war planners argued that the United States would have to send ground troops to assure an ultimate victory in Indochina. They estimated that seven American combat divisions would be needed if China stayed out of the conflict and that twelve divisions would be required if China became involved.

Admiral Radford then asked the Joint Chiefs of Staff to consider the question of committing American air and naval units to save the French forces at Dien Bien Phu. During a meeting on March 31, General Ridgway argued emphatically against the proposed bombing raid. He reasoned that, even if Operation Vulture proved successful, a victory at Dien Bien Phu would not decisively affect the overall military situation in Indochina. Yet Radford persisted. On April 2, he asked the JCS to reconsider the issue of an atomic attack against the Vietminh to turn the tide of battle at Dien Bien Phu. Both the chief of naval operations and the commandant of the Marine Corps sided with Ridgway in registering their dissent. Only the Air Force chief was willing to give even qualified support for the proposed atomic strike. The JCS therefore concluded that the United States should not respond favorably if France requested American military intervention in Indochina.

Nevertheless the Eisenhower administration proceeded to seek congressional support for possible American military action in Indochina. On April 3, Secretary Dulles invited a bipartisan group of House and Senate leaders to a confidential meeting at the State Department. Dulles showed the senators and representatives a State Department proposal for a congressional resolution empowering the president to use air and naval forces in Southeast Asia. But the legislators made it clear that they would not approve American military intervention in Vietnam until Dulles had obtained firm commitments from allied governments to participate in joint combat operations with the United States. Expressing the unanimous feeling of the group, one legislator declared, "We want no more Koreas with the United States furnishing 90 percent of the manpower." It was the sense of the meeting that the United States should not fight alone and that Dulles should attempt to secure cooperation from Great Britain and other nations. If definite commitments for united military action could be obtained, the consensus of the group was that a congressional resolution along the lines Dulles had drafted could be passed.

The meeting reinforced Eisenhower and Dulles in their desire for united action rather than unilateral intervention. On April 4, the French government officially requested that the United States implement Operation Vulture to lift the siege of Dien Bien Phu. But Eisenhower reaffirmed his determination not to authorize military action without congressional approval and British participation. The president said he would also require assurance that the French would continue fighting in Indochina and grant complete independence to the Associated States. Dulles thereupon informed the French government on April 5 that the United States had decided against military involvement except on a multilateral basis. In a personal letter to Prime Minister Winston Churchill on the same day, Eisenhower asked Great Britain to join the United States in a coalition of nations to help France defeat the Vietminh. The National Security Council and the President's Special Committee on Indochina also urged that maximum diplomatic pressure should be placed on France not to withdraw from the war.

Eisenhower and Dulles wanted to internationalize the Indochina conflict. During a National Security Council meeting on April 6, the president said that he would seek congressional authorization for intervention if a united military front could be established. Eisenhower and his top advisers agreed that the Joint Chiefs of Staff should prepare contingency plans for military operations in Indochina. After the meeting, Dulles immediately departed for England and France in hopes of organizing a multinational military grouping. But he was destined to be disappointed. When he arrived in London, Dulles found that the British opposed military action in Indochina until the chances for a reasonable peace settlement had been explored at the Geneva Conference. Then Dulles learned in Paris that, while the French insisted on maintaining their imperial rule in Indochina, they wanted an American air strike on Dien Bien Phu only to strengthen their negotiating position at Geneva.

This was unacceptable to Eisenhower. Although he advocated united action to prevent the spread of communism in Southeast Asia, Eisenhower refused to consider unilateral intervention on behalf of French colonialism in Indochina. The president was deeply annoyed with the French, and he blamed their military failures on their refusal to grant independence to Vietnam, Cambodia, and Laos. Democratic spokesmen in the Senate gave vent to similar feelings. Senator John F. Kennedy of Massachusetts warned that American military aid would not enable the French to defeat rebel forces that had popular support. Senator Lyndon B. Johnson of Texas agreed. He therefore opposed "sending American G.I.s into the mud and muck of Indochina on a blood-letting spree to perpetuate colonialism and white man's exploitation in Asia." Eisenhower felt the same way, and on April 26 he told congressional leaders that it would be a "tragic error to go in alone as a partner of France."

The American decision not to carry out Operation Vulture sealed the fate of the French garrison at Dien Bien Phu. Giap had ordered human wave assaults against the French defenders in the early days of the battle, but when his losses mounted he instructed his troops to dig a vast network of trenches around the French fortress. Although American military leaders urged Navarre to send a large number of soldiers to reinforce Dien Bien Phu, he lacked the necessary manpower because many of his forces were tied down in military operations elsewhere in Vietnam and Laos. The Vietminh, in the meantime, tunneled closer and closer until they were able to overrun the French positions at the point of fixed bayonet. Finally, on May 7, after fifty-five days of resistance, the French surrendered at Dien Bien Phu. This humiliating defeat, which cost Navarre more than 16,000 troops, signaled the end of the French war effort in Indochina.

The Indochina phase of the Geneva Conference began just one day after the last French gun fell silent at Dien Bien Phu. Pham Van Dong, the spokesman for the Vietminh, hoped to turn Giap's great military victory into an equally impressive political triumph at the peace table. He demanded that France withdraw completely from his country and leave the Vietnamese alone to resolve their differences. He also insisted that France recognize the communist-backed resistance movements in Cambodia and Laos. But China and Russia exerted pressure on the Vietminh to accept a compromise settlement. While the Russians hoped to assure the survival of a French government that opposed the creation of an EDC with West German participation, the Chinese sought to prevent the emergence of a strong Vietnamese empire on their southern frontier. Chou En-lai, the top Chinese delegate at Geneva, persuaded the Vietminh to drop their demand that the Pathet Lao and the Free Khmer rebels occupy parts of Laos and Cambodia. He also convinced the Vietminh to agree that Vietnam should be temporarily divided and then reunified following general elections. Pham Van Dong wanted to hold the elections only six months after the cease-fire, but Russian Foreign Minister Vyacheslav Molotov used his influence to delay the elections for a full two years.

The cease-fire arrangement, worked out at Geneva in July 1954, provided for the temporary partition of Vietnam along the seventeenth parallel. The accords stressed that the demarcation line should not be "interpreted as constituting a political or territorial boundary." The French and Vietminh agreed that a Demilitarized Zone (DMZ) 10 kilometers wide would be established along the seventeenth parallel and that the Vietminh forces would be regrouped north of the DMZ while the French troops moved south of the buffer area. Both sides also agreed that general elections would be held in July 1956 to reunify the country. Disappointed that the political settlement at Geneva did not reflect their military superiority in Vietnam, the Vietminh delegates felt betrayed by the Chinese. Pham Van Dong complained to an aide that Chou En-lai "has double-crossed us." Realizing that it would be difficult to expel the French from Vietnam without Chinese military aid, the Vietminh had been compelled to settle for half of the loaf at Geneva. They could only hope to get the other half in the future either by casting ballots or by firing bullets.

Eisenhower and Dulles were not as displeased as the Vietminh with the Geneva Accords. They know that Ho Chi Minh would easily win in the political arena if elections were held in the near future, but they believed that the two-year delay would give them enough time to build a separate state in southern Vietnam. During the peace conference, Dulles told congressional leaders that the United States would have to assume the responsibility for defending the southern half of Vietnam along with Laos and Cambodia. Dulles explained that it would be necessary for the United States to draw the line against the advance of communism and provide economic and military aid to the noncommunist countries in Indochina. He also said that the United States would have to organize a strong regional defense association to protect Southeast Asia. Both he and Eisenhower felt confident that, without the taint of French colonialism, the United States could establish an independent noncommunist nation in southern Vietnam.

Their determination to prevent the spread of communism in Southeast Asia was rooted in their continuing desire to keep Japan in the capitalist orbit. American leaders repeatedly warned that the Japanese might become dependent upon Red China if they did not have access to noncommunist markets in Southeast Asia. "Japan's population," Dulles explained in June 1954, "depends for its livelihood upon foreign trade. Trade is offered by the Communists—at a price. The price is that Japan—the only industrial power in Asia—should cease to cooperate with the United Nations and with the United States." A few days later, during a private discussion with congressional leaders, Eisenhower emphasized the same point. "If we don't assist Japan, gentlemen, Japan is going Communist," he lectured. "Then instead of the Pacific being an American lake, believe me it is going to be a Communist lake."

The Birth of a Client State

Ngo Dinh Diem was the man around whom the United States would struggle to build a new nation to serve as a bulwark against the spread of communism in Southeast Asia. Diem was born in 1901 and reared in a conservative Vietnamese family with strong religious and political feelings. Back in the seventeenth century, his ancestors had been among the earliest Vietnamese converts to Catholicism. His father, a well-educated mandarin who had come to resent the foreign domination of Vietnam, quit working for the government and began participating in anti-French nationalist activities. Diem inherited from his father a deep hostility toward French imperialism along with a fierce religious fervor. Hence he grew up to be both an ardent nationalist and a devout Catholic who hated communism. While Diem wanted to oust the French from his country, he stood against a radical revolution that would alter the traditional economic and political structure of Vietnam. In short, Diem was a Vietnamese patriot with conservative views about government and society.

Ngo Dinh Diem, like Phan Boi Chau before him, became one of the most prominent noncommunist nationalists in Vietnam. During his youth, Diem never learned to feel comfortable with members of the opposite sex, and while he was attending a Catholic school the young puritan contemplated becoming a priest. But he finally decided to enter a local French school of law and public administration to prepare himself for a government job. Soon after graduation in 1926, Diem became a provincial governor, and in 1933 Emperor Bao Dai appointed him minister of the interior. But Diem accused the emperor of being a tool of the French, and after only three months he resigned from his high government post. And when Bao Dai offered to make him prime minister in 1949, Diem rejected the offer because he regarded the emperor as a French puppet. Instead he created a new political party to serve as the nucleus for the emergence of a Third Force standing between the polar extremes of French colonialism and Vietnamese communism. But the party remained small.

Unable to attract many supporters to his brand of nationalism in Vietnam, Diem looked to the United States for patronage. He left home in 1950, and after visiting the Vatican he spent two years living in a Maryknoll seminary in New Jersey. Taking advantage of his location on the East Coast, Diem made frequent trips to New York and Washington where he became acquainted with prominent Catholics like Francis Cardinal Spellman and Senator John F. Kennedy. His great opportunity soon came. While the statesmen at Geneva were preparing to partition

Vietnam, Bao Dai decided to appoint Diem as prime minister of the southern portion of the country. The playboy summoned the puritan to Paris in June 1954 and persuaded him to kneel before a crucifix and swear that he would defend southern Vietnam against both the communists and the French. Diem then hurried back to Vietnam. When he landed at the Saigon airport on June 26, Diem received a warm welcome from a small group composed mostly of Catholics. The new prime minister expected the South Vietnamese people to obey him just as if he had been appointed by God to govern them. Never willing to abandon the idea that he had a mandate from heaven to rule South Vietnam as he saw fit, Diem typically responded to queries about his policies by saying that he knew what was best for his people.

Even though his paternalistic attitudes ran counter to democratic principles, Eisenhower and Dulles decided to support Diem. They hoped to keep Vietnam permanently divided and to help Diem establish an independent noncommunist regime south of the seventeenth parallel. Right after the conclusion of the Geneva Conference, American leaders set out to rebuild the economy of South Vietnam. They were motivated by three considerations. First, if the South Vietnamese people enjoyed prosperity under Diem, they would be less likely to join the communist movement. Second, if the South Vietnamese received financial aid from the United States, they would obtain dollars that could be used to purchase Japanese goods. Third, if South Vietnam became a successful showcase for capitalism, the North Vietnamese might be induced to abandon their commitment to communism. While the minimum American goal was to erect a stable capitalist regime in South Vietnam, the maximum American objective was to spark a counterrevolution in North Vietnam and thereby roll back the tide of communism to the Chinese border.

Besides promoting economic reconstruction in southern Vietnam, Eisenhower and Dulles quietly dispatched Colonel Edward G. Lansdale to Saigon to organize a covert campaign aimed at weakening the Vietminh regime in Hanoi. Lansdale had served with the Office of Strategic Services during World War II, and later he advised the president of the Philippines on how to suppress the Huk rebels. Upon his arrival in Vietnam in June 1954, Lansdale used Central Intelligence Agency (CIA) funds to set up the Saigon Military Mission composed of American soldiers and intelligence agents. Lansdale infiltrated small paramilitary units across the DMZ on missions to sabotage railroads and bridges in northern Vietnam. These undercover teams not only tried to destroy transportation facilities, but they also employed psychological warfare techniques in an effort to destabilize the Vietminh government. They likewise recruited secret squads of South Vietnamese commandos and trained them to foment unrest among the North Vietnamese. But these clandestine operations failed to stimulate a popular uprising against Ho Chi Minh.

Colonel Lansdale and his staff, while striving to weaken the Vietminh, simultaneously worked to strengthen the Diem regime by encouraging a mass exodus of Vietnamese civilians from the northern to the southern half of their country. Taking advantage of the Geneva Agreements which allowed for the free movement of population within Vietnam, American intelligence operatives directed a propaganda campaign at Catholics with slogans proclaiming that "Christ has gone South" or that "The Virgin Mary has departed from the North." American agents also spread rumors that the United States might bomb the communists in the north and that the only way to escape atomic destruction was to flee to the south. The propaganda barrage produced tangible results. Between August 1954 and May 1955, more than 800,000 Vietnamese living above the seventeenth parallel were induced to migrate below that demarcation line. The United States Navy furnished transportation for many of those who chose to leave the north, and the American government provided $282 million to help pay the cost of resettling them in the south.

These political refugees provided a hard-core group of supporters for the Diem government in Saigon. Most were Catholics who had strongly opposed the Vietminh and their struggle for national liberation. In fact, many were either civil servants who had worked under Bao Dai or auxiliary soldiers who had fought for the French. Vietnamese nationalists resented the role that many Catholics had played in the French colonial regime. "Vietnamese Catholics," they complained, "are the claws by which the French crab has been able to crawl across and devour our land." About half of the northern Catholic community moved below the seventeenth parallel, and as a result the size of the southern Catholic population more than doubled. These Catholics, numbering approximately 1 million, helped Diem maintain political power by serving as both government officials and military officers in the new order emerging in southern Vietnam.

While Diem was integrating these Catholics into his regime, Dulles was busy organizing a regional defense association that treated the seventeenth parallel as a permanent political boundary rather than as a temporary line for the regroupment of opposing military forces. Dulles hurried to Manila in September 1954 to persuade other countries to join with the United States in establishing a legal basis for united military action in Indochina. The Manila conference produced the Southeast Asia Treaty Organization (SEATO) to protect Cambodia, Laos, and southern Vietnam against either an attack from northern Vietnam or internal subversion. Along with the United States, the SEATO alliance included Great Britain, France, the Philippines, Australia, New Zealand, Pakistan, and Thailand. Conspicuous in their absence from the organization were India, Burma, and Indonesia. The SEATO members agreed to consult with one another about how to meet any common danger that might arise in Southeast Asia. But they did not pledge themselves to defend any country or government in the region. After the Senate ratified the SEATO pact, however, Eisenhower and his successors in the White House claimed that they had congressional sanction for American military intervention to check the spread of communism in Indochina.

In the meantime, the United States maneuvered to block the peaceful reunification of Vietnam. American intelligence sources predicted in August 1954 that the Vietminh would easily win if free elections were held in Vietnam according to the schedule agreed upon at Geneva. Two weeks later, the National Security Council concluded that the United States should make every effort to prevent a communist victory in Vietnam through general elections. But the State Department hoped to achieve that goal without publicly admitting that Washington was attempting to undermine the Geneva Accords. Dulles therefore cabled the American embassy in Saigon in April 1955 that Diem should demand election safeguards that the communists would reject. Not wanting the Vietminh to appear as the sole champions of reunification, the NSC decided on May 17 that Diem should agree to consultations regarding proper voting procedures and that the United States should then help him blame the ultimate failure for holding elections on the communists. But Diem refused to discuss the issue with Ho Chi Minh. On August 9, in response to calls from Hanoi for talks to prepare the groundwork for a political contest, Diem announced that there could be no elections as long as the communists ruled northern Vietnam.

Eisenhower and Dulles had already decided that the United States should help organize a new South Vietnamese army to buttress the Diem regime. Dulles explained to American military planners that the only purpose for building a South Vietnamese army was to help Diem maintain internal security and that any external threat from the North Vietnamese would have to be countered by either American or SEATO forces. Although the Joint Chiefs of Staff were reluctant to assume the task of training an indigenous army for a weak and unstable government,

Dulles argued that the best way to strengthen the anticommunist regime in Saigon was to assist in creating an efficient South Vietnamese military force. Dulles assured American military authorities that a small native army of about 50,000 South Vietnamese would be adequate because its mission would be limited to suppressing political subversion. Eisenhower agreed. "What we want," he told the NSC in October 1954, "is a Vietnamese force which will support Diem."

President Eisenhower decided to send General J. Lawton Collins to South Vietnam as his personal representative to help stabilize the Diem regime. When General Collins arrived in Saigon in November 1954, he was appalled by the chaotic political situation confronting him. Collins found that General Nguyen Van Hinh, the commander of the Bao Dai army, had been openly talking about forming a new government to replace Diem. With French backing, General Hinh was pushing Prince Buu Hoi as his candidate for prime minister. But American officials firmly opposed Buu Hoi because he favored holding elections to reunify Vietnam. They therefore informed General Hinh that, in the event of a coup against Diem, the United States would not provide financial support for the new government in South Vietnam. Realizing that his candidate could not survive without American economic aid, Hinh decided to abandon his plans for a coup. Bao Dai also succumbed to American pressure. Four days after Collins arrived in Saigon, the emperor ordered Hinh to Paris and dismissed him from the army.

But if Prince Buu Hoi could no longer challenge Diem, General Collins remained concerned about the continuing political instability in South Vietnam. The Cao Dai and Hoa Hao religious sects refused to merge their militias into the regular army, and the Binh Xuyen gang would not give up control of gambling, prostitution, and opium in Saigon. In early March 1955, these three heavily armed factions issued an ultimatum demanding the formation of a new government in South Vietnam. Collins became increasingly alarmed, and on April 9 he cabled Dulles that the United States should replace Diem with a coalition government that could unify the powerful factions. But Dulles replied that any change in political leadership might be for the worse. Thus Diem continued to receive strong American support. With the help of Lansdale and the use of large bribes, Diem was able to induce a majority of Cao Dai and Hoa Hao military leaders to rally to his side. Then Dulles persuaded Diem to attack the Binh Xuyen, and by May 2 his army had succeeded in driving the gangsters out of Saigon.

After extending his control over the religious sects and crushing the Binh Xuyen, Diem moved swiftly to consolidate his political power. He called for a national referendum to determine whether South Vietnam should remain a monarchy with Bao Dai as emperor or become a republic with himself as president. In the elections held under the supervision of his own police force in October 1955, Diem claimed that 98.2 percent of the voters had cast their ballots for him to replace Bao Dai as the chief of state. Fraud was extensive, with many electoral districts recording more votes for Diem than there were registered voters. American advisers had cautioned Diem that a 60 percent majority would look more credible, but he wanted his victory to appear like a mandate from heaven. Diem thereupon established a dictatorship rather than a democracy in the new Republic of Vietnam. To placate American officials, he created a national assembly in March 1956, but this legislative body remained powerless. Diem knew that he could resist American pressure to broaden his political base because Eisenhower and Dulles regarded his government as a crucial bastion against the spread of communism in Southeast Asia. So if Diem served as a mandarin under the aegis of the United States, he was a puppet who frequently pulled his own strings.

Despite his refusal to reform, Diem received American aid to build a South Vietnamese army needed to support his regime. The withdrawal of the French Expeditionary Corps from Indochina beginning in March 1955 meant that the Army of the Republic of Vietnam (ARVN) would have to be larger than originally planned. In addition to serving as an internal police force, ARVN would have to be strong enough at least to delay an attack from North Vietnam until American or SEATO forces could come to the rescue. The American Military Assistance Advisory Group, headquartered in Saigon, assumed the responsibility for building ARVN into a force that could shield South Vietnam against a massive communist assault across the seventeenth parallel. To accomplish that objective, the MAAG officers fashioned ARVN after the American forces that had successfully fought conventional conflicts during World War II and in Korea. The new South Vietnamese army, like the old French Expeditionary Corps, became a heavily equipped, road-bound force. As a result, ARVN was totally unprepared to cope when an insurgency erupted within South Vietnam.

The Revolt in the Rice Fields

While American military advisers were training South Vietnamese soldiers to repel an external attack, Ho Chi Minh and his communist associates in Hanoi were struggling to promote economic reconstruction in the area above the seventeenth parallel. They aimed to transform North Vietnam from a backward agricultural colony into a modern industrial country by following the Soviet model for economic development. The North Vietnamese communists began by nationalizing French companies and converting native businesses into producer cooperatives. Although they accepted some financial and technical assistance from Russia and China, Ho and his comrades were determined to achieve economic independence. Therefore they sent thousands of North Vietnamese students and workers to Russia and China to receive technical and professional training. They also chose to purchase industrial equipment rather than consumer goods with the money that they obtained from exporting raw materials. Their austerity program, which imposed a low standard of living on their own people for the sake of economic growth, soon put North Vietnam on the road to becoming the most industrialized nation in Southeast Asia.

Land reform became a central part of the drive to rebuild North Vietnam. The communist leaders in Hanoi hoped to turn the large mass of landless peasants into small farmers with enough acreage to grow surplus crops. These farmers would then be able to sell agricultural commodities to their urban neighbors and thereby earn money to buy factory goods produced in nearby cities. Besides creating a home market for domestic industry, the land reform program provided a way for the communists to consolidate their political power in North Vietnam. Many landlords and rich peasants were either imprisoned or killed, and their property was confiscated and redistributed to poor peasants. This process enabled the communists to eliminate a dangerous social class and to gain popular support. But the campaign got out of control, and consequently many landowners were ruthlessly accused of crimes that they did not commit. Finally, in August 1956, Ho Chi Minh called off the land reform program and released thousands of innocent landholders from prison.

In the meantime, while the North Vietnamese were pulling themselves up by their own bootstraps, the South Vietnamese continued to depend upon American financial support. The United States gave the Saigon government almost $1 billion between 1955 and 1959, yet South Vietnam remained economically underdeveloped. Believing that Diem needed a strong army to maintain control over the South Vietnamese people, American officials channeled large amounts of money into military rather than civilian projects in South Vietnam. In fact, 78 percent of all the American financial aid to South Vietnam was used for military purposes while only 1.25 percent went into industry and mining. Diem added to the problem by importing large qualities of consumer goods rather than machinery needed for industrial development. Diem resisted American advice to reduce spending on consumer items because he feared that a lower standard of living would create social unrest and thereby endanger his regime. Despite the massive infusion of American capital into South Vietnam, therefore, Diem did little to lay the foundations for achieving economic independence.

But the American economic aid package did help Diem win political support in the urban areas of South Vietnam. Most of the American funds used to subsidize the Diem regime were funneled into the commercial import program. After receiving free dollars from the United States, the Saigon government sold them to local importers for South Vietnamese piasters at about half of the official exchange rate. The commercial import program provided Diem with the means to pay most of the cost of his military forces and civil servants without having to impose high income taxes on the South Vietnamese middle class. The privileged merchants used their cheap dollars to import a vast array of consumer goods that allowed the urban middle class to enjoy a high standard of living. Besides producing an artificial prosperity in South Vietnam, the commercial import program enabled the select group of merchants to reap huge profits, and those who received importing licenses from the government became staunch supporters of both Diem and his American sponsors.

Although the United States supplied the Saigon government with four times more military aid than economic assistance, the South Vietnamese army still did not become a strong and effective fighting force. Diem promoted officers because they were loyal to him even if they were incompetent on the battlefield. Hence his officer corps was riddled with favoritism and nearly devoid of patriotism. Many senior ARVN officers had fought on the French side during the recent war, and almost none of them had participated in the anticolonial resistance movement. To make matters worse, the South Vietnamese army was corrupt to the core. Many officers regarded military service as an opportunity to enrich themselves rather than an obligation to defend their country. Although their pay was extraordinarily high by Asian standards, ARVN officers often supplemented their regular income by embezzling funds and selling drugs. Those in the lower ranks of the armed forces frequently robbed the very peasants they were supposed to protect. In short, the South Vietnamese army was basically a mercenary force, primarily designed to help Diem maintain his police state.

While depending upon his army for internal security, Diem sought political support from the affluent landlords in the fertile Mekong Delta. Many rich landowners had sympathized with the French during the war, and the Vietminh had confiscated their large holdings and distributed small plots to a great number of poor peasants. After Diem came to power in South Vietnam, however, he would not allow these peasants to keep the land that they considered their own unless they paid high prices to compensate the former owners. Few peasants could afford to buy the land, and as a result most of the property was returned to the original holders. Since Diem refused to implement a land reform program that would alienate the powerful landlords, only 2.5 percent of the landholders owned 50 percent of the acreage under cultivation in the Mekong delta. Most peasants in the area remained tenant farmers who had to pay high land rents ranging from one-third to one-half of their total rice crop. So the old problem of landlordism continued to generate peasant discontent in South Vietnam.

The Diem regime, supported by the great landlords and wealthy merchants, attempted to crush all political opposition. Although the Geneva Agreements promised amnesty for everyone who had participated in the war, Diem immediately launched a campaign against the Vietminh to prevent them from organizing a political challenge to his government. He stopped at nothing in an effort to suppress the Vietminh soldiers and political cadres who had been born and raised in the south and had decided to remain there after the war ended. Peasants were dragooned into mass meetings and pressured into informing against Vietminh members and sympathizers, and before long a large number of political dissidents were either executed or sent to concentration camps. In the spring of 1956, a South Vietnamese government official acknowledged that between 15,000 and 20,000 people had been incarcerated for the purpose of "reeducation." Diem did succeed in smashing many Vietminh cells, but his brutal treatment of former war heroes alienated large segments of the South Vietnamese population.

Although Diem posed in republican dress, his regime was a repressive dictatorship. Real power in South Vietnam remained in the hands of Diem and his three brothers who ruled the country through the secret Can Lao party, which was deeply entrenched in the armed forces and the civil service. Fearing that the Vietminh would win positions in local governments throughout South Vietnam, Diem decided in 1956 to abolish the traditional practice of holding elections for village councils and to appoint local officials who were loyal to him. Many of those appointed to office were Catholic refugees from the north, some were corrupt, and most held the common people in contempt. Diem also made sure that only his supporters would be allowed to run for the national assembly, and his secret police, headed by his brother Ngo Dinh Nhu, used intimidation to assure huge election victories for his candidates. People who questioned his authority were imprisoned while newspapers that criticized his government were shut down. In other words, Diem employed physical coercion rather than social reform in order to maintain political control over the South Vietnamese populace.

But his repressive policies triggered a revolutionary upheaval within South Vietnam. Until July 1956, the Vietminh fighters and organizers who had stayed in the south following the Geneva Agreements could hope that there would be a peaceful reunification of Vietnam as a result of general elections. After that date had passed, however, the Vietminh leaders in the south decided to resort to violence in order to achieve their long-cherished goal of national reunification. Thus a revolt from below erupted inside South Vietnam. The insurgents were soon joined by native southerners who had remained in the north after the Geneva Accords to receive special training in the art of revolutionary warfare. These Vietminh veterans were not outside invaders with strange manners and different accents, and when they returned home they rejoined families and friends in a familiar environment. Together with other indigenous southerners, they engaged in an energetic campaign to recruit new members for their struggle against Diem, and during 1957 the rebel ranks swelled as more and more southern peasants joined the insurgency.

Ho Chi Minh and his colleagues in Hanoi, however, were reluctant to become involved in a military struggle to liberate South Vietnam. These leaders of the Lao Dong, or Workers Party (formerly the Communist Party), feared that renewed warfare would undermine their effort to promote economic development in North Vietnam. They also worried that the United States might intervene if northern soldiers were sent to help the southern rebels. In November 1956, therefore, the northern communists told their southern comrades that they should use peaceful means to grasp power. Yet many southerners, hounded by secret police, began agitating for a policy of armed rebellion rather than peaceful resistance. Hanoi responded in November 1957 with a clear message that the time was not yet ripe for armed insurrection. But Diem became increasingly successful in his repressive measures during the next year, and as more and more insurgents were captured or killed, southern pressure for a change in policy grew apace. Finally, in February 1959, the Lao Dong leaders authorized the use of military force but only in support of the political struggle against the Saigon government. Hanoi gave clear instructions that the goal should be to topple the Diem regime by a general uprising rather than through guerrilla warfare.

Meanwhile Diem continued to implement policies that fanned the flames of insurgency in South Vietnam. During 1957, he began establishing large Vietnamese settlements in the Central Highlands at the expense of mountain tribesmen who were pushed off lands that they needed for their slash-and-burn agricultural methods. The ethnic Vietnamese from the coastal lowlands viewed the mountaineers as savages, and in late 1958 the CIA reported that there was growing tribal discontent with the Saigon government. Worse yet, in May 1959, Diem started forcing peasants to resettle in fortified agrovilles in an effort to separate them from the rebels in the surrounding countryside. The peasants resented being forced to relocate away from their ancestral burial grounds and their family rice paddies. The agroville program was eventually abandoned, but not before it had spawned an enormous amount of hostility in rural areas against the Diem regime. As a result, more and more South Vietnamese peasants responded favorably to the rebel promise that better days would come after the downfall of Diem.

After resorting to violence to assure their own survival, the southern insurgents became increasingly bold in their efforts to bring down the Diem regime. The rebels assassinated about 700 local government officials in 1958, and the number of political assassinations in South Vietnamese villages leaped to about 1,400 two years later. During the last half of 1959, moreover, the insurgents shifted from hit-and-run operations to large-scale attacks against exposed units of the South Vietnamese army. They also intensified their drive to win support from the rural population of South Vietnam. Diem responded to the rising tide of revolution by launching a propaganda campaign designed to discredit the South Vietnamese insurgents. Although many of the old Vietminh veterans and the new recruits to the revolutionary cause were not communist, Diem claimed that anyone who opposed his government was by definition a communist. Thus he began referring to the indigenous rebels as Vietcong (meaning Vietnamese communist) rather than as Vietminh (meaning Vietnamese nationalist). The term Vietcong (VC) soon gained widespread currency and helped justify American efforts to counter the insurgency in South Vietnam.

Meanwhile the communist leaders in Hanoi felt compelled to accommodate their policies to maintain control over the revolutionary movement in South Vietnam. Although they had decided in May 1959 to construct a route through Laos (later known as the Ho Chi Minh Trail) to move men and supplies southward, they continued to warn against rash adventures in South Vietnam. The Lao Dong cautioned in March 1960 that the southern insurgents were not yet ready for a direct revolution against Diem. But the impatient southerners could not be restrained by Hanoi. In April 1960, a group of noncommunists in Saigon issued a manifesto demanding that Diem make sweeping reforms, and as the pace of the revolution accelerated the Lao Dong decided to authorize direct action aimed at overthrowing the Diem regime. Finally, in December 1960, the southern rebels formed the National Liberation Front (NLF) to rally their compatriots behind a program calling for a coalition government in Saigon and the gradual reunification of Vietnam through peaceful negotiations. The new organization, like the old Vietminh, included a large number of noncommunists who were willing to take their instructions from communists in order to achieve their nationalist goals.

American leaders had by then become apprehensive about the situation in South Vietnam. Disappointed with the performance of the South Vietnamese army, they decided in May 1959 to begin sending American advisers on military missions with ARVN units. Although Ambassador Elbridge Durbrow argued that Diem needed to make reforms in order to gain enough popular support to defeat the insurrection in South Vietnam, most American military advisers continued to view the problem in battlefield terms. Despite their narrow perspective, however, American military authorities began to lose their sense of complacency about the armed forces buttressing the Saigon government. They also began to realize that the immediate danger to the Diem regime came from the revolution in South Vietnam and not from a massive invasion from North Vietnam. In the summer of 1960, therefore, the United States belatedly shifted the emphasis of its military training program away from conventional warfare and toward counterinsurgency. American military planners quite logically concluded that the way to defeat an insurgency was to engage in counterinsurgency. But while the United States was finally beginning to apply appropriate military measures to fight the symptoms of the problem, it was not doing much in the political arena to combat the causes of the revolution in South Vietnam.

Despite the change in military orientation, political conditions in South Vietnam remained chaotic. A State Department intelligence report warned in August 1960 that South Vietnamese army officers were becoming increasingly discontent about the promotion of incompetent commanders and the influence of the Can Lao party on military affairs. The report also noted that criticism of the Diem regime had mounted among government officials who were upset about the activities of Ngo

Dinh Nhu and his wife. "Should a coup materialize," the report concluded, "the immediate and principal objective would probably be to oust the Nhus and their entourage and then leave Diem with the alternative of either continuing in office with reduced power or resigning." Ambassador Durbrow promptly encouraged Diem to take steps to reduce the prospects for a coup. He advised Diem to remove the unpopular Nhu from his position of power in the government and to alter the nature of the Can Lao party. But Diem refused to diminish the authority of his brother or to change the character of the principal instrument that the Ngo family used to rule South Vietnam.

When it became clear that Diem would not make any meaningful reforms, the disgruntled military officers decided to stage a coup against his regime. The rebels struck in November 1960, but fundamental disagreements over their ultimate objectives helped foil their effort to grasp power. While some of the conspirators aimed to get rid of Diem along with Nhu, others wanted to keep Diem as a figurehead in a new government after eliminating his brother. The American embassy in Saigon, hoping to prevent bloodshed, urged both Diem and the coup leaders to settle their differences through negotiations. With rebel troops surrounding his palace, Diem maneuvered to buy time by promising to make far-reaching concessions. The rebel officers took the bait and agreed to enter into discussions. Then Diem took advantage of the opportunity to order loyal troops to Saigon to quell the rebellion. But the coup attempt had almost succeeded, and the event seriously damaged the relationship between the Ngo brothers and their patrons in Washington. Believing that some American officials had encouraged the rebels, Diem and Nhu became ever more suspicious and distrustful of the United States.

FOUR

The Summons of the Trumpet

What I am concerned about is that Americans will get impatient and say, because they don't like events in Southeast Asia or they don't like the Government in Saigon, that we should withdraw. That only makes it easier for the Communists. I think we should stay. We should use our influence in as effective a way as we can, but we should not withdraw.

President John F. Kennedy, 1963

The Global Domino Theory

President John F. Kennedy was determined to defeat the growing communist challenge to the liberal capitalist world system. In his inaugural address delivered in January 1961, Kennedy set the tone for the beginning of a bold American foreign policy. His manner was vigorous and energetic; his words were militant and defiant: "We shall pay any price, bear any burden, meet any hardship, support any friend, oppose any foe to assure the survival and success of liberty." Just two weeks earlier, Premier Nikita S. Khrushchev had belligerently pledged that the Soviet Union would support wars of national liberation. And Radio Hanoi, in a broadcast coinciding with the bellicose statement from Moscow, announced the formation of the National Liberation Front to direct the forces of revolt against the Ngo Dinh Diem regime in Saigon. In his response to these ominous developments, Kennedy called upon the

American people to join with him in launching a New Frontier. "Now," the youthful president exhorted, "the trumpet summons us."

The Kennedy administration confronted a wave of social revolutions that threatened to destroy the institution of private property and the principle of free trade throughout large parts of Asia, Africa, and Latin America. While Patrice Lumumba was leading a struggle in the Congo against the old order of colonialism, Fidel Castro was engaged in a campaign to transform Cuba into a showcase for communism in the heart of the Caribbean basin. Kennedy and his advisers feared that radicals would gain control of revolutionary movements elsewhere in the Third World, adopt a communist model for economic development, and place severe restrictions upon international commercial and financial transactions. In an effort to encourage leaders in underdeveloped countries to follow a capitalist recipe for material accumulation, Professor Walt W. Rostow of the Massachusetts Institute of Technology wrote a book entitled *The Stages of Economic Growth: A Non-Communist Manifesto.* Kennedy agreed with his prescription for the Third World, and shortly after winning the presidential election in November 1960 he selected Rostow to serve as a top national security aide.

Kennedy and his advisers planned to employ a dual diplomacy in an attempt to keep Third World countries functioning within the framework of the liberal capitalist international order. On the positive side, they intended to offer the economic carrot to eradicate the conditions of poverty that provided seedbeds for the growth of communism in underdeveloped areas. Programs of financial and technical assistance were devised to induce political leaders in the Third World to maintain their allegiance to capitalism. On the negative side, Kennedy and his aides aimed to use the military stick to defeat revolutionary movements that threatened to bring communist regimes to power in underdeveloped countries. Counterinsurgency programs were organized to teach American soldiers effective methods for combating guerrilla forces operating in tropical regions. In short, if the Peace Corps failed to do the job, the Green Berets stood ready for action.

Growing apprehensions about revolutionary upheavals in the Third World had produced a significant metamorphosis in the domino theory by the time Kennedy entered the White House. During the 1950s, American policymakers feared that the fall of Indochina to communism would lead to the loss of the rest of Southeast Asia as a market for Japan. But by the 1960s, they also worried that the fall of Indochina to communism would lead to the loss of Africa and Latin America as markets for the United States and its European trading partners. Thus the old formula, "so goes Vietnam, so goes Malaya and Indonesia" became the new refrain, "so goes Vietnam, so goes Guatemala and the Congo." As the domino theory assumed global dimensions, South Vietnam loomed large as the testing ground for wars of national liberation. The communist leaders in North Vietnam hoped to receive ample military supplies from China where Mao Tse-tung was busy portraying the United States as a paper tiger. "South Vietnam is the model of the national liberation movement of our time," General Vo Nguyen Giap declared. "If the special warfare that the United States imperialists are testing in South Vietnam is overcome, then it can be defeated anywhere in the world."

Determined to protect American economic and strategic interests around the world, Kennedy and the New Frontiersmen made preparations to combat the communist menace in Southeast Asia. They intended to refute Mao by demonstrating that the United States had the ability and resolve to prevent Giap from directing a successful war of national liberation in South Vietnam. American leaders feared that rebel groups throughout the Third World would be emboldened if the United States appeared weak and hesitant in the face of the communist challenge in South Vietnam. Thus they felt compelled to maintain the prestige and credibility of the United States as a vital part of their commitment to perpetuate the Pax Americana.

During his last months in the White House, however, President Dwight D. Eisenhower regarded Laos rather than South Vietnam as the most dangerous trouble spot in Indochina. The United States had been supporting a right-wing regime in Laos, but in 1960 Laotian neutralists joined hands with the Pathet Lao communist rebels in an effort to oust the American-sponsored government. By the end of the year, North Vietnam and the Soviet Union were giving substantial aid to the anti-American forces, and Eisenhower was seriously considering the option of military intervention. On the eve of his retirement in January 1961, Eisenhower briefed president-elect Kennedy about the menacing situation in Laos. The fall of Laos would endanger Thailand, Cambodia, and South Vietnam, he warned, and if the United States did not draw the line in Laos, all of Southeast Asia might be lost to communism. Having thus defined Laos as the key domino in the whole region, Eisenhower advised Kennedy that the United States should attempt to persuade its SEATO allies to undertake multilateral action. But if they refused to comply with American wishes, Eisenhower concluded, the United States might have to resort to unilateral intervention as a last desperate effort to save Laos.

After taking the oath of office on the next day, Kennedy gave serious thought to the question of whether or not the United States should dispatch combat troops to Laos. But the new president was given pause when he learned that a large American task force could not be deployed in Laos unless the United States withdrew troops from Europe just as a crisis concerning Berlin was becoming increasingly acute. Kennedy realized that the American strategic reserve would be inadequate to meet other contingencies that might occur anywhere around the world if the United States become involved in a major military operation in Laos. Hence he chose to negotiate rather than fight. The United States subsequently agreed to participate in a peace conference in Geneva, and in May 1961 a cease-fire was arranged for the contending forces in Laos. Although shooting continued in the mountains in the eastern part of the country, a peace settlement was finally concluded in July 1962 at Geneva. The treaty stipulated that Laos would be neutralized under a coalition government representing communist as well as conservative elements.

But if this compromise temporarily ended the turmoil in Laos, the situation in South Vietnam remained very serious. A few days after his inauguration in January 1961, President Kennedy read an alarming report prepared by General Edward G. Lansdale about the steady growth of the insurgency in South Vietnam and the increasing problems of the shaky Ngo Dinh Diem regime in Saigon. Lansdale predicted a large-scale Vietcong offensive before the end of the year and warned that, if the communists won in South Vietnam, they would have easy pickings in the remainder of Southeast Asia because the toughest anticommunist forces in the region would be gone. The loss of South Vietnam, he asserted, would be "a major blow to U.S. prestige and influence, not only in Asia but throughout the world." Lansdale made two important policy recommendations. First, he advocated a major American effort to defeat the Vietcong drive to gain control of South Vietnam. Second, he argued that Ambassador Elbridge Durbrow should be transferred from his post in Saigon because Diem believed that he had sympathized strongly with the leaders of the recently aborted coup.

President Kennedy was impressed by the Lansdale memorandum, and he quickly demonstrated his readiness to take steps to prevent the South Vietnam domino from toppling. Following a meeting with a small group of his closest advisers on January 28, Kennedy approved an additional $42 million in American aid to fund an expansion of the Army of the Republic of Vietnam. The president also decided to replace Ambassador Durbrow with Frederick E. Nolting who was sent to Saigon to carry out the difficult assignment of getting along with Diem. Three months later, on April 27, an interagency work group warned that South Vietnam was nearing a decisive phase in its battle for survival as an independent non-communist nation. Kennedy quickly responded to this report by dispatching another 100 American military advisers to South Vietnam along with 400 Special Forces troops to teach ARVN units counterinsurgency techniques. Besides authorizing an increase in American military personnel in South Vietnam, Kennedy decided to sponsor a program of covert operations against North Vietnam. The United States soon began to infiltrate undercover teams of South Vietnamese across the seventeenth parallel to sabotage North Vietnamese installations and to agitate against the communist government in Hanoi. At the same time, the United States initiated a secret war in Laos by arming and training Meo tribesmen for attacks against the Ho Chi Minh Trail.

Yet many American military leaders thought that the United States would have to take even more forceful actions to prevent South Vietnam from falling into the hands of the National Liberation Front. The Joint Chiefs of Staff did not believe that the dispatch of Green Berets and the expansion of the Military Assistance Advisory Group (MAAG) would be sufficient to subdue the Vietcong, and in May 1961 they formally recommended that the United States should immediately deploy regular military forces in South Vietnam. Kennedy quickly instructed Vice President Lyndon B. Johnson to raise the question in Saigon, but Diem indicated that he did not want American combat troops except in the case of overt aggression from North Vietnam. Critics were already referring to the Saigon government as the "American-Diem" regime, and Johnson reported that the introduction of a large number of troops from the United States would intensify anticolonial emotions in South Vietnam. Endeavoring to reassure Diem that he could count on American support, Johnson publicly described him as "the Winston Churchill of Southeast Asia." But the vice president was less enthusiastic when a reporter later asked in private if he really meant what he had said. "Shit," Johnson drawled, "Diem's the only boy we got out there."

Not long after Johnson left Saigon, alarming reports reached Washington about sharply escalating Vietcong attacks in the Mekong delta. The insurgents mounted three assaults in units of more than 1,000 men during September 1961, and on one occasion they briefly occupied a provincial capital just fifty-five miles from Saigon. In an intelligence estimate made on October 5, the Central Intelligence Agency calculated that the rebel forces had grown from about 4,000 to around 16,000 during the past year and a half. The CIA noted that 80 to 90 percent of the Vietcong soldiers were local recruits and that 10 to 20 percent were southerners who had gone north for training before returning home via mountain trails through Laos. Unable to find evidence of any communist-bloc military equipment in South Vietnam, the CIA concluded that the Vietcong guerrillas obtained their arms from small local arsenals and by capturing them from ARVN units.

The Second Indochina War

During a Lao Dong party conference, convened by the Central Office for South Vietnam in the autumn of 1961, communist leaders reviewed the progress of their revolutionary movement. The Central Committee of the party observed that forms of limited guerrilla warfare and partial uprisings had set the stage for the beginning of a period of prolonged political crisis in South Vietnam. "The revolutionary forces will be rapidly built and developed and forms of revolutionary government will appear in localities everywhere," it predicted, "and a general offensive and general uprising of the people will break out, overthrow the U.S.-Diem regime and liberate the South." To hasten that process, the Central Committee outlined a plan of action for the National Liberation Front. Political struggle was to remain primary in the cities, but in the plains region political and military struggle were to be placed on the same level, and in the mountainous areas military struggle was to become primary. The Central Committee concluded that the revolutionary forces should be prepared not only to take advantage of future coup attempts against the Saigon government but also to cope with "the possibility of armed intervention by bringing troops of U.S. imperialism and its lackeys into the South."

Already thinking along such lines, President Kennedy decided to send a mission, headed by Walt Rostow and his personal military adviser General Maxwell D. Taylor, to assess the situation in South Vietnam. Kennedy made it clear during a meeting in early October 1961 that the group should weigh the need for the deployment of American combat troops to deal with the Vietcong. Upon their arrival in Saigon a week later, Taylor and Rostow found that South Vietnam was suffering from a double crisis in confidence: doubt that the United States was determined to save Southeast Asia and doubt that Diem could defeat the communists with the defensive tactics he was employing. After completing their two-week tour of the country, Taylor and Rostow recommended a series of specific measures that the United States should take to prevent a further deterioration of the situation in South Vietnam. They advocated the training and equipping of the Civil Guard and the Self-Defense Corps to relieve the regular South Vietnamese army of static assignments, together with the provision of considerably more American helicopters and light aviation to increase the mobility of ARVN units for offensive operations. They also urged the expansion of MAAG and the introduction of American military personnel to perform difficult tasks such as air reconnaissance and special intelligence that were beyond the capacity of the South Vietnamese forces.

Further, although Diem still opposed the introduction of American combat troops, Taylor and Rostow proposed the dispatch of an 8,000-man military task force to South Vietnam. The ostensible purpose of the unit would be to assist in repairing the extensive damage caused by flooding in the Mekong delta. But under the cloak provided by the humanitarian activity of engineers and medics, American infantrymen would conduct combat operations against the Vietcong. Taylor and Rostow argued that the presence of American soldiers would raise morale in South Vietnam and demonstrate the resolution of the United States to resist communism in Southeast Asia. They concluded that the task force would not only furnish an emergency reserve to back up ARVN in the case of a heightened military crisis in South Vietnam but also serve as an advance party if more American ground troops were needed to stem the tide in the future.

Secretary of Defense Robert S. McNamara and the Joint Chiefs of Staff thought that the United States should go well beyond these recommendations. In a memorandum sent to President Kennedy in early November 1961, they warned that the introduction of only 8,000 American soldiers in the context of flood relief would neither convince the communist leaders in Hanoi that the United States meant business nor tip the scales decisively against the Vietcong guerrillas. Thus they reasoned that the initial dispatch of American troops should be accompanied by a definite commitment to prevent the fall of South Vietnam to communism and by a warning to Ho Chi Minh that the United States would retaliate against North Vietnam if he continued to support the Vietcong rebels. While not quite sure how many American troops would be needed to put ARVN on the road to victory, McNamara and the JCS assured Kennedy that no more than about 205,000 American ground forces would be required even in the event that both North Vietnam and Red China intervened overtly in South Vietnam. They therefore supported the Taylor-Rostow recommendations but only as the first steps toward the fulfillment of American objectives.

Taking a contrary stand, the State Department opposed sending any American combat troops to South Vietnam. Secretary of State Dean Rusk doubted that the deployment of a small American task force would have a decisive influence if Diem remained unwilling to make essential political and military reforms. While attaching great importance to checking the spread of communism in Southeast Asia, Rusk was reluctant to make a major commitment of "American prestige to a losing horse." Under Secretary of State Chester Bowles and ambassador-at-large W. Averell Harriman likewise questioned the viability of the Saigon government. Their skepticism about the Diem regime led them to advocate a diplomatic rather than a military solution. In a memorandum to Kennedy delivered on November 11, Harriman proposed a peace settlement based upon the 1954 Geneva Accords. But he warned that, if Diem continued to be "repressive, dictatorial and unpopular," South Vietnam would not in any case long remain an independent noncommunist country.

Beset by divided counsel, Kennedy was in a quandary about what should be done. Yet it soon became clear that he was firmly opposed to a negotiated settlement. In a brief presented to Rusk and McNamara on November 14, Kennedy asserted that the basic issue was not whether Diem was a good ruler but whether the United States would remain passive while North Vietnam continued supporting the guerrillas in South Vietnam. "If we postpone action in Vietnam to engage in talks with the Communists," he concluded, "we can surely count on a major crisis of nerve in Vietnam and throughout Southeast Asia." But while he wanted to show the strength and determination of the United States, the president balked at committing American ground forces and embarking upon what might become an unending program of military escalation. "The troops will march in, the bands will play, the crowds will cheer," he grumbled, "and in four days everyone will have forgotten. Then we will be told we have to send in more troops. It's like taking a drink. The effect wears off, and you have to take another."

Thus rejecting the alternatives of either negotiating a peace settlement or deploying a task force, Kennedy decided to take a middle course. The president explained at a National Security Council meeting on November 15 that he would approve a substantial increase in American military aid for South Vietnam but that he wanted to defer the combat option for future consideration. The State Department immediately notified Ambassador Nolting that the United States would not at the present time introduce combat troops into South Vietnam. But he was also informed about contingency plans for the dispatch of American ground forces should North Vietnam pursue a policy of direct military intervention below the seventeenth parallel. A week later, on November 22, the State Department instructed Nolting to tell Diem that, in an effort to arrest the military and political deterioration in South Vietnam, the United States proposed to do the following: send more military advisers and assume greater control over combat operations; provide more helicopters and light aircraft along with pilots to fly them; and supply additional equipment and personnel to gather intelligence and to execute bombing and strafing missions.

But Nolting ran into a stone wall when he indicated that the United States expected Diem to reciprocate both by broadening the base of his government to win popular support and by overhauling the command structure of his army to create an effective military organization. Diem replied that the quid pro quo aspects of the American proposals "played right into the hands of the communists" by making his regime appear subservient to a foreign country. Arguing that the United States was "putting the cart before the horse" by demanding that he implement political reforms, Diem stressed that first he would have to provide military security for the South Vietnamese people in order to regain their allegiance. Nolting immediately backed away from a confrontation with Diem. In a cable to Washington, he suggested that the United States should emphasize the need for governmental efficiency rather than political reform in negotiations with Saigon. Kennedy quickly came to the same conclusion. Convinced that he could not find another South Vietnamese leader as capable as Diem, Kennedy decided to furnish the additional military assistance without insisting upon basic reforms in return.

Kennedy also agreed with Nolting regarding the issue of how American military escalation should be justified before the bar of world opinion. Nolting had already anticipated the eventual need to increase the number of United States military advisers in South Vietnam far beyond the limits established in 1954 at Geneva. Thus he had recommended that the American government should announce that it could no longer be bound by those restrictions because of the failure of international controls to prevent North Vietnam from violating them. Kennedy ultimately directed the State Department to prepare a White Paper that would rationalize whatever breach in the Geneva Agreements he might make by charging that North Vietnam was already disregarding them with impunity. Released in December 1961, the official State Department brief was entitled *A Threat to the Peace: North Vietnam's Efforts to Conquer South Vietnam.*

So advertised as a response to North Vietnamese aggression, the American military buildup in South Vietnam proceeded apace. The United States began shipping a vast array of equipment and supplies in an effort to enhance the combat effectiveness of the South Vietnamese army. Before long, a steady stream of helicopters, fixed-wing aircraft, trucks, armored personnel carriers, howitzers, mortars, machine guns, petroleum, napalm, herbicides, and other items were flowing across the Pacific and pouring into South Vietnam. Waves of American military specialists also splashed ashore in order to train South Vietnamese soldiers and show them how to use the weapons arriving from the United States. The number of American military advisers stationed in South Vietnam jumped from less than 700 in January 1961 when Kennedy became president to more than 3,000 by the end of his first year in office. The swift military expansion prompted the United States to replace MAAG in February 1962 with a new organization called the Military Assistance Command, Vietnam (MACV). Under the supervision of General Paul A. Harkins, who ran MACV from his headquarters in Saigon, the number of American military specialists in South Vietnam continued to grow by leaps and bounds, reaching 9,000 in January 1963 and exceeding 16,000 by the end of the year.

This massive infusion of men and weapons from the United States provided an immediate boost to the morale and effectiveness of the South Vietnamese army. The helicopters quickly gave ARVN the upper hand in the fight against the guerrillas. "Roaring in over the treetops, they were a terrifying sight to the superstitious Viet Cong peasants," a State Department official later recalled. "In those first few months, the Viet Cong simply turned and ran—and, flushed from their foxholes and hiding places, and running in the open, they were easy targets." At the same time, in the flat stretches of the Mekong delta, armored personnel carriers were chasing down fleeing guerrillas like hounds pursuing rabbits in an open prairie. The speed and mobility of the new American equipment enabled the South Vietnamese army to take the offensive, and during the spring of 1962 it appeared that ARVN had gained the edge. But it would soon become evident that the tide of the battle had only temporarily turned against the rebels.

For if ARVN had assumed the initiative against the guerrillas, the revolution against the Diem regime continued to gain momentum in the South Vietnamese countryside. The situation in Long An province, which occupies a strategic position separating Saigon from the rice fields of the Mekong delta, provides a case in point. Between 1961 and 1963, as more and more peasants decided to defy government authority, land tax collections declined from 50.6 percent to 40.3 percent in Long An. Large numbers of peasants in the province also refused to report for induction into the South Vietnamese army. Many parents preferred an illegal status for their sons rather than having them conscripted by the government for military service in some distant part of the country, and many young men and boys who wished to avoid the draft turned to the insurgents for protection from the government and ultimately joined the Vietcong. As a result, between 1962 and 1963, both the number of armed rebels in Long An and the size of the area that they controlled in the province increased more than 10 percent.

One reason for the growing peasant alienation in Long An and other provinces was the widespread corruption of the Diem regime. More concerned about their own wealth than the welfare of the South Vietnamese people, Ngo Dinh Nhu and his wife exerted an increasing influence in the government as the ruling clique in Saigon kept shrinking until only members of the Ngo family held power. The Nhus set a bad example of nepotism and corruption for the political and military pawns of the Ngo family oligarchy. Although Diem personally may have found the resulting waste and graft distasteful, he never did anything to root out the corruption and brutality that surrounded him. Diem realized that the survival of his regime depended upon the secret police that Nhu used as an instrument to control the people of South Vietnam. Diem also understood that he could not punish or dismiss lazy and corrupt officials without destroying his own base of support.

While tolerating corruption within his government as a means of retaining power, Diem stubbornly resisted American suggestions that he should clean house. American leaders had hoped that their huge military assistance program would give them leverage to induce Diem to make essential reforms. But they soon learned that, while Diem wanted American military aid, he did not want political advice from the United States. Confident that he was indispensable to his American patrons, he rejected their pleas to broaden his government as he relied more and more upon Nhu for guidance. Diem also acted contrary to American recommendations by tightening rather than relaxing government controls in South Vietnam. Besides prohibiting all types of public gatherings unless they were approved in advance, the Saigon regime imposed a rigorous censorship on all material written in the country. The veteran *Newsweek* correspondent Francois Sully, for example, was expelled from Saigon because he made critical remarks about Madame Nhu.

Like a giant octopus, the Diem regime had long tentacles extending out from the palace in Saigon and reaching down to the villages and hamlets in the most remote areas of South Vietnam. The centrally appointed province and district chiefs selected local notables to serve as hamlet chiefs and members of the village councils, and these subordinate officials at the lowest levels of government dutifully carried out policies established in Saigon. Although theoretically impartial bodies, the village councils under Diem were actually controlled by the landlords and used to collect taxes and exploit the peasants. Local officials often embezzled government funds and extorted money from peasants, and efforts by honest administrators to promote clean government were usually frustrated by central authorities. "Naturally, I would try to salvage as many corrupt officials as I could," one province chief recalled. "Hopeless cases I would send back to Saigon with the reasons why I refused to have such an individual in my province. But frequently the very reason these people were in the government was that they had relatives or friends back in Saigon, who would just 'lose' my reports, and the individual would end up getting a better assignment than he had in the first place. It often happened that in the place of a corrupt official I would receive a corrupt official who had been thrown out of another province and then assigned to me."

The Growth of the Vietcong

But the roots of the revolution in the rice paddies of South Vietnam ran a great deal deeper than mere complaints about official corruption. Rather it was the land issue that remained the single most important factor in turning the rural population against the Saigon government. During the war against the French and their client Bao Dai, the Vietminh had destroyed the status quo in the countryside when they instituted a land reform program. The peasants had seen the landlords flee and their large holdings divided into small plots and distributed to the landless. After the United States helped Diem consolidate his power in Saigon, however, the status quo was restored in rural South Vietnam. The landlords returned to repossess their property in areas secured by government troops. But as the Vietcong extended their control over the countryside, they launched another land reform program. Once again the landlords were chased away and their holdings were given to the landless, and it was a lesson that the communists would not allow the peasants to forget.

Communist cadres told the peasants in liberated areas that the revolution was directed against feudalism as well as imperialism. Because the local landlords were sponsored by the American-Diem regime, they lectured, the peasants needed to support the struggle against the American imperialists and their lackeys in Saigon in order to retain the land that had been taken from the old owners and given to them. The communists warned that, if the imperialists won the war, the big landlords would come back and the peasants would return to their former condition of servitude. Only by sending their sons into the National Liberation Front army and paying taxes to support the rebel forces, the cadres concluded, could the peasants assure the defeat of the imperialists and thereby win the right to keep their land. Buttressed by recent developments in South Vietnam, their arguments prompted more and more peasants to contribute to the Vietcong cause.

The economic assistance programs financed by the United States did little to dissuade many peasants in South Vietnam from cooperating with the revolutionary movement. Maintaining its conservative disposition, the Diem regime used American funds to promote economic development rather than to redistribute property ownership among different social classes. The construction of roads and canals added to the productive capacity of the country as a whole, but these developmental projects did nothing to shift the allocation of wealth and power within South Vietnam. While the communist insurgents sponsored a program of progressive taxation and land redistribution, the Saigon government imposed a regressive tax structure and a reactionary land policy. The contrast was clear even to the least sophisticated peasants. Committed to preserving the traditional social order in South Vietnam, Diem was unable to win the hearts and minds of the peasants.

Nor could the American-sponsored strategic hamlet program win the war at the rice roots level. Like the earlier agroville arrangement, the strategic hamlet program brought peasants from scattered villages together into fortified settlements surrounded by moats and barbed-wire fences. The proponents of the plan had two purposes. First, by separating the peasants from the guerrillas, they aimed to cut the rebels off from their source of food, intelligence, and manpower. Second, by providing schools, fertilizer, and medical care in compensation for the burdens of forced relocation, they hoped to persuade the peasants that the Saigon government offered better living conditions than the Vietcong. But much of the money furnished by the United States for social and economic services ended up in the pockets of corrupt officials. And the displaced peasants resented having to build new homes away from their rice fields and ancestral graves. Disenchanted peasants often welcomed rebel agents into the strategic hamlets at night, and eventually the Vietcong overran many of the settlements. While failing to prevent the guerrillas from living off the rural population, the strategic hamlet program added to the mounting discontent in the countryside.

The South Vietnamese army employed a variety of military tactics that compounded the problem. Operating in the confusing conditions engendered by a bitter civil war, ARVN soldiers did not always successfully distinguish between armed insurgents and innocent civilians. Peasants suspected of sympathizing with the Vietcong were frequently shot, and villages suspected of harboring guerrillas were often strafed and bombed. At the same time, it was customary for the forces of the Saigon government to torture prisoners held for questioning about possible rebel connections. The widespread use of napalm and defoliants, sanctioned by the United States, likewise failed to discriminate between friend and foe. Besides doing extensive ecological damage, these lethal chemicals sometimes injured or killed women and children as well as crops and animals. Many of these military measures proved to be counterproductive as they made it easier for the Vietcong to mobilize the masses.

The armed forces of the National Liberation Front and the Republic of Vietnam presented sharply contrasting images in the eyes of the peasants. On the one hand, the troops serving under Diem acted a lot like those who had fought for the French. They routinely patrolled hamlets during the day, grabbed a few chickens for lunch, and then disappeared before dark. Despite American efforts to get them to treat civilians with respect, ARVN soldiers continued to plunder the people they were sent to protect. "Up to the very end," General Lansdale lamented after the war, "the army was still stealing from the population." On the other hand, the NLF guerrillas resembled those who had fought against the French. The Vietcong, like the Vietminh, dressed in black pajamas, used hit-and-run tactics, and set up their own governments, which not only collected taxes and conscripted young men but also provided the peasants with educational services and medical care. Having watched their fathers expel the French and Bao Dai from the northern half of Vietnam, they dedicated themselves to liberating the rest of their country from the yoke of the American-Diem dictatorship. Thus the Vietcong guerrillas, unlike the ARVN regulars, were ready and willing to die for their cause.

During the autumn of 1962, the tide of the battle began to turn against the South Vietnamese army. The fighting had become increasingly bloody as ARVN battalions, following American advice, tried to close with and kill the NLF forces. In classic textbook fashion, the Saigon government troops would sweep into an area, establish blocking positions, and then attempt to encircle and liquidate the Vietcong. But these aggressive "search and destroy" operations led to heavy losses for ARVN as well as NLF units. Apparently worried that high casualty rates would result in intensified political agitation against his regime, Diem hastily ordered his military commanders to limit their losses on the battlefield. They responded by employing "search and avoid" maneuvers designed to leave an escape route for the Vietcong. While ARVN officers were becoming increasingly cautious, moreover, the insurgents were rapidly overcoming their fear of the noisy American helicopters hovering overhead. The rebels learned to remain camouflaged in their hiding places and to hold their fire until the helicopters landed to discharge ground forces. More and more of the slow aircraft were shot down with small arms, and their landing parties were frequently mauled during the ensuing ambush. And as the Vietcong guerrillas became increasingly bold, they quickly regained the initiative against their opponents.

The battle of Ap Bac epitomized the fundamental shift in the fortunes of the war. In early January 1963, a large ARVN force of 2,500 soldiers attacked a small group of 200 guerrillas near the village of Ap Bac, located in the Mekong delta only fifty miles from Saigon. The troops fighting for Diem not only were equipped with amphibious personnel carriers and artillery, but they were also supported by American bombers and helicopters. Yet the Vietcong battalion managed to kill sixty-one attackers and wound over 100 more, to shoot down five helicopters and damage nine others, and then to escape almost intact through a big hole that the Saigon government troops had intentionally left open. Despite having the advantages of superior numbers and firepower, the ARVN force had blown the opportunity to corner and crush the rebels. The failure revealed all of the deficiencies of the South Vietnamese army: its lack of aggressiveness, its hesitancy about taking casualties, its lack of battlefield leadership, and its almost nonexistent chain of command. The American military advisers who had taken part in the fighting were disgusted by the poor performance of their ARVN pupils. The battle of Ap Bac, more than any other setback, convinced them that Diem was not willing to buy victory with blood.

The official American response to this deteriorating military situation sowed the seeds for a widening chasm between rhetoric and reality or what later came to be called the "credibility gap." Believing that no other South Vietnamese leader was capable of filling Diem's shoes, both Ambassador Nolting and General Harkins made repeated pronouncements claiming that ARVN forces were winning the war. Harkins even went so far as to describe the battle of Ap Bac as a victory for the Saigon government. But while the American embassy and MACV continued to exude great optimism about the progress of counterinsurgency, the American press corps in Saigon began to challenge the official line.

Correspondents such as David Halberstam of the *New York Times* and Neil Sheehan of United Press International, while denouncing the Diem regime as corrupt and repressive, argued that ARVN was losing the war. Diem reacted angrily. Some American reporters were forced to leave South Vietnam, and others had their phones tapped and their writings censored. When Halberstam refused to mute his criticism, President Kennedy tried unsuccessfully to get the *New York Times* to recall him.

Despite their public posture of complacency, however, American officials worried privately about their relations with the Diem regime. The rapid arrival of American civilian and military advisers and their growing assertiveness in South Vietnam soon began to alarm Diem. Tension between Washington and Saigon mounted in April 1963 when Ambassador Nolting reported that Diem opposed plans for an expanded and deepened American advisory effort. Nolting admitted that the proliferation and zeal of the American advisers were creating the impression that South Vietnam had become a "protectorate" of the United States. Warning that Diem might demand a reduction in the number of Americans stationed in his country, Nolting proposed that the United States should threaten to cut military aid to Diem to convince him that "we mean business." Diem ultimately withdrew his objection to American plans to send more personnel to South Vietnam but not before policymakers in Washington had become increasingly concerned about the pliability of their protégé in Saigon.

American apprehensions about conditions in South Vietnam were greatly heightened when the long-smoldering issue of religious discrimination suddenly burst into flames. Diem had from the very outset of his rule in Saigon regarded the Catholic refugees from North Vietnam as the core of his constituency. Believing that these anticommunist Catholics could be trusted, Diem appointed them to high positions in the government and military in return for their personal loyalty. Many ambitious South Vietnamese natives got the message, and in the hope of securing better jobs they conveniently converted to Catholicism. As a result, most district and province chiefs were Catholics who often exercised authority over a completely Buddhist populace. The Buddhists increasingly complained that Diem was discriminating against them. Constituting a large majority of the population of South Vietnam, they charged that the Catholics who made up only 10 percent of the population held a disproportionate share of political and military offices. In brief, the Buddhists resented the fact that they had become second-class citizens in a country once dominated by their religion.

Finally, in the spring of 1963, an act of religious discrimination provoked a political crisis that shook the very foundations of the Diem regime. The trouble began on May 8 when thousands of Buddhists assembled in Hué to celebrate the 2,527th birthday of the founder of their religion. The Catholic deputy province chief sought to restrain them by enforcing an old decree that prohibited the flying of religious flags. A week earlier, however, he had allowed Catholics in the same city to display papal banners to commemorate the twenty-fifth anniversary of the ordination of Diem's brother Archbishop Ngo Dinh Thuc. The blatant inconsistency dismayed the Buddhists of Hué, and several thousand of them gathered peacefully in protest. After failing to disperse the demonstrators, the Catholic deputy province chief ordered his troops to fire into the crowd. Nine people were killed on the spot. Buddhists throughout the country protested and demanded that the officials responsible for the massacre at Hué be punished. But Diem ignored their demands. Adding insult to injury, he made the preposterous claim that a Vietcong bomb had caused the deaths even though thousands of people had witnessed the government troops firing on the crowd.

Reacting with remarkable speed and skill, the Buddhist leaders proceeded to organize a massive protest movement. They agitated among relatives, sponsored numerous rallies, and distributed leaflets denouncing religious persecution. On May 30, while hundreds of Buddhist monks staged a demonstration in Saigon, thousands of their colleagues began a fast in the pagodas at Hué. The United States promptly urged Diem to conciliate the Buddhists, but he merely created an innocuous committee to investigate their complaints. Then the Buddhists exploded a bombshell. On June 11, at a busy intersection in Saigon, an elderly monk sat down on the street and crossed his legs, and while he pressed his hands together in prayer, his companions doused him with gasoline and set him ablaze. An Associated Press correspondent, who had been tipped off in advance by Buddhist militants, arrived with a camera in time to photograph the martyr just as a sheet of flames enveloped his body. On the next day, a ghastly picture of the burning monk appeared on the front page of newspapers and on television screens around the world. The American people were horrified. Having been told that the United States was defending democracy in South Vietnam, they wondered what the Saigon government had done to drive the venerable religious leader to sacrifice his life.

President Kennedy, a Catholic himself, became increasingly embarrassed and disturbed about the treatment of the Buddhists in South Vietnam. While Diem continued to do nothing to mollify the distressed

Buddhists, several more monks burned themselves to death. Madame Nhu, the beautiful and haughty Dragon Lady, publicly ridiculed the immolation of the monks. "Let them burn," she jeered, "and we shall clap our hands." Her husband was equally scornful. "If the Buddhists want to have another barbecue," he declared, "I will be glad to supply the gasoline." American policymakers began thinking in private that Nhu and his wife should be removed from positions of influence, and on June 27 Kennedy announced that Henry Cabot Lodge would replace Nolting as the American ambassador in Saigon. But before Nolting left his post, thousands of students took to the streets of Saigon to denounce the Diem regime. Nolting therefore decided to make one last effort to reason with Diem. During his farewell visit on August 14, Diem assured him that no further repressive actions would be taken against the Buddhists.

This promise was broken a week later when Nhu unleashed his Special Forces against the Buddhists. Striking without warning shortly after midnight on August 21, Nhu's men raided and ransacked the pagodas in Saigon, Hué, and other cities throughout South Vietnam. Several monks were killed, many others were injured, and more than 1,000 were arrested. The brutal assaults outraged people from all walks of life. The South Vietnamese ambassador in Washington resigned in protest while the foreign minister in Saigon quit his post and shaved his head in the fashion of a Buddhist monk. The sons and daughters of middle-class families were equally outspoken in their criticism of the government. Students at the University of Saigon began a massive demonstration against the Diem regime on August 24, and more than 4,000 of the protesters were carted off to jail before the rally could be subdued. As the unrest spread, the Buddhist movement grew stronger and became more political. Soon the most militant Buddhist leaders began harboring dark thoughts about overthrowing Diem.

The Plot to Topple Diem

Dissident South Vietnamese army officers had already begun plotting a coup against Diem. On the Fourth of July 1963, General Tran Van Don met with Lieutenant Colonel Lucien Conein, a top CIA operative in South Vietnam. General Don hinted that a coup was in the making, and he asked Conein how the United States would react if the conspirators attempted to depose Diem. But the disgruntled army officers remained hesitant until the brutal crackdown against the Buddhists provided them with both an opportunity and an excuse to move against the government. When news of the pagoda raids reached Washington, the State Department immediately ordered Henry Cabot Lodge to hurry to South Vietnam to appraise the situation. Ambassador Lodge arrived in Saigon on August 22 and promptly confirmed reports that certain army officers had inquired if the United States would support a coup. But Lodge cautioned that the military opposition to the government lacked cohesion. On the next day, Conein reported to Washington that General Don did not seem to think that there was enough support among the officer corps to overthrow Diem. The CIA agent concluded that Don appeared "not to know what to do next."

President Kennedy hastily decided to provide General Don and his associates with the answer. On August 24, he authorized the State Department to cable Ambassador Lodge that the American government could not tolerate the fact that Nhu had maneuvered himself into a commanding position in Saigon. The State Department instructed Lodge to give Diem a chance "to rid himself of Nhu and his coterie," and to replace them with the best military and political personalities available. But if Diem remained obdurate, the State Department explained, "we must face the possibility that Diem himself cannot be preserved." The ambassador was also instructed to tell key military leaders that the United States would find it impossible to continue supporting the South Vietnamese government unless immediate steps were taken to release the arrested Buddhist monks. Moreover, after informing the appropriate military commanders that the United States was prepared to abandon Diem if he refused to remove Nhu, Lodge was to assure them of direct American support during any interim period of breakdown of the central government. Finally, the State Department directed that Lodge and his colleagues "urgently examine all possible alternative leadership and make detailed plans as to how we might bring about Diem's replacement if this should become necessary."

Lodge quickly carried out his instructions. But when he met Diem for the first time on August 26, the ambassador could hardly believe his eyes. "I could see a cloud pass across his face," Lodge recalled years later, "when I suggested that he get rid of Nhu and improve his government." Immediately after his frigid encounter with Diem, the ambassador asked Conein to contact the coup leaders. But General Duong Van Minh told the CIA agent that the rebel generals would remain cautious until they had visible evidence that the United States would not betray them. General Minh urged a severance of economic aid to the Diem government as a sign of American determination to support the coup group. Hoping to encourage the waffling generals, Lodge appealed to Washington on August 29 for permission to give them the green light that Minh had requested. "We are launched on a course," he cabled, "from which there is no respectable turning back: the overthrow of the Diem government." Stressing that the chance of bringing off a coup "depends at least as much on us" as on the generals, Lodge urged that the United States should make an "all-out effort" to get the insurgents to "move promptly."

President Kennedy responded positively to these recommendations. In a cable on August 29, the State Department instructed Lodge to have Harkins reassure the generals that the United States would support a coup that appeared to have a good chance of success. But while establishing liaison with the coup planners, Harkins was to explain that American military forces would not assist them in toppling the Diem regime. The State Department also authorized Lodge to announce at the proper time a suspension of American aid to the Saigon government. Lodge was to use his own discretion in giving the generals the signal that they were waiting to receive from Washington. In a strictly private message later on the same day, Kennedy pledged his support for Lodge but advised him to disengage if he thought the coup would fail. "We will do all that we can," Kennedy promised, "to help you conclude this operation successfully."

But when fears that Nhu had gotten wind of their plans led some of the conspirators to waver, General Minh and his key supporters abruptly called off the coup. Lodge then reasoned that the United States should attempt to work out an accommodation with Diem. In a cable on August 31, the ambassador proposed an arrangement calling for Madame Nhu and Archbishop Thuc to leave the country and for Nhu to limit his role in the government. Secretary of State Dean Rusk agreed that these steps should be taken to improve the situation in South Vietnam. Chairing a meeting of top American policymakers to consider the suggestions received from Lodge earlier in the day, Rusk asked "if anyone present had any doubt but that the coup was off." Only Paul Kattenburg, a junior State Department officer, thought that American officials might still be able to engineer a coup against Diem. Warning that the United States would be thrown out of South Vietnam within a year if Washington attempted to live with the repressive Saigon regime, Kattenburg stated that "at this juncture it would be better for us to make the decision to get out honorably." But Rusk promptly dismissed such thoughts and concluded that the basis of American policy should be "that we will not pull out of Vietnam until the war is won, and that we will not run a coup."

American military leaders were relieved that the political maneuvering in Saigon had come to naught and that they could now get back to the job of helping ARVN defeat the Vietcong. General Harkins, while overseeing military operations from his headquarters at MACV, always maintained a cautious attitude toward the idea of a coup. Although Harkins had come to favor ousting Nhu, he remained opposed to the removal of Diem from his seat of power. Harkins feared that the downfall of Diem would create a political vacuum in Saigon and thereby undermine the war effort against the Vietcong. His superiors in Washington shared his apprehensions. Both Secretary of Defense McNamara and General Taylor, currently the chairman of the Joint Chiefs of Staff, worried that a coup against Diem would work to the advantage of the Vietcong by causing political chaos in Saigon. Doubtful that the plotting generals could provide adequate political leadership for South Vietnam, McNamara and Taylor hoped that the United States could reestablish friendly relations with Diem and return to the task of winning the war.

President Kennedy concurred. Although the vicious persecution of the Buddhists during the summer of 1963 had presented him with a golden opportunity to withdraw from South Vietnam without losing face, Kennedy chose merely to make a temporary retreat to his earlier policy of urging Diem to mend his ways. He clarified his position on September 2 in a widely publicized television interview with Walter Cronkite of CBS. Asserting that the South Vietnamese government had gotten out of touch with the people and that the repression of the Buddhists was very unwise, the president stated that he did not think that ARVN could win the war unless Diem made a greater effort to obtain popular support. "With changes in policy and perhaps with personnel," he suggested, the Saigon regime would be able to regain the support of the people. Kennedy admitted that more than forty Americans had already been killed in combat with the Vietcong. "But I don't agree with those who say we should withdraw," he emphasized. "That would be a great mistake."

The president reiterated his views on September 9 in a television interview with Chet Huntley and David Brinkley of NBC. After referring to the difficulties with the Buddhists, he explained that the United States was attempting to persuade the Saigon government to take steps to win back popular support. But Kennedy said that he did not think that it would be helpful at the present time to reduce American aid to South Vietnam. Nor did he believe that there was any reason to doubt the validity of the domino theory. If South Vietnam fell, Kennedy declared, it would "give the impression that the wave of the future in Southeast Asia was China and the Communists." He therefore insisted that the

United States must not disengage from South Vietnam: "What I am concerned about is that Americans will get impatient and say, because they don't like events in Southeast Asia or they don't like the Government in Saigon, that we should withdraw. That only makes it easier for the Communists. I think we should stay. We should use our influence in as effective a way as we can, but we should not withdraw."

But President Kennedy soon had reason to fear that the United States might be asked to leave by the South Vietnamese government itself. Although Diem agreed that Madam Nhu and Archbishop Thuc should make extensive trips abroad, he refused to remove Nhu from his position of authority. Lodge therefore concluded on September 11 that an accommodation with Diem was now out of the question. Widespread reports that Nhu was seriously negotiating with the North Vietnamese convinced many in Washington that Lodge was right. Roger Hilsman, the assistant secretary of state for Far Eastern affairs, summarized their arguments. In a memorandum presented to Rusk on September 16, Hilsman asserted that it would be futile to pursue a policy of reconciliation toward the Saigon regime because Nhu had already decided to approach Hanoi. He reasoned that the minimum goal of Nhu would be to sharply reduce American influence in South Vietnam and to avoid any meaningful concessions that would go against his mandarin outlook. "The maximum goal," Hilsman warned, "would be a deal with North Vietnam for a truce in the war, a complete removal of the U.S. presence, and a 'neutralist' or 'Titoist' but still separate South Vietnam."

Meanwhile, as American officials were becoming increasingly worried about the possibility of a rapprochement between Saigon and Hanoi, the South Vietnamese generals were reviving their plans for a coup against the Diem regime. General Minh informed Conein on October 5 that the conspirators needed assurances that the United States would not thwart their effort to overthrow the government. Although he and the other generals did not expect any American support for their coup, Minh explained, they would need American military and economic aid after they seized power. Kennedy immediately decided to give the generals the assurances that they sought. "While we do not wish to stimulate a coup," Lodge was instructed on October 6, "we also do not wish to leave impression that U.S. would thwart a change of government or deny economic and military assistance to a new regime if it appeared capable of increasing effectiveness of military effort, ensuring popular support to win war and improving relations with U.S." A few days later, Conein conveyed the message to Minh. The generals received further encouragement during the following weeks when the United States not only announced that economic aid to the Diem regime would be suspended but also threatened that funds for the Special Forces of the South Vietnamese government would be cut unless they were taken away from Nhu and transferred to the field.

After flashing the green light to the generals, however, Kennedy began to have second thoughts. The White House was still haunted by memories of the American-sponsored assault at the Bay of Pigs and the subsequent failure to bring down Castro and reintegrate Cuba into the liberal capitalist world system. Kennedy feared that an American-backed coup attempt against Diem would likewise end in disaster and that he would be held responsible for another embarrassing fiasco. "We are particularly concerned about the hazard that an unsuccessful coup, however carefully we avoid direct engagement, will be laid at our door by public opinion almost everywhere," National Security Adviser Mc-George Bundy cabled Lodge on October 25. "Therefore, while sharing your view that we should not be in a position of thwarting a coup, we would like to have the option of judging and warning on any plan with poor prospects of success." Cabling Lodge again on October 30, Bundy expressed fears that the balance of forces in Saigon were approximately equal and that the possibility of either prolonged fighting or even defeat could be disastrous for American interests. Bundy concluded that, if the coup leaders could not show that their prospects for a quick success were good, "we should discourage them from proceeding since a miscalculation could result in jeopardizing U.S. position in Southeast Asia."

Lodge and Harkins were working at cross-purposes in Saigon during the autumn of 1963. Analyzing the problem in South Vietnam primarily in military terms, Harkins had recently tried to dissuade the rebel generals from implementing their coup plans. Harkins cabled Washington on October 30 that in his opinion there were "no generals qualified to take over" if Diem were dumped. Thus he recommended that the United States should try to "win the military effort as quickly as possible" and then let the South Vietnamese "make any and all changes they want." Defining the problem in South Vietnam fundamentally as a political matter, however, Lodge had not abandoned his doubts that the war could be won under a government headed by Diem. He therefore cabled Washington on October 30 that, rather than discouraging the coup leaders, the United States should provide them with funds to buy off any potential opposition. "My general view is that the United States is trying to bring this medieval country into the twentieth century," Lodge explained with characteristic American arrogance. "We have made considerable progress in military and economic ways, but to gain victory we must also bring them into the twentieth century politically, and that can only be done by either a thoroughgoing change in the behavior of the present government or by another government."

Kennedy remained content to have Lodge decide whether he should make a last-minute effort to stop or delay the coup. In a second cable to the ambassador on October 30, Bundy indicated that he should base his decision on his own judgment regarding the likelihood of success or failure. "If you should conclude that there is not clearly a high prospect of success," he instructed Lodge, "you should communicate this doubt to generals in a way calculated to persuade them to desist at least until chances are better." "But once a coup under responsible leadership has begun," Bundy explained, "it is in the interest of the U.S. Government that it should succeed." It was a foregone conclusion that Lodge would do nothing to discourage the coup leaders, and on November 1 they struck. As the coup got under way, the rebel generals asked Conein to come to their headquarters and maintain telephone contact with the CIA office in Saigon. Conein brought a bag of money with him in case the insurgents needed any funds to accomplish their objective. With the balance of forces overwhelmingly against him, Diem offered to negotiate, but rather than falling into that trap again, the generals brutally murdered both Diem and Nhu.

News of the slaying of the Ngo brothers produced great jubilation throughout South Vietnam. In Saigon, elated crowds danced in the streets, destroyed statues of Diem, and decorated victorious soldiers with garlands of flowers. The celebration spread rapidly into the countryside where happy peasants released their pent-up hostility by demolishing the hated strategic hamlets. Ambassador Lodge was especially delighted when he heard about the death of the dictators. A day after the coup, the Brahmin from Boston invited the triumphant generals to his office in Saigon to congratulate them for ending the rule of the Vietnamese mandarin who had refused to remake himself in the image of his American patrons. Lodge assured the new leaders of South Vietnam that their government would immediately receive economic assistance and diplomatic recognition from the United States. In a cable he sent to Washington a few days later, Lodge optimistically predicted that the overthrow of Diem would shorten the war against the Vietcong.

With the strings of his puppet in Saigon severed, President Kennedy was also hopeful about the prospects for a more effective war effort in South Vietnam. On November 6, he cabled his appreciation to Lodge for a job well done. "Your own leadership in pulling together and directing the whole American operation in South Vietnam in recent months has been of the greatest importance," Kennedy praised. "As you say, while this was a Vietnamese effort, our actions made it clear that we wanted improvements, and when these were not forthcoming from the Diem Government, we necessarily faced and accepted the possibility that our position might encourage a change of government." But the youthful president did not live to see the fate of South Vietnam following the death of Diem. A few weeks later, Kennedy himself was assassinated while traveling down the streets of Dallas in an open car. Vice President Johnson was suddenly elevated to the pinnacle of power in Washington, and now it would be his turn to answer the summons of the trumpet.

FIVE

The Master of Deceit

So just for the moment I have not thought we were ready for American boys to do the fighting for Asian boys. . . . We are not going north and drop bombs at this stage of the game.

President Lyndon B. Johnson, 1964

Political Disorder in South Vietnam

When Lyndon B. Johnson became president following the assassination of John F. Kennedy in November 1963, he pledged to continue the policies of his fallen predecessor. Johnson demonstrated his intentions by retaining Kennedy's top foreign affairs counselors: Dean Rusk as secretary of state, Robert McNamara as secretary of defense, and McGeorge Bundy as national security adviser. These men shared the same basic assumptions and general outlook that had guided the diplomacy of the Kennedy administration. They all believed that foreign markets were needed to absorb surplus American products and to assure full employment for workers in the United States. They all feared that revolutionary upheavals in underdeveloped countries would undermine the liberal capitalist world system and retard the flow of international commerce. They all subscribed to a global version of the domino theory, which held that indigenous revolutions in Southeast Asia could spread by example into Africa and Latin America. And they all viewed the defense of South Vietnam as a test of their resolve to sustain the Pax Americana.

From the very outset of his administration, President Johnson made it clear that he was determined to draw the line against the spread of communism in South Vietnam. "I am not going to lose Vietnam," he asserted within hours after taking the oath of office on November 22. "I am not going to be the President who saw Southeast Asia go the way China went." Two days later, after listening to Henry Cabot Lodge describe the situation in South Vietnam, Johnson instructed the ambassador to return to Saigon and tell the generals who had replaced Diem that the United States would make good on its promise to provide them with economic and military assistance. The president, like his principal advisers, believed that the way the United States responded to the communist challenge in Southeast Asia would have profound consequences all around the planet. A few months after he entered the White House, Johnson told a veteran American diplomat that a firm stand against communism in South Vietnam would ensure international order and stability by demonstrating that the United States would resist violent changes in the status quo.

Despite his determination to defend the New Frontier throughout the Third World, however, Johnson confronted a rapidly deteriorating situation in South Vietnam. State Department officials had hoped that the removal of Diem and Nhu would restore political harmony in South Vietnam, but as American military leaders had feared, Saigon soon plunged into the throes of political instability. Shortly after the death of the Ngo brothers, the coup leaders established a twelve-member Military Revolutionary Council headed by General Duong Van Minh. But rather than organizing an effective war effort against the Vietcong, the members of the military junta bickered endlessly among themselves. The ruling generals were unable to bring the Buddhists and Catholics together into a strong anticommunist coalition. Nor were they able to build a solid base of support in the countryside where the strategic hamlet program lay in shambles. In early December 1963, the senior American representative in Long An reported that since the summer three quarters of the 200 strategic hamlets in the province had been destroyed either by the Vietcong or by their own occupants. "The only progress made in Long An province," he concluded, "has been by the Vietcong."

Ho Chi Minh and his comrades in Hanoi hoped to take advantage of the political disorder in Saigon following the overthrow of Diem and his family. Meeting in December 1963, the Central Committee of the Lao Dong party decided to promote a military buildup in South Vietnam to tip the balance of forces in favor of the Vietcong. "We must strive to attain victory step by step," the Central Committee resolved, "and gradually push back the enemy before reaching the General Offensive and Uprising to win complete victory." The communist leaders in Hanoi not only authorized the infiltration of more men and weapons into South Vietnam, but they also directed the National Liberation Front to launch a political campaign to weaken the new government in Saigon. While the members of the Military Revolutionary Council were struggling to consolidate their power, therefore, the NLF put forth a conciliatory manifesto calling for a cease-fire, general elections, and the formation of a coalition government representing "all forces, parties, tendencies and strata of the South Vietnamese people." The NLF advocated the establishment of an independent South Vietnam that would pursue a neutralist policy until reunification with North Vietnam could eventually be carried out "step by step on a voluntary basis."

Although President Johnson and his advisers assumed that the military junta in Saigon would remain firmly opposed to communism, they feared that the growing antiwar sentiment in South Vietnam might impel the feuding generals to make an accommodation with the National Liberation Front. American leaders contemplated an alarming scenario: negotiations between the contending political groups in Saigon might lead to a halt in the fighting and the emergence of a coalition government; and the new regime might bend to popular pressure in favor of neutralism and demand the withdrawal of American military personnel from South Vietnam. "Neutralism," Ambassador Lodge cabled the State Department in early December 1963, "is always present in varying degrees here in South Vietnam." Lodge and his colleagues in Washington became increasingly worried that the ultimate consequences of a movement toward neutralism would be a complete collapse of the anticommunist forces in South Vietnam, a reunification with North Vietnam, and the triumph of communism in the rest of Southeast Asia and elsewhere in the Third World.

After a brief visit to South Vietnam, Secretary of Defense McNamara reported to President Johnson on December 21 that conditions had deteriorated to a far greater extent than Americans realized. "The situation is very disturbing," he warned. "Current trends, unless reversed in the next two to three months, will lead to neutralization at best and more likely to a Communist-controlled state." McNamara pointed out that the Vietcong had made substantial progress since the coup against Diem.

"The Vietcong now control very high proportions of the people in certain key provinces, particularly those directly south and west of Saigon," he noted. "In these key provinces, the Vietcong have destroyed almost all major roads, and are collecting taxes at will." But McNamara thought that the new government in Saigon was the greatest source of concern. He observed that the military junta "is indecisive and drifting" and that military operations "are not being effectively directed because the generals are so preoccupied with essentially political affairs." McNamara ended his gloomy assessment on an ominous note. "We should watch the situation very carefully, running scared, hoping for the best, but preparing for more forceful moves if the situation does not show early signs of improvement."

The Joint Chiefs of Staff shared his anxiety about conditions in South Vietnam and his readiness to unleash American military power to subdue the Vietcong insurgents. In a memorandum prepared for McNamara in January 1964, they pressed for bolder actions to accomplish American objectives in Southeast Asia. The JCS regarded the conflict in South Vietnam as "the first real test of our determination to defeat the communist wars of national liberation formula." Believing that South Vietnam occupied a pivotal position in the worldwide confrontation between capitalism and communism, they warned that a Vietcong victory would damage American prestige and credibility throughout Asia and have "a corresponding unfavorable effect upon our image in Africa and Latin America." The JCS complained that the United States was fighting under self-imposed restrictions by keeping the war within the boundaries of South Vietnam and by avoiding the direct use of American combat forces. They thought that the time was fast approaching when Uncle Sam would have to take off his gloves and strike his enemy with a combination of punches.

Determined to score a victory in South Vietnam, the Joint Chiefs of Staff recommended that the United States should be ready to take the following actions: give the head of MACV responsibility for the total American program in South Vietnam, induce the Saigon government to turn over the tactical direction of the war to the American military commander, persuade the rulers of South Vietnam to conduct overt ground operations in Laos to impede the flow of men and material from North Vietnam, arm and aid South Vietnamese forces in the aerial bombing of critical targets in North Vietnam and in the mining of sea approaches to that country, advise and support South Vietnamese units in conducting large-scale commando raids inside North Vietnam, and if necessary commit additional American forces in support of combat action within

South Vietnam. "It is our conviction," the JCS concluded, "that any or all of the foregoing actions may be required to enhance our position in Southeast Asia."

A week later, on January 30, a group of young officers headed by General Nguyen Khanh overthrew the divided and ineffective military junta in Saigon. Some of the rebel officers had supported the ouster of Diem but now felt insufficiently rewarded under the Minh regime while others who had been close to Diem feared that they would lose their positions if Minh and his cohorts remained in power. General Khanh himself was also motivated by personal ambition, but he justified his actions by claiming that the leading members of the Military Revolutionary Council were preparing to make an agreement with the National Liberation Front. While the coup against Minh was in progress, Khanh informed Lodge that he was eager to turn to the United States for political advice. "It is safe to say," the CIA promptly reported from Saigon, "that Khanh's group will be essentially pro-American, anti-communist and anti-neutralist in general orientation." President Johnson welcomed the news, and on February 2 he sent Khanh a warm note promising that the United States would support his government.

Khanh quickly demonstrated his desire to cooperate fully with the United States. After revamping the Military Revolutionary Council and promoting several young officers to key positions in his new regime, he yielded to American wishes and retained Minh in a figurehead capacity to make it appear that no basic change in the government had taken place. Khanh then proceeded to work closely with the United States in carrying out military operations against the Vietcong, and in early February 1964 he began participating in an enlarged American-directed program of covert action against North Vietnam. This scheme, code-named Operation Plan 34 Alpha, involved intelligence overflights, the dropping of propaganda leaflets, and commando raids. While some American-trained South Vietnamese units parachuted into North Vietnam on sabotage missions, others attacked facilities along the North Vietnamese coast from patrol boats provided by the United States. The OPLAN 34 A program also included electronic espionage missions conducted by American destroyers in the Gulf of Tonkin to pinpoint the location of radar stations and antiaircraft networks in North Vietnam. These maritime surveillance operations, code-named De Soto patrols, were initiated in anticipation of future air and naval attacks against North Vietnam.

In a long memorandum prepared for President Johnson on the first day of March 1964, Assistant Secretary of Defense William P. Bundy recommended that the United States should also begin taking overt military actions against North Vietnam. After discussing the situation with his brother McGeorge, he argued that American forces should first blockade the port of Haiphong and then bomb roads and railroads, power stations and industrial plants, and military training camps in North Vietnam. Bundy explained that one purpose of the blockade and bombing campaign would be to get North Vietnam to stop or at least cut down the shipment of supplies to the Vietcong. He also hoped that such a demonstration of American determination to prevent the spread of communism in Southeast Asia would stiffen the Khanh government and "discourage moves toward neutralism in South Vietnam." Although he admitted that the proposed military measures would normally require a declaration of war, Bundy warned that an attempt to induce Congress to declare war might spark a major political controversy in the United States. He therefore suggested that President Johnson should circumvent the constitutional requirement for a legislative declaration of war by obtaining a congressional resolution freeing him to take punitive action against North Vietnam.

As pressure for overt military action against North Vietnam increased, Secretary of Defense McNamara made another trip to Saigon to assess the situation in South Vietnam. McNamara found that conditions had grown much worse since his last visit, and on March 16 he reported to President Johnson that about 40 percent of the countryside was under Vietcong control or predominant influence. McNamara pointed out that, while ARVN desertion rates were high and increasing, the Vietcong were recruiting energetically and effectively. He also noted that the North Vietnamese were supplying the Vietcong with a growing assortment of Chinese weapons including recoilless rifles, machine guns, rocket launchers, and mortars. Despite the enhanced military capability of the Vietcong, however, McNamara still believed that the greatest problem in South Vietnam was the uncertain viability of the Saigon government. "Large groups of the population are now showing signs of apathy and indifference," he warned. "There is a constant threat of assassination or of another coup, which would drop morale and organization nearly to zero."

McNamara urged that the United States should do everything possible to help Khanh build up his base of support and root out the Vietcong. He recommended that American officials at all levels "should continue to make it clear that we fully support the Khanh government and are totally opposed to any further coups." McNamara also recommended that the United States should provide funds for a substantial increase in the size of the South Vietnamese armed forces. If the Khanh regime succeeded in taking hold in the next few months, he added, the United States might want to exert graduated military pressure against North Vietnam to undermine the confidence of the Vietcong and to bolster the morale of the ruling clique in Saigon. But McNamara advised against bombing North Vietnam at the present time. "Unless and until the Khanh government has established its position, and preferably is making significant progress in the South," he argued, "an overt extension of operations in the North carries the risk of being mounted from an extremely weak base which might at any moment collapse and leave the posture of political confrontation worsened rather than improved."

President Johnson concurred. After approving a mobilization plan to put South Vietnam on a war footing, he cabled Lodge on March 17 that the United States had agreed that ARVN ground troops should begin cross-border penetrations into Laos to impede the flow of military equipment down the Ho Chi Minh Trail. But the president indicated that he would reserve judgment regarding the question of launching overt American military attacks against North Vietnam. Three days later, on March 20, Johnson cabled Lodge that for the moment any overt measures against North Vietnam would be premature. Johnson explained that "our planning for action against the North is on a contingency basis" and that the immediate task in the South "is to develop the strongest possible military and political base for possible later action." He added the United States expected a showdown between China and Russia in the near future and that an American bombing campaign against North Vietnam would be more practicable after a Sino-Soviet rift. Worried that in the meantime the South Vietnamese government might negotiate a peace settlement calling for the withdrawal of American military personnel, Johnson instructed Lodge to explain to authorities in Saigon that his mission was "precisely for the purpose of knocking down the idea of neutralization wherever it rears its ugly head."

While holding the decision to bomb North Vietnam in abeyance, President Johnson and his top foreign policy advisers were eager to do everything they could to shore up the Khanh regime in South Vietnam. "In our efforts to help the Vietnamese to help themselves, we must not let any arbitrary limits on budget, or manpower, or procedures stand in our way," Johnson cabled Lodge on April 28. "You must have whatever you need to help the Vietnamese do the job, and I assure you that I will act at once to eliminate obstacles or restraints wherever they may appear." But the military junta in Saigon did not make much progress either in building a solid base of popular support or in gaining the initiative against the Vietcong. In a cable to Lodge on May 21, Secretary of State Rusk revealed his growing exasperation with Khanh and his cohorts. "Is there any way we can shake the main body of leadership by the scruff of the neck and insist that they put aside all bickering and lesser differences in order to concentrate upon the defeat of the Viet Cong?" Rusk asked. "Can we find some way by which General Khanh can convince larger segments of the people that they have a stake in the success of his leadership against the Viet Cong?" Rusk searched for an answer. "Somehow we must change the pace at which people move," he concluded, "and I suspect that this can only be done with a pervasive intrusion of Americans into their affairs."

The Gulf of Tonkin Affair

Several American leaders wanted to go further and employ military force against North Vietnam. During a conference held in Honolulu in early June 1964, Lodge joined with the Joint Chiefs of Staff in advocating the aerial bombardment of North Vietnam. Specialists in the Pentagon drew up a list of ninety-four targets for potential air strikes in North Vietnam while a small group of civilian officials in Washington prepared a rough draft of a congressional resolution empowering the president to commit American military forces anywhere in Southeast Asia. William P. Bundy, currently the assistant secretary of state for Far Eastern affairs, outlined the arguments in favor of such a resolution. "The situation in South Viet-Nam," he reasoned on June 12, "could deteriorate to the point where we had to consider at least beginning stronger actions to the north in order to put greater pressure on Hanoi and lift morale in South Viet-Nam." Bundy concluded that the proposed resolution would demonstrate American firmness and provide "complete flexibility in the hands of the Executive in the coming political months."

Not wanting to look like a warmonger on the eve of the presidential election, Johnson decided to take a different tack. He asked the Canadian government to send J. Blair Seaborn on a secret mission to persuade the communist leaders in North Vietnam to stop supporting the Vietcong insurgents. During a confidential meeting in Hanoi on June 18, Seaborn warned Prime Minister Pham Van Dong that the United States held North Vietnam directly responsible for the guerrilla war in South Vietnam. He hinted that the United States would reward the North Vietnamese with economic assistance if they agreed to confine their energy to developing their own resources. Seaborn also implied that the United

States would punish the North Vietnamese with devastating attacks if they continued to support the Vietcong rebels. But Pham Van Dong replied that a just solution to the war would require an American withdrawal from Indochina, the participation of the National Liberation Front in a coalition government in Saigon, and the peaceful reunification of Vietnam. Asserting that his people were determined to carry on the struggle, he confidently predicted that they would eventually achieve their goals.

Despite his failure to intimidate the rulers of North Vietnam, President Johnson was not about to abandon his efforts to assure the survival of an independent noncommunist regime in South Vietnam. Johnson demonstrated his desire to infuse greater vigor into the counterinsurgency campaign in South Vietnam on June 20 when he promoted the resolute and energetic General William C. Westmoreland to replace the ever-optimistic Harkins as the commander of MACV. The number of American military advisers serving under Westmoreland was quickly increased by more than 4,000. And when Lodge resigned his position as ambassador to seek the Republican nomination for president, Johnson appointed General Maxwell D. Taylor to take charge of the American embassy in Saigon. The American economic aid package was rapidly expanded after Taylor began his new job on July 2, and before long the United States was pouring money into South Vietnam at a rate of nearly $2 million a day.

The American-directed program of covert harassment and naval surveillance was also pressed forward with great vigor against North Vietnam. On July 31, South Vietnamese commandos carried out clandestine OPLAN 34 A raids against two islands a few miles off the coast of North Vietnam. The American destroyer *Maddox*, operating under explicit orders on the next day, conducted a De Soto mission of electronic espionage in the same general vicinity. The North Vietnamese mistakenly concluded that the *Maddox* was running cover for the South Vietnamese commandos, and on August 2 three North Vietnamese torpedo boats attacked the American destroyer. As the small craft swiftly approached his ship, Captain John J. Herrick directed his crew to commence firing while he radioed the *Ticonderoga* for air support. Only one bullet struck the *Maddox* before jet planes from the aircraft carrier arrived overhead to help sink one of the North Vietnamese boats and cripple the other two. "The other side got a sting out of this," Secretary of State Rusk told reporters. "If they do it again, they'll get another sting."

Rather than attempting to avoid another clash with North Vietnamese patrol boats, American leaders continued to authorize provocative actions in the Gulf of Tonkin. Commander-in-Chief for the Pacific Admiral Ulysses G. Sharp ordered the *Maddox*, together with the *Turner Joy*, to resume operations and to repel any further attacks. As the two American destroyers zigzagged off the North Vietnamese coast on August 3, South Vietnamese commandos returned to the area and raided communication facilities along the North Vietnamese shore. Captain Herrick soon reported to his superiors in Hawaii that intercepts of communist radio messages indicated that the North Vietnamese thought that the De Soto operations were tied in with the commando forays. Wanting to steer away from probable trouble, he proposed that the *Maddox* and *Turner Joy* should retreat to the open sea. But Admiral Sharp ordered both destroyers to continue their maneuvers "to assert our legitimate rights in these international waters." Rusk promptly cabled Saigon to explain to Ambassador Taylor how Washington viewed the situation: "We believe that present OPLAN 34 A activities are beginning to rattle Hanoi, and MADDOX incident is directly related to their efforts to resist these activities. We have no intention of yielding to pressure."

American statesmen and seamen were fully prepared for a second incident in the Gulf of Tonkin. As the *Maddox* and *Turner Joy* proceeded cautiously in anticipation of another ambush, their crews carefully scanned sonar instruments in an effort to pick up noise from the propellers of any North Vietnamese patrol boats that might be lurking in the area. The two destroyers began getting distorted radar beams in the midst of a violent thunderstorm on the night of August 4, and the anxious American sailors began firing wildly into the dark. After calling for air support, Captain Herrick reported to Honolulu that the *Maddox* and *Turner Joy* were engaged in battle. But he soon had second thoughts. Not a single sailor on either American ship had seen or heard any enemy gunfire, and none of the pilots from the *Ticonderoga* had been able to detect any trace of enemy boats. Herrick promptly reported that "no actual sightings" had been made and that "freak weather effects" may have caused the erratic radar blips. He therefore suggested that a "complete evaluation" of the episode should be made before any further actions were taken.

Despite the lack of solid evidence for the supposed second attack in the Gulf of Tonkin, President Johnson seized the opportunity to implement contingency plans that had been temporarily shelved. Johnson appeared on television screens across the nation just before midnight on August 4 and solemnly announced that the United States was retaliating against North Vietnam for "repeated acts of violence" directed at American forces. While he was speaking, American jets flew sixty-four sorties against North Vietnamese naval bases and nearby oil storage facilities. His aides had already broadened their earlier draft of the proposed congressional resolution to give him wide discretionary authority to deploy American military forces in Southeast Asia. A few days later, Johnson privately expressed his own doubts about the alleged second attack on American seamen. "Hell," he confided to one of his advisers, "those dumb, stupid sailors were just shooting at flying fish." But Johnson was not about to forego the chance to obtain bipartisan support for whatever military action he might desire to take in the future. Johnson wanted a congressional resolution that would strengthen the morale of the Saigon government and authorize him to exercise unlimited American military power in Southeast Asia.

President Johnson and Secretary of State Rusk made a concerted effort to mobilize support for the resolution in the Senate. During private meetings with a select group of senators, Johnson and Rusk claimed that they sought no wider war but that they wanted to convince the North Vietnamese that Americans were united in their determination to safeguard South Vietnam. J. William Fulbright, the chairman of the Foreign Relations Committee, agreed to shepherd the resolution through the Senate. But he faced a small number of skeptical colleagues. Fearful of giving the president a blank check to take whatever action that he deemed necessary, Senator Gaylord Nelson of Wisconsin began preparing an amendment to the resolution to indicate that Congress opposed any direct American military involvement in Southeast Asia. But Fulbright told Nelson that Johnson desired unanimous backing for the permissive measure simply to frighten Ho Chi Minh and his comrades in Hanoi into stopping their support for the insurgency in South Vietnam. Having been assured that the president had no intention of sending American combat troops to Vietnam, Nelson finally decided against introducing a restrictive amendment to the resolution.

Only two isolated senators continued to oppose the maneuver to grant the president the power to make war in the absence of a congressional declaration of war. Charging that the reported incidents in the Gulf of Tonkin were the inevitable consequence of an aggressive American policy in Southeast Asia, Ernest Gruening of Alaska pleaded with his colleagues not to authorize the president to send "American boys into combat in a war in which we have no business." So did Wayne Morse of Oregon. "I believe that history will record that we have made a great mistake in subverting and circumventing the Constitution of the United States," Morse declared. "Future generations will look with dismay and great disappointment upon a Congress which is now about to make such a historic mistake." But his warnings were cast aside. On August 7, with the House voting 416 to 0 in favor and only Gruening and Morse dissenting in the Senate, Congress passed the Gulf of Tonkin Resolution. The joint resolution authorized the president "to take all necessary measures to repel any armed attack against the forces of the United States and to prevent further aggression."

President Johnson had proved himself to be the master of deceit. His spokesmen had withheld critical information about the South Vietnamese commando assaults along the North Vietnamese coast, and they had described the American destroyers as the targets of deliberate communist aggression while engaging in routine patrols in international waters. In so doing, they had helped the president gain an almost unanimous endorsement for the unlimited exercise of executive power from a badly misled Congress. Johnson was delighted with the broad authority that the Gulf of Tonkin Resolution had given him. "Like grandma's nightshirt," he later quipped, "it covered everything." Johnson had not only obtained a free hand to pursue a militant policy in Southeast Asia, but he had also prepared the way for his victory in the fast approaching presidential election. By taking a firm but restrained stand against what were portrayed as unprovoked attacks on the high seas, the president won widespread support from the American people. His ratings in the Harris public opinion poll skyrocketed from 42 to 72 percent overnight. Thus Johnson had succeeded in outmaneuvering Barry Goldwater, the hawkish Republican nominee for president, on the potentially disruptive war issue.

The Rhetoric of Restraint

Johnson projected himself as the peace candidate for the Democratic party as the 1964 presidential campaign got under way. Not wanting to jeopardize his strong position in the polls, he proceeded with caution immediately after the Tonkin Gulf affair. Johnson temporarily suspended both the De Soto patrols and the American-sponsored clandestine attacks along the North Vietnamese coast. But while he assumed the posture of a dove in an effort to maintain the support of moderate voters across the country, Goldwater cast himself as a hawk who wanted to go all out to achieve a quick victory against the forces of communism in Southeast Asia. Taking advantage of the militant rhetoric of his Republican adversary, Johnson shrewdly implied that Goldwater was an irresponsible fool. "Some others are eager to enlarge the conflict," Johnson

declared in a campaign speech on August 12. "They call upon us to supply American boys to do the job that Asian boys should do. They ask us
to take reckless action which might risk the lives of millions and engulf
much of Asia and certainly threaten the peace of the entire world." He
warned that "such action would offer no solution at all to the real problems of Vietnam."

Renewed political turmoil in South Vietnam gave President Johnson
additional reason to remain cautious. As the apprehension grew that
North Vietnam might retaliate for the Tonkin Gulf air strikes, Khanh
jumped at the chance to consolidate his power in Saigon. He hastily
declared a state of emergency, severely limited civil liberties, and
sharply restricted the press. On August 16, Khanh moved to oust Minh
as chief of state by introducing a new constitution that eliminated the
position of his principal rival. Khanh simultaneously announced that he
would assume the new post of president while remaining chairman of the
Military Revolutionary Council. These abrupt moves sparked an explo-
sive reaction in Saigon. Streaming into the streets, Buddhist militants
and their student allies led massive demonstrations against Khanh. The
angry Buddhists demanded that he establish a civilian government,
assure religious freedom, and schedule elections for the coming year.
Retreating in the face of the mounting protest movement, Khanh
announced that he would revise the new constitution and relax government controls. But these modest concessions failed to satisfy the Buddhists, and they continued to press for major reforms.

Americans on the scene were alarmed about the political uproar in
Saigon. As the Buddhists became increasingly assertive in their confrontations with Khanh, American observers feared the emergence of a coalition government that would seek neutralist goals. "War weariness and a
desire for a quick solution to the long struggle against the Viet Cong may
be an important factor underlying the current agitation," the CIA warned
on August 25. "The confused situation is extremely vulnerable to
exploitation by the Communists and by the proponents of a negotiated
settlement." American officials became even more anxious when they
learned that malcontents within the armed forces were plotting a coup
against Khanh. Ambassador Taylor worked hard to discourage the con-
spiring officers and to help Khanh solidify his position. But machina-
tions within the officer corps continued, and Taylor remained
pessimistic about the future. "We should not delude ourselves," he
cabled from Saigon on September 2, "that we can put together any
combination of personalities that will add up to a really effective
government."

President Johnson promptly ordered Ambassador Taylor to return to Washington to participate in a full review of American policy. During a conference at the White House on September 7, the president and his top advisers considered the option of embarking upon an accelerated program of military action against North Vietnam. General Earle Wheeler, the chairman of the Joint Chiefs of Staff, argued that the United States should launch a bombing campaign against North Vietnam as soon as possible. He and his colleagues believed that only significant military pressure on North Vietnam could provide the psychological boost necessary to attain political stability in South Vietnam. But Taylor wanted to postpone the bombardment of North Vietnam until Khanh had time to strengthen his military position against the Vietcong. Fearing the development of a popular front that would demand the withdrawal of American forces from South Vietnam, Taylor concluded that beginning around December 1 the United States would have to direct escalating pressure against North Vietnam. "If we leave Vietnam with our tail between our legs," he warned, "the consequences of this defeat in the rest of Asia, Africa and Latin America would be disastrous."

Two days later, on September 9, Johnson met once again with his top advisers to discuss what actions the United States should take to assure the survival of an independent noncommunist South Vietnam. Secretary of Defense McNamara reported that there was an important division among the Joint Chiefs of Staff. The air force and marine corps representatives believed that the situation in South Vietnam would continue to deteriorate unless immediate air strikes were launched against North Vietnam. But General Wheeler, together with the army and navy representatives, now agreed with Ambassador Taylor that it was important not to overstrain the currently weakened Saigon government by drastic action in the immediate future. While acknowledging that this was his view, Taylor emphasized that sooner or later the United States would indeed have to act more forcefully against North Vietnam. John McCone, the director of the CIA, likewise argued that a sustained air attack against North Vietnam would be dangerous at present because of the weakness of the South Vietnamese government. While agreeing that the decision to bombard North Vietnam should be delayed, Secretary of State Rusk suggested that by December the deepening Sino-Soviet split might make the Chinese communists more reluctant to respond aggressively to bolder American moves in Southeast Asia.

The president and his advisers were preoccupied with the problem of political disorder in South Vietnam. When Johnson asked whether the United States could stop the internal feuding in Saigon, Taylor replied that it would be difficult to accomplish much with "a group of men who turned off their hearing aids in the face of appeals to the public weal." He explained that the present rulers of South Vietnam "regularly estimated matters in terms of their own personal gains and losses." When Johnson asked him to compare Khanh and Diem in regard to popular support, Taylor responded that the South Vietnamese people did not care for either one. McNamara was equally concerned about the internal discord in South Vietnam. He emphasized the importance of funneling American economic aid into the urban areas to lower the level of student and Buddhist pressure and to increase the political base of support for the government. Endorsing this judgment, McCone stated that the CIA was "disturbed by the prospect that the internal movement toward negotiations might be increasing and that there was some sign also of anti-American feeling in South Vietnam."

President Johnson asked if anyone present doubted whether South Vietnam was worth all the effort that would be necessary to achieve American objectives in Southeast Asia. "We could not afford to let Hanoi win," Ambassador Taylor replied, "in terms of our overall position in the area and in the world." General Wheeler reported that the Joint Chiefs of Staff were in unanimous agreement with that assessment. "If we should lose in South Vietnam, we would lose Southeast Asia," he declared with considerable force. "Country after country on the periphery would give way and look toward Communist China as the rising power of the area." McCone and Rusk concurred that the United States must not allow the South Vietnam domino to fall into the clutches of communism. Then, after watching his aides reach a consensus, Johnson said that in his opinion the United States should not take extensive action against North Vietnam until the government in South Vietnam could be strengthened. "With a weak and wobbly situation," he reasoned, "it would be unwise to attack until we could stabilize our base." Johnson ended the September 9 meeting by asking Wheeler to explain to his colleagues on the JCS that "we would be ready to do more when we had a base."

But the political structure in South Vietnam continued to rest upon shaky foundations. On September 13, a group of disgruntled officers led their forces into Saigon in an effort to wrest control from Khanh. American officials raced to the rescue, however, when Khanh requested their help. The Voice of America announced that the United States backed Khanh, and General Westmoreland persuaded some of the rebel officers to remove their troops from Saigon. Although the coup attempt quickly collapsed, Khanh concluded that he would have to broaden his base of support to gain leverage against his military rivals. Khanh realized that the Buddhist monks were the only noncommunist leaders with a large following in South Vietnam, so in an attempt to win their favor he yielded to their demands for a civilian government. On September 26, Khanh created the High National Council composed of seventeen elderly civilians and charged them with the task of selecting a chief of state. The council of elders proceeded to set up a civilian administration, but Khanh retained real power in his hands. Although American officials feared that the Buddhists might ultimately push Khanh toward neutralism, they saw no alternative except to continue supporting him.

Meanwhile, during the final phase of his campaign for reelection in the autumn of 1964, President Johnson continued telling the American people what he thought they wanted to hear. Johnson assured his audiences on numerous occasions that he sought no wider war in Southeast Asia. Yet his campaign speeches often contained escape clauses tailored to keep his options open. While addressing a crowd in New Hampshire on September 28, for example, Johnson stated that he would consider attacking North Vietnam "only as a last resort" to prevent a communist takeover in South Vietnam. "We are not going north and drop bombs," he proclaimed, adding the qualifying phrase, "at this stage of the game." Johnson also indicated that he wanted to be very careful with regard to the situation in the South. "So just for the moment," he hedged, "I have not thought we were ready for American boys to do the fighting for Asian boys." The American people registered their approval of this rhetoric of restraint at the polls on November 3. As a result, Johnson crushed Goldwater by the largest vote margin ever scored in a presidential election in the history of the United States. The spectacular Democratic landslide kept Johnson in the White House and gave his party huge majorities in both chambers of Congress.

Under Secretary of State George W. Ball was the only high American official who took a private position that jibed with the public posture of the president. In October 1964, Ball prepared a long memorandum that argued forcefully in favor of negotiation rather than escalation. He not only challenged the contention that an American air offensive against North Vietnam would improve morale in South Vietnam, but he also questioned whether a bombing campaign would compel Hanoi to stop supporting the insurgency against the Saigon government. Ball warned that North Vietnam might retaliate by pouring a large number of combat troops into South Vietnam. If the United States responded in kind, he reasoned, China might intervene with unlimited manpower. Ball cautioned that the spreading military conflict might lead to a nuclear holocaust. "Once on the tiger's back," he wrote, "we cannot be sure of picking the place to dismount." To enable the United States to avoid becoming involved in a process of mutual escalation, he advocated a political solution to the military struggle. Ball suggested that the United States should encourage the organization of a neutralist South Vietnamese government that would negotiate a settlement with the National Liberation Front. If the likely communist takeover of South Vietnam were postponed for a substantial period of time, he concluded, the damage to the global prestige of the United States would be minimized.

Shortly after his smashing victory over Goldwater on November 3, Johnson created a National Security Council Working Group to study American options in Southeast Asia. The members of the Working Group, chaired by William Bundy, held frequent sessions before they formulated a range of possibilities for the president to consider. The representative for the Joint Chiefs of Staff advocated an all-out air offensive against North Vietnam to impede the flow of military supplies into South Vietnam and to compel Hanoi to stop supporting the Vietcong insurgents. But many civilians on the committee feared that a massive bombing campaign might provoke North Vietnam to send combat units into South Vietnam and spur China to intervene in the war. On November 21, the Working Group prepared a position paper that outlined three broad courses of action for the United States to take in Southeast Asia. Option A called for reprisal actions against North Vietnam for any spectacular attack by the Vietcong within South Vietnam. Option B required a systematic program of rapidly increasing military pressures against North Vietnam. Option C demanded slowly graduated military moves first against infiltration routes in Laos and than against targets in North Vietnam. In short, rather than urging a negotiated settlement along the lines advocated by George Ball, the Working Group presented three formulas for military escalation.

Before returning to Washington to help shape the final recommendations for the president, Ambassador Taylor set forth his views in a comprehensive memorandum. Taylor emphasized the lack of an adequate political base in South Vietnam. "It is impossible to foresee a stable and effective government under any name in anything like the near future," he observed. "We sense a mounting feeling of war weariness and hopelessness that pervade South Vietnam." In contrast, Taylor marveled at the continued strength of the Vietcong guerrillas. "Not only do the Vietcong units have the recuperative power of the phoenix, but they have an amazing ability to maintain morale." Taylor argued that the United States should make a concerted effort to change the situation before it was too late. To raise morale in Saigon, he reasoned, the United States should be ready to bomb selected targets in North Vietnam in retaliation for any outrageous Vietcong attack in South Vietnam. If a satisfactory government could be established in Saigon, he concluded, Washington should be prepared to embark upon "a methodical program of mounting air attacks" in order to induce Hanoi not only to stop aiding the Vietcong guerrillas but also to pressure them into ending the revolution in South Vietnam.

President Johnson met with his top foreign policy advisers on December 1, 1964 to discuss what actions the United States should take in Southeast Asia. His senior advisers advocated an air offensive to be implemented in two stages. Phase I called for bombing raids against infiltration routes in Laos plus reprisal strikes against targets in North Vietnam in response to any dramatic Vietcong actions in South Vietnam. Phase II provided for a program of gradually extended air attacks against North Vietnam. But the president refused to authorize provocative actions against Hanoi until the government in Saigon demonstrated more stability. Reluctant to hit North Vietnam unless South Vietnam was able to take a punch in return, Johnson said he did not want "to send a widow woman to slap Jack Dempsey." He stressed that the South Vietnamese must put their house in order before the United States provoked the North Vietnamese dragon. Johnson agreed that Operation Barrel Roll, a secret bombing campaign against infiltration trails in Laos, should begin promptly. But he was not yet ready to approve the implementation of either Phase I or Phase II plans for the bombing of North Vietnam.

Two days later, on December 3, President Johnson spelled out his position in instructions to Ambassador Taylor. "There are certain minimum criteria of performance in South Vietnam which must be met," he explained, "before new measures against North Vietnam would be either justified or practical." Johnson insisted that South Vietnamese leaders should be capable of maintaining law and order in the principal centers of population and be able to carry out effective counterinsurgency operations in the countryside. He also demanded that the Saigon government "must have the means to cope with the enemy reactions which must be expected to result from any change in the pattern of our operations." While American air strikes against North Vietnam could contribute to the campaign against the Vietcong, the president argued, they could not in and of themselves end the guerrilla war in South Vietnam. Even if Hanoi stopped aiding the Vietcong, he reasoned, it would be necessary to have a stable and effective government in Saigon to defeat the revolutionary forces in South Vietnam. Johnson therefore instructed Taylor to inform the political and military leaders in Saigon that continued American support for South Vietnam depended upon the establishment of governmental stability and national unity. Taylor was authorized to promise an increase in American military aid if they demonstrated political cohesion and improvement in fighting the Vietcong.

But Ambassador Taylor was unable to foster harmony among the various civilian and military factions in South Vietnam. Shortly after he returned to his post in Saigon, the Buddhists began staging demonstrations against Prime Minister Tran Van Huong and his recently installed civilian government. General Khanh and a group of young officers headed by Air Vice Marshal Nguyen Cao Ky feared that the political disturbances might provide an opening for General Minh to worm his way back into power. They promptly began plotting to protect their position. Alarmed by rumors of an impending coup, Taylor invited General Nguyen Van Thieu, Air Vice Marshal Ky, and a few other young officers to dinner on December 8 and warned them that chronic disorder in Saigon might discourage Congress from increasing aid to South Vietnam. Despite his threats, the Young Turks soon demanded that the High National Council pass a law requiring the immediate retirement of Minh and eight other Old Guard generals accused of fomenting unrest. But the civilian leaders refused to yield, and on December 20 Khanh and his cohorts on the Military Revolutionary Council abolished the High National Council. While allowing Huong to remain as the prime minister, they set up a new Armed Forces Council as the real authority in Saigon.

Taylor was furious. He promptly summoned Ky and Thieu along with two other young officers to the American embassy and gave them a humiliating lecture. Taylor reminded the officers that he had recently told them over dinner that their American patrons were tired of coups. "Apparently I wasted my words," he scolded. "Now you have made a real mess. We cannot carry you forever if you do things like this." But once again his threats fell upon deaf ears. Taylor lost all patience when against his wishes Khanh announced to the press that the Armed Forces Council had dissolved the High National Council. The angry ambassador told Khanh that he should resign and leave the country. But Khanh was not about to quit, and he publicly denounced Taylor for meddling in the internal affairs of South Vietnam. Despite their reliance on American aid, Khanh and his colleagues remained convinced that the United States needed them as pawns in the struggle to prevent the spread of communism in Southeast Asia. Thus Taylor, like Lodge before him, learned that Americans lacked leverage in dealing with their weak Asian clients.

But a stunning Vietcong attack on Americans stationed in South Vietnam soon raised the question of whether or not the United States should launch Phase I reprisal air strikes against North Vietnam. On Christmas Eve 1964, Vietcong agents planted a bomb in the Brinks Hotel, which housed American officers on duty in Saigon. The resulting explosion killed two Americans and injured thirty-eight others. On December 30, Taylor urged Johnson to authorize retaliatory bombing raids against North Vietnam. But the president refused to sanction any action that might provoke a strong communist reaction. South Vietnam had yet to demonstrate greater political stability or military capability, and Johnson remained skeptical about the effectiveness of American air power. "I have never felt that this war will be won from the air," he replied to Taylor on December 30, "and it seems to me that what is much more needed and would be more effective is a larger and stronger use of rangers and special forces and marines, or other appropriate military strength on the ground and on the scene." Johnson indicated that he was now prepared to permit American troops to engage in combat to strengthen ARVN units. "Although I know that it may involve the acceptance of larger American sacrifices," he emphasized, "I myself am ready to substantially increase the number of Americans in Vietnam if it is necessary to provide this kind of fighting force against the Viet Cong."

The Decision to Bomb North Vietnam

A major military setback for the Saigon government during the first week of 1965 suggested the need for the United States to do something fast to stave off a complete collapse in South Vietnam. On January 2, two crack companies of ARVN rangers walked into a Vietcong ambush inside a rubber plantation near the village of Binh Gia. The South Vietnamese field commanders threw two of their best battalions into the engagement. Although the ARVN units and their American advisers were supported by tanks, artillery, and helicopters, however, they suffered a devastating defeat. General Wheeler reported in a secret memorandum on January 5 that there had been 445 ARVN and 16 American casualties compared with just 132 Vietcong losses during the battle of Binh Gia. Despite the relative superiority of ARVN in force size, firepower, and air mobility, Wheeler warned, the Vietcong might now feel strong enough to compete in a war of movement because of their better sources of intelligence, more intimate knowledge of the terrain, and greater control over the local population.

On January 6, only four days after the Binh Gia disaster, Taylor sent the president a somber assessment of current political and military conditions in South Vietnam. The ambassador pointed out that he was confronted with a seriously deteriorating situation characterized by continued political turmoil, lethargy in the counterinsurgency program, and the loss of morale throughout the country. "Unless these conditions are somehow changed and trends reversed," he warned, "we are likely to face a number of unpleasant developments ranging from anti-American demonstrations, further civil disorders, and even political assassinations to the ultimate installation of a hostile government which will ask us to leave while it seeks accommodation with the National Liberation Front and Hanoi." Opposed to the introduction of American combat troops into South Vietnam, Taylor advocated a program of graduated air attacks to sap the will of the enemy in North Vietnam. "With regard to your feeling that this guerrilla war cannot be won from the air," he wrote, "I am in entire agreement, if we are thinking in terms of the physical destruction of the enemy." But Taylor assumed that a sustained bombing campaign would have a profound psychological impact upon the communist leaders in Hanoi. "As practical men," he concluded, "they cannot wish to see the fruits of ten years of labor destroyed by slowly escalating air attacks."

Taylor then advocated implementing a two-staged bombing program against North Vietnam to help turn the situation around in South Vietnam. He argued that the president should be prepared to approve Phase I reprisal air strikes against North Vietnam to lift morale in South Vietnam. To give an added boost to spirits in South Vietnam, Taylor continued, American representatives should indicate their intention of joining with Saigon officials in planning for Phase II bombing operations designed to deter Hanoi. Taylor wanted to make a conditional commitment: if the South Vietnamese government attained a certain level of performance, the United States would initiate a gradually escalating air war against North Vietnam. "Hopefully," he explained, "by such action we could improve the government, unify the armed forces to some degree, and thereupon move into the Phase II program without which we see little chance of breaking out of the present downward spiral." Therefore Taylor asked for permission to begin joint planning with authorities in Saigon and to give a conditional pledge to carry out a sustained bombing campaign against North Vietnam.

President Johnson agreed to meet Taylor halfway. In a message cabled to the ambassador on January 7, Johnson indicated that he was now inclined to adopt a policy of prompt and clear reprisal against North

Vietnam in response to any spectacular Vietcong attacks in South Vietnam. He also gave Taylor permission to start joint planning for sustained air operations in the future. But the ambassador was not to make any commitment with regard to the timing or scale of Phase II bombing. In planning for this contingency with Saigon officials, Taylor was to make it very clear that American decisions concerning a gradually escalating air campaign against North Vietnam would depend upon their progress in achieving political stability in South Vietnam. "My decisions on Phase II," Johnson emphasized, "will necessarily be affected by performance in earlier activities." In short, while he was now ready to launch retaliatory Phase I bombing strikes, the president was still not prepared to embark upon a graduated program of air attacks against North Vietnam.

Taylor worked hard during the next week to promote a stable political base in Saigon. By threatening to withhold American funds earmarked for a major expansion of the South Vietnamese military establishment, he induced General Khanh and the Armed Forces Council to agree to continue backing Tran Van Huong as prime minister. He subsequently prevailed upon Huong to add four of the Young Turk officers to his cabinet. Then, after persuading the South Vietnamese military leaders to raise draft levels, Taylor agreed to release the American funds required to increase the size of the armed forces under their command. But these moves provoked an explosion in the major cities of South Vietnam. Beginning on January 19, the Buddhists and their student allies led huge demonstrations against the Huong government. The protestors accused Taylor of misconduct and demanded that he should be recalled. They also sacked United States Information Service buildings in Saigon and Hué. As the demonstrations took an increasingly bitter anti-American tone, Taylor warned Washington that Khanh might arrange a marriage of convenience with the Buddhists directed toward the overthrow of Huong.

The political disorder rocking South Vietnam during the first month of 1965 prompted McGeorge Bundy and Robert McNamara to urge President Johnson to abandon his preconditions for bombing North Vietnam. On January 26, Bundy prepared a long memorandum that he and McNamara presented to the president the next morning. "Both of us are now pretty well convinced that our current policy can only lead to disastrous defeat," Bundy explained. "What we are doing now, essentially, is to wait and hope for a stable government." But he and McNamara had come to the conclusion that there was not much chance for the emergence of such a government in South Vietnam unless the United States employed military force against North Vietnam. "The underlying difficulties in Saigon arise from the spreading conviction that the future is without hope for anti-Communists," Bundy argued. "Our best friends have become somewhat discouraged by our own inactivity in the face of major attacks on our own installations." Acknowledging that Dean Rusk still sought a way to make the present wait-and-see policy work, Bundy warned that he and McNamara believed that this passive course could "only lead to eventual defeat and an invitation to get out in humiliating circumstances."

President Johnson received an additional prod on January 27 when he heard that another coup had occurred in Saigon. With Buddhist support, Khanh had ousted Huong and taken charge of the government in behalf of the Armed Forces Council. "The most sinister aspect of this affair," Taylor immediately warned the president, "is the obvious danger that the Buddhist victory may be an important step toward the formation of a government which will eventually lead the country into negotiations with Hanoi and the National Liberation Front." Johnson was inclined to judge the situation in the same way. "I am determined," he quickly replied, "to make it clear to all the world that the U.S. will spare no effort and no sacrifice in doing its full part to turn back the communists in Vietnam." Five days later, on the second of February 1965, Taylor advised the president that the United States should no longer demand the establishment of a stable government in South Vietnam as a prerequisite for bombing North Vietnam. Taylor concluded that only the initiation of sustained air operations against North Vietnam offered the slightest hope of preventing the eventual appearance in Saigon of a neutralist government that would seek a negotiated settlement and ask the United States to withdraw from South Vietnam.

The opportunity to begin Phase I reprisal air raids came shortly after Taylor had summarized the argument for bombing North Vietnam. On February 7, Vietcong soldiers attacked an American army barracks and helicopter base near the South Vietnamese market town of Pleiku, located in the Central Highlands. Eight Americans were killed, more than 100 others were wounded, and ten aircraft were destroyed. President Johnson hastily convened the National Security Council, and after a brief discussion he announced that the United States would strike back against North Vietnam. Johnson had finally overcome his reluctance to take bold action. Using the Vietcong assault at Pleiku as a pretext, he ordered the immediate implementation of Operation Flaming Dart, a tit-for-tat retaliatory bombing of a previously selected target in North Vietnam. Three American aircraft carriers, poised to strike from the Gulf of Tonkin, launched forty-nine jets to bomb a North Vietnamese army camp.

In a long memorandum presented to the president on February 7, McGeorge Bundy urged that the United States should move beyond Phase I retaliatory bombing raids and step toward a Phase II program of gradually escalating air operations. "The situation in Vietnam is deteriorating, and without new U.S. action defeat appears inevitable," he warned. "We believe that the best available way of increasing our chance of success in Vietnam is the development and execution of a policy of sustained reprisal against North Vietnam." Bundy suggested that at the outset American officials might wish to relate their air attacks to highly visible Vietcong acts such as the Pleiku incident. But he thought that once the bombing program was clearly underway it should not be necessary to connect each specific act against North Vietnam to a particular outrage in South Vietnam. Bundy stressed that the United States should cite the whole Vietcong campaign of violence in the south to justify air action against the north. "We are convinced that the political values of reprisal require a continuous operation," he explained. "Episodic responses geared on a one-for-one basis to 'spectacular' outrages would lack the persuasive force of sustained pressure."

Bundy argued that the main reason for bombing North Vietnam was to influence the course of the struggle in South Vietnam. He predicted that a sustained reprisal policy would produce a sharp increase in optimism among noncommunist groups throughout South Vietnam and thereby provide the United States with an opportunity to exert greater influence in pressing for a more effective government in Saigon. Bundy also speculated that such a demonstration of American determination might have a substantially depressing effect upon the morale of Vietcong cadres in South Vietnam. "We emphasize that our primary target in advocating a reprisal policy is the improvement of the situation in South Vietnam," he stated. "The immediate and critical targets are in the South—in the minds of the South Vietnamese and in the minds of the Viet Cong cadres." Bundy admitted that a policy of sustained reprisal bombing might not succeed in changing the course of the contest in South Vietnam. "What we can say is that even if it fails, the policy will be worth it," he concluded. "A reprisal policy—to the extent that it demonstrates U.S. willingness to employ this new norm in counter-insurgency—will set a higher price for the future upon all adventures of guerrilla warfare, and it should therefore somewhat increase our ability to deter such adventures."

President Johnson promptly agreed to launch a sustained bombing campaign against North Vietnam. During the morning of February 8, Johnson called a meeting of the National Security Council to consider the Bundy memorandum. A few of those present expressed reservations about the wisdom of military escalation, but Johnson decided to endorse the graduated bombing program that had been outlined in early December. "It is our hope," he declared, "that current U.S. action may pull together the various forces in Saigon and thus make possible the establishment of a stable government." On that evening, Johnson cabled Taylor that he was now ready to apply escalating pressure against North Vietnam in an effort to promote the building of a minimum government in South Vietnam. "I have today decided," he informed Taylor, "that we will carry out our December plan for continuing action against North Vietnam." Five days later, on February 13, the president formally authorized a program of sustained bombing against North Vietnam.

But Taylor did not believe that the Khanh regime provided an adequate political foundation in South Vietnam for the projection of American air power against North Vietnam. Fearing that Khanh would negotiate a settlement with the National Liberation Front, Taylor had already begun courting ambitious ARVN officers in an effort to promote a coup in Saigon. But Khanh continued to exercise his authority, and on February 14 he prevailed upon the Armed Forces Council to appoint Phan Huy Quat as the new prime minister of South Vietnam. Although Khanh had succeeded in installing a civilian government subject to his own domination, he did not have time to consolidate his position. On February 19, two dissident ARVN officers led their troops into Saigon in a bid to grab power. But Air Vice Marshall Ky refused to support the rebels, and they promptly agreed to withdraw from Saigon on the condition that Khanh be removed as the head of the South Vietnamese military establishment. Ky and Thieu jumped at the chance to get rid of Khanh. On February 20, they persuaded the Armed Forces Council to oust Khanh and to maintain Quat as a figurehead prime minister. Thus the veneer of a civilian government remained in South Vietnam, and Taylor now felt that the political ground had been prepared for sustained American air operations against North Vietnam.

American leaders immediately launched a propaganda campaign designed to win public support for a policy of military escalation. At a press conference held on February 25, Secretary of State Rusk told reporters that there could be no peace talks until the communist regime in Hanoi agreed to respect the political independence and territorial integrity of South Vietnam. His aides had already begun gathering evidence to convince the American people that North Vietnam was carrying out a carefully conceived plan of aggression against South Vietnam. To help the State Department officials prove their case, the CIA took more than 100 tons of communist bloc weapons from its warehouses, loaded them on a boat, sunk the vessel just off the coast of South Vietnam, and then invited reporters to inspect what was described as a cargo of arms lost by a North Vietnamese ship during a firefight. The State Department incorporated this phony evidence in a White Paper drafted to justify the continuous bombardment of North Vietnam. Published on February 27, the document was entitled *Aggression from the North: The Record of North Viet-Nam's Campaign to Conquer South Viet-Nam.*

Three days later, on March 2, 1965, the United States embarked upon a program of gradually escalating air attacks against North Vietnam. Operation Rolling Thunder, as its code name suggests, started with a soft rumble and slowly grew into a deafening roar. American planes flew more than 3,600 sorties against North Vietnamese targets during April as the tempo of the air war accelerated. From the outset, President Johnson insisted on maintaining tight control over the bombing campaign. "They can't even bomb an outhouse," he boasted, "without my approval." But when the initial attacks achieved only meager results, Johnson expanded the list of targets and authorized the use of napalm to ensure greater destructiveness. A violent cascade of American explosives rained down on North Vietnam as the pace of Rolling Thunder quickened during the next eight years. Indeed, between March 1965 and January 1973, the United States dropped three times more tonnage of bombs on North Vietnam than had been dropped on Europe, Asia, and Africa during the entire course of World War II.

As Rolling Thunder got under way in the spring of 1965, the Johnson administration encountered growing pressure for a negotiated settlement. United Nations Secretary General U Thant proposed a preliminary conference to lay the foundation for a peace treaty, and seventeen non-aligned nations issued an urgent plea for immediate negotiations. Even England and Canada, two of the staunchest allies of the United States, joined in the drive to promote a peaceful solution to the military struggle in Vietnam. At the same time, the massive aerial attack against North Vietnam provoked the beginning of an antiwar movement in the United States. Professors at some major American universities conducted teach-ins to provide information about the nature of the Vietnam conflict, and students on various college campuses held small demonstrations to protest against the bombardment of North Vietnam. But the burgeoning peace movement was not confined to the academic community. Prominent Democratic Senators such as Frank Church, Mike Mansfield, and George McGovern called upon the president to search for a negotiated settlement, and a few influential newspapers and political columnists joined the crusade against the war.

President Johnson moved quickly to counter his domestic and foreign critics. His public relations campaign began on March 25 when he announced that the United States would strive to achieve a just settlement to the Vietnam conflict. "I am ready," he declared, "to go anywhere at any time, and meet with anyone whenever there is promise of progress towards an honorable peace." Two weeks later, in a speech at Johns Hopkins University, he told his audience that the United States was prepared to enter into "unconditional discussions" in an effort to achieve peace in Vietnam. Johnson also said that he would be willing to ask Congress for $1 billion to help promote the economic development of Southeast Asia. But the president affirmed that the United States would do everything necessary to prevent North Vietnam from conquering South Vietnam. "Our objective," he stressed, "is the independence of South Viet-Nam." Shortly after his address at Johns Hopkins, his White House aides began sending apologists to speak at other universities in an attempt to check the spread of antiwar sentiment among student groups.

Contrary to the rhetoric emanating from the White House, however, President Johnson had no desire to begin serious peace talks until he could strengthen his bargaining position. The president remained firmly committed to maintaining a separate noncommunist South Vietnam, and he had no intention of compromising with North Vietnam on this fundamental issue. Johnson did not even bother to respond when Hanoi advanced a four-point program on April 13 to serve as the basis for negotiations with the United States. The peace plan called for the withdrawal of American military personnel from South Vietnam, the termination of hostile actions against North Vietnam, the formation of a coalition government in Saigon with National Liberation Front participation, and the peaceful reunification of Vietnam without any foreign interference. Johnson and his senior advisers feared that, if Washington accepted these proposals, the result would be a united Vietnam under communist domination. Thus they concluded that the United States would have to take stronger military measures before opening a dialogue with North Vietnam.

President Johnson thereupon made a concerted effort to build domestic support for a program of military escalation. On May 4, he asked Congress for an additional $700 million to sustain the struggle against communism in South Vietnam. Johnson made it clear that he would regard a vote for the appropriation as an endorsement of his policies in Southeast Asia. Not wanting to be charged with refusing to support American troops already in the field, Congress approved the request by an overwhelming margin that provided Johnson with a basis for

The Escalating Military Stalemate

If the Communist world finds out we will not pursue our commitments to the end, I don't know where they will stay their hand.

Secretary of State Dean Rusk, 1965

The Dispatch of American Ground Troops

President Johnson and his principal foreign policy advisers decided to wage only a limited war in Southeast Asia. Their basic objective was to maintain South Vietnam as an independent noncommunist nation and thereby to discourage revolutionary movements elsewhere in the Third World. They were not willing to launch an all-out military crusade against North Vietnam in an effort to roll back the forces of communism to the Chinese border. The president and his civilian advisers feared that Red China would intervene, if necessary, to prevent the complete defeat of North Vietnam. The White House was still haunted by memories of Chinese troops fighting American soldiers to a stalemate in Korea, and Johnson did not want the United States to become engaged once again in a ground war against the immense armies of communist China. Nor did he want to sacrifice his domestic welfare program by authorizing unlimited military operations in Southeast Asia. Consequently, although his military advisers often urged bold moves, the president would not approve either an American invasion of North Vietnam or an unrestricted bombing campaign against Hanoi and the rest of the Red River basin.

While carefully orchestrated to avoid a confrontation with China, the initiation of the air war against North Vietnam in February 1965 paved the way for the introduction of American ground troops into South Vietnam. General William C. Westmoreland and his subordinates at MACV anticipated Vietcong attacks against American airfields in retaliation for the bombardment of North Vietnam, and on February 22 Westmoreland asked for two marine battalions to protect the vulnerable air base at Danang. But his proposal was opposed by the American embassy in Saigon. In a cable to the White House, Ambassador Maxwell D. Taylor warned that once the United States committed combat units in South Vietnam it would be very difficult to hold the line against future troop deployments. "Intervention with ground forces would at best buy time," he predicted, "and would lead to ever increasing commitments until, like the French, we would be occupying an essentially hostile foreign country." But President Johnson approved Westmoreland's request despite Taylor's reservations, and on March 8 a contingent of 3,500 marines dressed in full battle regalia splashed ashore near Danang. Welcomed by pretty South Vietnamese girls passing out leis of flowers, the two marine battalions were the first American combat troops deployed on the Asian mainland since the Korean War.

The dispatch of these foot soldiers marked a crucial change in the role of the United States in the Vietnam War. Although the initial marine mission was limited to the static defense of the air base at Danang, pressure quickly mounted for the deployment of additional American combat forces and for the commencement of offensive operations against the Vietcong. General Harold K. Johnson, the army chief of staff, hurried to Saigon to find out what more could be done to improve the military situation in South Vietnam. Upon his return to Washington on March 14, General Johnson urged the deployment of a full American army division to reinforce ARVN units in the field. But Ambassador Taylor expressed grave concern about the proposal to increase the involvement of the United States in counterinsurgency operations. Cabling the president on March 17, Taylor warned that the introduction of large numbers of American ground troops might encourage the South Vietnamese to lie down on the job and pass the military burden to the United States. He also cautioned that the arrival of an American infantry division in South

Vietnam would make it look like the United States was assuming "the old French role of alien colonizer and conqueror."

But two weeks later, while in Washington for consultations, Taylor was dismayed to find that the president and most of his top advisers were on the verge of sending more American combat troops to South Vietnam. General Westmoreland had asked for the immediate commitment of two American army divisions and for permission to use them in offensive operations in the Central Highlands. Besides endorsing this request, the Joint Chiefs of Staff pressed for the dispatch of one South Korean division to help pursue the Vietcong. Although Taylor was against these proposals, he realized that those advocating the deployment of additional ground forces were in the saddle. Thus Taylor argued that, if American soldiers were to be committed to combat, they should be restricted to enclaves along the coast of South Vietnam. Rather than employing United States troops in search and destroy operations deep in the jungles of the interior, he insisted, Westmoreland should confine them to the task of protecting American air bases and other installations near the seaboard.

But at a high-level meeting held in the White House on April 1, 1965, President Johnson took another significant step toward full-scale warfare. He decided to give General Westmoreland two more marine battalions plus an air squadron and 18,000 to 20,000 support troops. Although the marines would be stationed in enclaves around the major American air bases, they were authorized to engage in offensive actions rather than to remain in static defensive positions. Yet Johnson tried to conceal this basic change in military mission from the American people. Hoping to avoid an adverse political reaction in the United States, he ordered that the new aggressive tactics should be employed as rapidly as possible but in ways that would minimize any appearance of a sudden change in policy. Westmoreland later criticized this lack of candor on the part of the president. "It was a masterpiece of obliquity," he charged. "To my mind the American people had a right to know forthrightly, within the actual limits of military security, what we were calling on their sons to do, and to presume that it could be concealed despite the open eyes of press and television was folly."

Though they feared media exposure, however, President Johnson and his senior advisers soon decided that the number of American combat forces deployed in South Vietnam should be more than doubled. And they succeeded in getting Taylor to go along with their plans. At an important conference held in Honolulu on April 20, Taylor joined with a group of top civilian and military leaders in advocating the rapid introduction of additional ground troops to fight the Vietcong. The conferees agreed that the United States could not expect to achieve a favorable settlement in South Vietnam by bombing North Vietnam. But they hoped to break the will of the North Vietnamese and the Vietcong by denying them victory in South Vietnam. Determined to hold the communists at bay while the authorities in Saigon were building up their armed strength, the conferees unanimously urged the dispatch of nine more American battalions to South Vietnam (bringing the United States troop level up to 82,000 men) along with one Australian and three South Korean battalions (bringing the third-country troop level up to 7,250 men). The president promptly approved their recommendations, yet he delayed the announcement of the troop increases for almost two months to cushion the shock of the escalation on public opinion.

But while American policymakers hoped to convince the communists that they could not win in South Vietnam, the tide of battle quickly turned against the forces of the Saigon government during the spring of 1965. American intelligence sources confirmed for the first time on April 21 that a regular North Vietnamese combat unit was operating in South Vietnam, and on May 11 the Vietcong began a vigorous offensive by overrunning a province capital located about fifty miles north of Saigon. During the ensuing weeks, several ARVN battalions were badly mauled in bloody engagements with aggressive Vietcong soldiers. The ineptness of the South Vietnamese army was blatantly demonstrated when two Vietcong regiments attacked a town in Phuoc Long province and the frightened ARVN officers fled in panic. As increasing battlefield losses and desertion rates weakened the South Vietnamese army, American officials worried that it might completely collapse in the face of the Vietcong offensive.

Americans stationed in Saigon were especially alarmed about the rapidly deteriorating military situation. In a cable to Washington on June 5, Ambassador Taylor reported that the communists were scoring one victory after another on the battlefields of South Vietnam. "The apparent aims of this campaign," he observed, "are to alter the balance of military forces in favor of the Viet Cong by inflicting maximum attrition on the government forces, including specifically the piecemeal destruction of regular ARVN ground combat units." General Westmoreland feared that without substantial American reinforcements the South Vietnamese army would not be able to stand up to the mounting communist pressure. "I see no course of action open to U.S.," he cabled Washington on June 7, "except to reinforce our efforts in SVN with additional U.S. or third country forces as rapidly as possible during the critical weeks ahead."

To prevent a swift defeat in South Vietnam, Westmoreland urged the immediate dispatch of an additional 32,000 American troops and nine South Korean battalions. The Joint Chiefs of Staff not only supported his recommendations, but they also advocated the deployment of ten more American battalions (bringing the United States troop level up to 150,000 men).

American apprehensions became even greater as the political situation in South Vietnam likewise went from bad to worse. On June 9, the Armed Forces Council decided to oust Prime Minister Phan Huy Quat and to form a new government headed by a committee of ten senior military officers. The junta installed Air Vice Marshal Nguyen Cao Ky as prime minister and General Nguyen Van Thieu as chief of state. Thus the veneer of civilian rule in South Vietnam was completely stripped away. Disturbed by the fact that Ky and Thieu possessed little political experience, Ambassador Taylor believed that he and his colleagues would have to help them handle public affairs. Policymakers in Washington were equally concerned about the nature of the new regime in Saigon. William Bundy later recalled that the Ky-Thieu directorate "seemed to all of us the bottom of the barrel, absolutely the bottom of the barrel." But even though they realized that Ky and Thieu were political novices without popular support, American officials were relieved to learn that the new leaders in Saigon intended to continue the fight against the Vietcong.

As Ky and Thieu took the reins of power, Westmoreland reiterated his request for reinforcements to avert a catastrophe in South Vietnam. He warned President Johnson on June 14 that desertion rates for the South Vietnamese army were inordinately high and that Vietcong units were destroying ARVN battalions faster than they could be reconstituted. Westmoreland saw no likelihood for achieving a quick victory against the Vietcong, but he advocated the active commitment of additional American ground troops as "a stop-gap measure to save ARVN from defeat." In a follow-up cable to Washington on June 22, Westmoreland estimated that the deployment of forty-four more American combat battalions would be sufficient to establish a favorable balance of forces in South Vietnam by the end of the year. But if the United States were to seize the initiative from the enemy, he concluded, further increments would be required in 1966 and thereafter. Westmoreland left President Johnson with a simple choice. He could either accept a certain defeat in South Vietnam or plunge the United States into a full-scale war.

At this critical point in the summer of 1965, Under Secretary of State George W. Ball was the only high-level Washington official who vigorously opposed a major increase in the number of American combat troops in South Vietnam. In a memorandum presented to the president on July 1, Ball expressed grave doubt that the United States could defeat the Vietcong. "No one," he declared, "has demonstrated that a white ground force of whatever size can win a guerrilla war—which is at the same time a civil war between Asians—in a jungle terrain in the midst of a population that refuses cooperation to the white forces (and the South Vietnamese) and thus provides a great intelligence advantage to the other side." Ball feared that an open-ended military commitment would lead to mounting American casualties and a well-nigh irreversible process of escalation. "Our involvement will be so great," he warned, "that we cannot—without national humiliation—stop short of achieving our complete objectives." Before committing American prestige to a protracted and bloody conflict of uncertain outcome, Ball concluded, policymakers in Washingon should "seek a compromise settlement which achieves less than our stated objectives and thus cut our losses while we still have the freedom of maneuver to do so."

In a memorandum prepared for the president on July 20, however, Secretary of Defense Robert S. McNamara argued that no peace settlement acceptable to the United States could be negotiated until after the application of additional American military force against the Vietcong. "The situation in South Vietnam is worse than a year ago," he observed. "The government is able to provide security to fewer and fewer people in less and less territory." McNamara reported that the Vietcong were pushing hard to dismember the country and to destroy the army buttressing the unpopular regime in Saigon. While some ARVN units had been mauled during combat and weakened by high desertion rates, he noted, the Vietcong seemed to be able to replace their losses and to increase their strength by drafting soldiers in areas under their control. McNamara also pointed out that the American bombardment of North Vietnam had been ineffective. "There are no signs that we have throttled the inflow of supplies for the VC or can throttle the flow while their material needs are as low as they are," he acknowledged. "Nor have our air attacks in North Vietnam produced tangible evidence of willingness on the part of Hanoi to come to the conference table in a reasonable mood."

McNamara concluded that the United States must demonstrate to the communists that the odds were against their winning the struggle in South Vietnam. He argued that a substantial increase in American military pressure against the Vietcong "would stave off defeat in the short run and offer a good chance of producing a favorable settlement in the longer run." McNamara therefore urged that the total American force level in South Vietnam should be brought up to approximately 175,000 men (or 200,000 if the South Koreans refused to commit nine more battalions). But he warned that the deployment of as many as 100,000 additional American troops might be necessary in early 1966 and even more thereafter. To be prepared for future troop deployments, McNamara recommended that Congress should be asked to authorize the call-up of approximately 235,000 men in the Reserves and National Guard. He also advised expanding the draft and extending the tour of duty for men already in the service in order to increase the size of the regular armed forces of the United States by approximately 375,000 men.

President Johnson invited his top advisers to the White House on July 21 to discuss the McNamara memorandum. When Johnson asked if anyone present opposed the course of action proposed by the secretary of defense, once again only George Ball registered a dissenting opinion. "This war will be long and protracted," he cautioned. "I truly have serious doubt that an army of westerners can successfully fight orientals in an Asian jungle." Ball argued that the best way to cut American losses in South Vietnam would be to maneuver the Saigon government into requesting that the United States leave. Although admitting that such a policy would probably lead to a communist takeover of South Vietnam, he concluded that other Asian nations would remain in the capitalist orbit. "But George," the president asked, "wouldn't all these countries say that Uncle Sam was a paper tiger, wouldn't we lose credibility breaking the word of three presidents, if we did as you have proposed?" Ball replied that a worse blow to American prestige would be to let everyone see that "the mightiest power on earth is unable to defeat a handful of guerrillas." But Secretary of State Dean Rusk clinched the argument in favor of escalation. "If the Communist world finds out we will not pursue our commitments to the end," he warned, "I don't know where they will stay their hand."

Regarding the Vietnamese conflict as a crucial test of their ability to counter wars of national liberation throughout the Third World, President Johnson and his principal advisers therefore determined that the United States must deploy whatever force level might be required to prevent the fall of the South Vietnam domino. But Johnson wanted to Americanize the war without antagonizing Congress and thereby hindering the enactment of legislation needed to fulfill his ambitious social welfare program. Hence he decided not to ask for authority to mobilize the Reserves or National Guard. In a nationally televised news conference on July 28, Johnson announced that the American force level in South Vietnam would be increased immediately to 125,000 men and that additional troops would be sent as requested by General Westmoreland. The president added that the number of Americans drafted into the armed services would soon be doubled. His announcement marked a fundamental turning point in the history of the Vietnam War. American boys would now attempt to do the job that Asian boys had failed to do.

The Protracted War of Attrition

As American forces assumed direct responsibility for the outcome of the war in Vietnam during the autumn of 1965, the United States implemented a military strategy that involved three interrelated actions. First, American pilots carried out a steadily escalating bombing campaign against military facilities and supply lines in North Vietnam. This air offensive was launched in an effort to impede the movement of men and material into South Vietnam and to induce the communist regime in Hanoi to stop supporting the Vietcong insurgents. Second, American troops conducted large-scale search and destroy operations against Vietcong regulars and North Vietnamese forces fighting in South Vietnam. These ground maneuvers were designed to kill enemy soldiers faster than they could be replaced and thereby to convince the communists that they could not win. Third, the United States assigned ARVN the task of holding territory that had been cleared by American combat units in South Vietnam. This so-called "other war" was aimed at pacifying the countryside while the Saigon government attempted to win the hearts and minds of the South Vietnamese people.

Although American troops were able to sweep through extensive areas controlled by communist forces in South Vietnam, however, the results of these actions were almost always transitory. The South Vietnamese army could not provide security in areas that had been penetrated by American soldiers. Nor could the Saigon government win popular support after the communist forces had been driven away. John Paul Vann, after serving as an adviser to the South Vietnamese army and a coordinator for the United States Operations Mission, put his finger on the basic problem. In a memorandum written in September 1965, Vann pointed out that despite lip service to the contrary the military junta in Saigon had not demonstrated a sincere interest in bettering the lot of the rural population. "Many patriotic and non-Communist Vietnamese," he explained, "were literally forced to ally themselves with a Communist dominated movement in the belief that it was their only chance to secure a better government." As a consequence, communist forces usually reoccupied areas soon after American troops had completed their clearing operations and moved into other regions to begin similar maneuvers.

When it became apparent that American ground operations were yielding little in terms of permanent territorial control, the United States began employing an overwhelming amount of firepower in an attempt to prevent the communists from utilizing the land and the people of South Vietnam. American artillery and B-52 bombers pounded the South Vietnamese countryside as more and more rural areas were defined as "free fire zones" subject to harassment and interdiction. American aircraft dropped more than 1 million tons of bombs on South Vietnam from 1965 to 1967 while American herbicides such as Agent Orange destroyed approximately half of the South Vietnamese timberlands. Besides disrupting communist base areas and logistical networks, the American bombs, shells, and defoliants forced a great many peasants in South Vietnam to flee from their villages and rice fields. About 4 million civilians, roughly 25 percent of the South Vietnamese population, sought safety in overcrowded cities or in refugee camps on their outskirts. Driven from their homes and farmlands by the American war machine, these displaced peasants harbored deep feelings of hostility toward the United States.

As death and destruction spread, Buddhist leaders gave vent to the rapidly growing antiwar sentiment in South Vietnam. But the monks did not openly articulate their intense desire for peace because they wanted to avoid a direct confrontation with the United States. During March 1966, the Buddhists and their student allies organized massive demonstrations in Danang, Hué, and Saigon. The protestors made immediate demands for the holding of free elections and the establishment of a civilian government to replace the military junta headed by Ky and Thieu. Although their ultimate objectives remained unstated, the Buddhists and their supporters looked forward to the creation of a neutralist government that would seek a political accommodation with the National Liberation Front and ask the United States to get out of South Vietnam. Their strong anti-American attitudes found expression in numerous banners calling for an end to the foreign domination of South Vietnam. Along with their American patrons, Ky and Thieu became increasingly alarmed when many ARVN soldiers stationed in the northern provinces showed their support for the democratic movement to elect a civilian government.

The military rulers of South Vietnam were determined to maintain their political authority and to sustain the war effort against the Vietcong. After obtaining American approval and support, Ky decided to suppress the Buddhists and those who had rallied around them in Danang, Hué, and Saigon. His troops moved into these Buddhist strongholds during May and June 1966, arresting several hundred monks and students. Then, as soon as order was restored, the military chiefs turned to the political arena to consolidate their power. They carefully selected a list of candidates, and in September 1966 elections were held for a constituent assembly. After deliberating for a few months, the assembly drafted a new constitution that disqualified anyone branded as a communist or neutralist sympathizer from running for president. The military junta subsequently decided that Thieu should replace Ky as the highest authority in Saigon, and in September 1967 Thieu was elected president by a small plurality of votes in a highly circumscribed contest.

The United States was by then waist deep in a bloody struggle that many had come to call "Mr. McNamara's War." After a brief visit to Saigon in November 1965, the secretary of defense made a bleak assessment of the military situation in South Vietnam. McNamara predicted a rapid expansion of communist forces both by heavy recruitment in South Vietnam and by increased infiltration from North Vietnam. To hold the line against the contemplated enemy buildup, McNamara recommended that the United States should intensify the bombing of North Vietnam and send a substantial number of additional troops to South Vietnam. He admitted that his recommendations might simply lead to a military standoff at a higher level. If President Johnson followed his advice, McNamara estimated that the American death rate in South Vietnam would reach 1,000 a month. He also calculated that the odds were even that the United States would still not achieve a victory. Yet McNamara concluded that the American force level should be brought up to 400,000 by the end of 1966 and that the deployment of 200,000 more American troops might be needed during the following year.

Acting on the advice of his influential defense secretary, Johnson carefully laid the political foundations for a sharp escalation in the American war effort. The president hoped to defuse his domestic and foreign critics by calling a temporary halt to the aerial bombardment of North Vietnam. During the bombing pause, which began on Christmas Eve 1965 and lasted for thirty-seven days, Johnson launched a dramatic peace offensive. He dispatched prominent envoys to more than forty different countries to spread the word that the United States desired peace. Hoping to convince the American people that he had explored every alternative to escalation, Johnson repeatedly insisted that he was ready to enter into discussions to bring an end to the fighting. But his peace gestures were bogus. Johnson was not willing to negotiate a peace settlement that would allow the formation of a neutralist government in Saigon and the reunification of Vietnam under communist leadership. Indeed, his public relations campaign was primarily designed to provide a justification for a major American military escalation.

During the months following the well-advertised bombing pause, Rolling Thunder gradually assumed massive proportions. The number of American air strikes grew from 25,000 to 108,000 between 1965 and 1967 while the tonnage of bombs dropped on North Vietnam increased from 63,000 to 226,000. The list of targets was simultaneously expanded to include supply depots, transportation networks, manufacturing plants, and power stations. The steadily intensifying air campaign against North Vietnam destroyed factories, disrupted agriculture, leveled cities, and scarred the countryside. Besides inflicting severe economic damage, the bombing raids maimed and killed many noncombatants in North Vietnam. American pilots did not direct their attacks against major population centers, but the huge payloads dropped from high altitudes by giant B-52 bombers seldom hit targets with pinpoint accuracy. Although American officials publicly maintained that civilian casualties were minimal, Secretary of Defense McNamara privately estimated that they were as high as 1,000 a month during peak bombing periods.

But the widespread bombardment did not destroy the morale of the North Vietnamese people. They responded to the American bombing onslaught in much the same way that the British had reacted to the Nazi air assault during World War II. Rather than disheartening the people of North Vietnam, the bombing missions seemed to stiffen their will to resist the American colossus. The North Vietnamese demonstrated remarkable determination in coping with the aerial attacks on their homeland. After evacuating many civilians from the cities, they constructed individual bomb shelters along the streets to protect those who remained to perform essential tasks. Small factories and storage facilities were dispersed across the countryside while trenches and tunnels were cut through rice paddies to safeguard peasants from shrapnel and napalm. Major roads were repaired within hours after bombs dotted them with craters, and damaged bridges were quickly replaced by bamboo pontoons and ferryboats. And while thousands of North Vietnamese worked full time to keep key transportation routes open, truck drivers traveled at night without headlights to avoid detection.

Although the American bombing attacks crippled industrial production in North Vietnam, Rolling Thunder had very little impact on the ground war in South Vietnam. The communist forces needed only about fifty tons of supplies per day to sustain their military operations in South Vietnam, and the bulk of the heavy equipment that they received came from a vast stockpiling area on the Chinese side of the Tonkin border. The Chinese shipped large quantities of arms and ammunition into Tonkin by rail and truck, and these materials were stored in scattered dumps until they could be reshipped to their final destination below the Demilitarized Zone. The Chinese also stationed 50,000 technicians and soldiers in North Vietnam to operate and defend their supply lines reaching southward. Despite the intensification of the American air campaign, therefore, North Vietnam continued to serve as a vital highway carrying ample amounts of weapons and munitions into South Vietnam.

Yet the United States paid a high price for the physical damage that Rolling Thunder caused in North Vietnam. In response to the American bombing campaign, the Soviet Union provided North Vietnam with anti-aircraft guns, surface-to-air missiles, Mig fighters, and sophisticated radar equipment. Thus American pilots encountered stiff resistance as they flew closer to Hanoi and Haiphong. Armed with Russian weapons, the North Vietnamese were frequently able to drive off American warplanes or shoot them down before they reached their targets. The United States lost more than 500 aircraft between 1965 and 1966 while the direct cost of the air war mounted to well over $1 billion. Summarizing the effectiveness of American air strikes conducted during 1966 the Central Intelligence Agency calculated that the United States spent nearly $10 on bombing missions and warplane replacements for each $1 in damage inflicted upon North Vietnam.

The United States was similarly engaged in an expensive big-unit ground war in South Vietnam. After making the momentous decision to dive into full-scale warfare in July 1965, President Johnson rushed logistical experts to South Vietnam to construct facilities to handle huge numbers of American troops and enormous quantities of military equipment. Soon supplies at the rate of 1 million tons a month were pouring into South Vietnam to provide American soldiers with a mighty arsenal of weapons and a vast array of luxuries rarely ever seen on a battlefield. The number of American combatants in South Vietnam simultaneously jumped from just under 185,000 at the end of 1965 to more than 485,000 by the end of 1967. As the American military buildup proceeded apace, General Westmoreland ordered his troops to conduct massive sweeps through the South Vietnamese countryside in an effort to entrap and eliminate main force enemy units. He sought to engage large concentrations of Vietcong and North Vietnamese soldiers in relatively unsettled areas where mobile American forces would be able to use maximum firepower while keeping civilian casualties to a minimum.

Despite their ability to move with tremendous speed, however, American troops seldom enjoyed the advantage of surprise. The mechanized American forces made a lot of noise, and they were often detected before they could pounce upon their prey. Upon hearing the roar of American vehicles charging down the roads, the Vietcong and North Vietnamese soldiers could choose to flee if they did not want to fight. Their ability to avoid combat was enhanced by information about American military plans that they received from agents who had worked their way into the highest ranks of the Saigon government and the South Vietnamese army. Aided by an impressive intelligence network, communist units could usually determine the location, timing, size, and duration of each battle that they fought against troops from the United States. If their casualties reached unacceptable levels, they could melt away into the jungle or retreat across the border into sanctuaries in Laos and Cambodia.

Although the communists were able to exercise control over the rate of their losses, General Westmoreland remained determined to pursue a strategy of attrition. He aimed to achieve a military victory by destroying enemy units faster than they could be replaced through either recruitment in South Vietnam or infiltration from North Vietnam. Engaged in a war without front lines, American army officers measured progress by counting cadavers rather than by taking and holding land. Their gruesome goal was to locate and liquidate the enemy. American field commanders sought a favorable kill ratio by exterminating a large number of enemy soldiers without losing a correspondingly high number of their own men. Having no territorial objectives to attain in South Vietnam, American ground troops found themselves pitted against hordes of Orientals in a killing contest on the Asian mainland.

With the body count serving as the primary index of success on the battlefields of South Vietnam, American army officers were not inclined to risk losing their men in close combat. Thus it became standard policy for the United States army to use foot soldiers to help find the foe and then to use an avalanche of fire in an attempt to annihilate him. As the motto "expend shells not men" was applied with a vengeance, the number of B-52 sorties in South Vietnam leaped from 60 a month in 1966 to over 800 a month in 1967. American infantry units were seldom prodded into practicing their traditional mission of closing with the enemy and destroying him in place. After making contact with Vietcong regulars or North Vietnamese forces, American ground troops generally fell back into a defensive perimeter to call for air strikes and artillery support. Large enemy units were therefore rarely pinned down by American infantrymen.

Given their ability to choose when and where to fight, the Vietcong and North Vietnamese maintained the strategic initiative throughout most of the war. The communists employed hit-and-run tactics with the hope that American troops would dissipate their energy in endless search and destroy operations. While avoiding major clashes unless having a clear numerical advantage, these elusive warriors were constantly darting out of tunnels and bunkers to ambush American patrols. They not only depended upon the element of surprise, but they also tried to maintain close and continuous contact when attacking isolated platoons so that American officers could not call for air strikes or artillery support without endangering their own men. To compensate for their military inferiority, the communists likewise relied upon an assortment of ingenious mines and booby traps that took a heavy toll on American grunts tramping through the rice paddies and along the jungle trails of South Vietnam.

As the number of casualties steadily mounted on both sides, the conflict became a protracted war of attrition. General Westmoreland clung to his assumption that American forces could sap the strength of the enemy by attacking him with a phalanx of fire. But General Giap remained confident that he could overcome American firepower with Vietnamese manpower. Although a great many of his men were killed or wounded, Giap continued to replace his losses with fresh troops. American intelligence experts estimated that the infiltration of North Vietnamese soldiers into South Vietnam increased from about 35,000 in 1965 to around 90,000 in 1967 even as the bombing of the Ho Chi Minh Trail grew in intensity. Giap had the capacity to match each American troop increment in South Vietnam with one of his own because approximately 200,000 potential recruits reached draft age every year in North Vietnam. Realizing that he could draw from a vast pool of men, Giap hoped to exhaust the patience of the American people in a prolonged struggle far away from their homeland.

President Johnson offered to make a deal with North Vietnam when he began to comprehend just what the United States was up against. In a letter to Ho Chi Minh in February 1967, Johnson indicated that the United States would cease bombing North Vietnam and refrain from augmenting its troop strength in South Vietnam as soon as North Vietnam stopped sending men and material into South Vietnam. He concluded that such acts of restraint on each side could set the stage for serious peace discussions. In a telegram to the American embassy in Saigon, Secretary of State Rusk explained the rationale underlying the proposal. "Deprived of additional men and of urgently needed equipment from the

North," he cabled, "we believe NVA/VC forces would be significantly weakened in concrete terms and would probably suffer serious adverse effects on their morale." But Ho Chi Minh refused to take the bait. He replied to Johnson that before peace talks could begin the United States would have to stop unconditionally its bombing raids and all other acts of war against North Vietnam. "The Vietnamese people will never submit to force," Ho declared. "They will never accept talks under the threat of bombs."

The American Antiwar Movement

With no end to the military struggle in sight, the American people found themselves paying an escalating price for the war in terms of both men and money. More than 13,000 Americans had died in Vietnam by the summer of 1967, and draft calls exceeded 30,000 each month. While deploying nearly a half million troops in South Vietnam, the United States was spending over $2 billion a month on the conflict. Yet President Johnson insisted that the United States could afford to support a comprehensive domestic welfare program while at the same time financing an open-ended war across the Pacific. Determined to build a Great Society at home without withdrawing from the New Frontier in Southeast Asia, Johnson decided in August 1967 that a 10 percent surtax needed to be placed upon individual and corporate incomes. The American people were subsequently forced to bear the burden of higher tax levies as well as continuously rising conscription quotas and death rates.

These mushrooming costs of the Vietnamese conflict made the American people increasingly critical of the Johnson administration. Only a few had objected in March 1965 when the United States began dispatching combat troops to South Vietnam. But when the American military effort failed to yield quick results, public support for the war gradually eroded. While some militants advocated even greater effort to achieve victory, most Americans simply did not understand why their country was plunging deeper and deeper into the quagmire in Southeast Asia. Nor were many in the United States willing to trust the rosy statements emanating from the White House. As the credibility gap produced a crisis of confidence, more and more Americans came to the conclusion that the decision to intervene in Vietnam had been a mistake. Their confusion and disenchantment continued to grow, and consequently by October 1967 public approval of the way President Johnson was handling the war had plummeted to only 28 percent.

As the struggle in South Vietnam became an escalating military stale-mate, the rippling antiwar movement in the United States swelled into a tidal wave that threatened to swamp the Johnson administration. Antiwar rallies on university campuses increased enormously during 1966 and 1967 in both size and intensity. Many older Americans joined hands with college students and marched side by side down the streets of New York, Washington, and other major cities in huge demonstrations protesting American military involvement in Vietnam. At the same time, numerous metropolitan newspapers shifted their editorials on the war from support to opposition. The antiwar campaign received strong back-ing from many prominent figures including Dr. Benjamin Spock, Muhammad Ali, Jane Fonda, Bishop Fulton J. Sheen, Joan Baez, and Dr. Martin Luther King, Jr. As more and more people joined the antiwar crusade, many young American men attempted to evade conscription by claiming to be conscientious objectors or fleeing to Canada. Some even preferred serving jail sentences over fighting in Vietnam.

Americans from different walks of life seriously debated whether or not the United States should remain involved in the Vietnam War. Many continued to accept the official State Department argument: the United States had a commitment to protect democracy in South Vietnam from a communist invasion from North Vietnam; and if South Vietnam fell to the forces of communism, China and Russia would be encouraged to sponsor aggression in other parts of the world. But an increasing number of Americans began to challenge the State Department position. Critics insisted that the Vietnam War could best be described as either a civil war or a social revolution rather than as a crucial front in the global struggle against communist aggression. They also charged that the United States was supporting a corrupt and repressive dictatorship in South Vietnam. Their accusations received strong support when Nguyen Cao Ky told American news reporters that Adolf Hitler had been his boy-hood hero.

Those opposed to the war questioned both the morality and rationality of American military action in Vietnam. Some argued from a humanitar-ian perspective that American bombs and shells were killing or maiming thousands of innocent civilians each month. Others argued on pragmatic grounds that the costs of the conflict far exceeded the benefits for the United States. Denying that the spread of communism in Southeast Asia would endanger the physical security of the United States, the peace advocates complained that the Vietnam War was diverting funds away from urgent domestic problems. General James M. Gavin, in his testi-mony before the Senate Foreign Relations Committee in February 1967, gave vent to the widespread belief that the United States had to choose between guns and butter. "I recommend that we bring hostilities in Vietnam to an end as quickly and reasonably as we can," he declared; "that we devote those vast expenditures of our national resources to dealing with our domestic problems; that we make a massive attack on the problems of education, housing, economic opportunity, lawlessness, and environmental pollution."

As the antiwar movement gained momentum, Secretary of Defense McNamara himself started to search for a way out of the conflict that had come to bear his name. He realized that the American bombing program had failed either to break the will of the communist leaders in North Vietnam or to prevent them from increasing the infiltration of soldiers and supplies into South Vietnam. In a memorandum prepared for President Johnson in October 1966, he warned that a more intensive bombardment of North Vietnam would provoke tremendous public criticism and "involve a serious risk of drawing us into open war with China." McNamara soon began to advocate restraint in the exercise of American military power in Southeast Asia. In private meetings, he urged Johnson to limit the area of bombing in North Vietnam and to place a ceiling on the level of American troops deployed in South Vietnam. McNamara also proposed a basic shift in American military operations away from pursuing Vietcong and North Vietnamese forces and toward controlling South Vietnamese population centers.

But General Westmoreland was still confident that his strategy of attrition would prove successful. During a meeting at the White House in April 1967, he warned President Johnson that without a major increase in American troop strength in South Vietnam the war might drag on for another five years or more. But the president seemed reluctant to escalate. "When we add divisions, can't the enemy add divisions," Johnson asked. "If so, where does it all end?" Westmoreland replied that during the last month it appeared that the "crossover point" had been reached in most parts of South Vietnam. Defining the "crossover point" as the moment when enemy attritions became greater than enemy additions, he argued that in the future United States forces would be destroying enemy units faster than they could be replaced. The more troops he had under his command, Westmoreland reasoned, the sooner he could win the war. Westmoreland calculated that he needed another 200,000 American soldiers in order to achieve a victory in the next two or three years.

The Joint Chiefs of Staff, besides supporting Westmoreland's request for additional troops in South Vietnam, advocated stepped-up attacks against North Vietnam. In a memorandum drafted in May 1967, the JCS recommended the interdiction of land and sea lines of communication entering and departing from the Hanoi-Haiphong area. They urged first the shouldering out of foreign ships from Haiphong by a series of air attacks around the port and then the mining of approaches to the harbor. In addition, they called for a systematic attack on the eight operational airfields in North Vietnam and an intensive bombing campaign against the roads and railroads extending down from China. But the Central Intelligence Agency responded negatively to these proposals. While acknowledging that such a program of mining and bombing would have serious economic consequences, the CIA concluded that it probably would not significantly weaken the military establishment in North Vietnam or prevent Hanoi from supporting the struggle against the Saigon government and its armed forces in South Vietnam.

President Johnson was torn by divided counsel. While Westmoreland and the JCS advocated the application of greater American military force, McNamara and the CIA expressed doubt that the strategy of attrition would work. Civilians in the Departments of State and Defense also warned that a major American escalation might provoke a massive Chinese intervention. Johnson responded to the barrage of conflicting advice by taking a middle course. To increase the pressure on North Vietnam, he decided in June 1967 to authorize expanded air strikes in the Hanoi-Haiphong region. But Johnson remained reluctant to call up the Reserves, and in July 1967 he approved only a 55,000 increase in American troop strength in South Vietnam instead of giving Westmoreland the 200,000 additional men he had requested. Thus Johnson proceeded with caution in hopes of achieving a victory without risking a war with China or adding fuel to the flames of the antiwar crusade in the United States.

Hoping to shore up the home front, Johnson summoned Westmoreland to Washington in November 1967 to assure the American people that his troops were making real progress in Vietnam. Westmoreland played his role to the hilt. In a command performance before Congress, he claimed that "we have reached an important point when the end begins to come into view." Westmoreland continued to exude great optimism during his campaign to win public support for the American war effort. In a television appearance, he said that the United States might be able to start withdrawing troops from Vietnam within two years or less. Westmoreland repeatedly professed to see "light at the end of the tunnel" in an attempt to convince the American people that his forces had the Vietcong and North Vietnamese on the run. "I hope they try something," he told an American journalist, "because we are looking for a fight." It would not be long before Westmoreland got his wish.

The Tet Offensive

During the summer of 1967, the communist leaders in Hanoi decided to abandon their protracted war strategy and make an all-out effort to win a quick victory. General Giap promptly began developing plans for a massive offensive scheduled to take place in the winter of 1968 after the rainy season ended. He aimed to precipitate a general uprising by launching a general offensive throughout South Vietnam. During Phase I, North Vietnamese soldiers would conduct aggressive operations near the borders of Laos and Cambodia in an attempt to draw American troops away from the centers of population in South Vietnam. During Phase II, after the United States had rushed forces to the mountainous regions on the periphery, the Vietcong would begin coordinated attacks on the major cities and towns sprinkled along the seacoast. Giap hoped that the South Vietnamese government and army would collapse during the urban assaults and that the South Vietnamese people would rise up and support the Vietcong insurgents.

The first phase of the offensive worked to perfection. In the autumn of 1967, Giap ordered North Vietnamese army units to go into action in remote areas along the western frontier of South Vietnam. His troops mounted a series of attacks, though they sustained heavy losses in order to accomplish their objective. While these bloody battles were raging, American intelligence reports indicated that about 40,000 North Vietnamese soldiers were converging on a small United States marine base located on the Khe Sanh plateau in the far northwest corner of South Vietnam. Westmoreland immediately sent reinforcements into the region, and he soon had half of his combat troops stationed in the northern sector of South Vietnam. Westmoreland looked forward to a decisive engagement. Delighted by the prospect of using American firepower on a large concentration on enemy soldiers, he eagerly drafted plans to deluge the North Vietnamese forces in a spectacular bombing cascade appropriately code-named Operation Niagara.

During the first month of 1968, Americans became fixated on Khe Sanh. The North Vietnamese attacked one of the hills serving as an outpost for the American Marines on January 21, and then they began a continuous shelling of the base at Khe Sanh. As the North Vietnamese assailants crept closer and closer to the beleaguered marines in approaching trenches and tunnels, Westmoreland assumed that Giap was maneuvering to grab as much territory as possible prior to the opening of peace negotiations just as he had done when fighting the French a decade and a half earlier. The American press noted that the similarities between Khe Sanh and Dien Bien Phu were striking in terms of both physical terrain and enemy tactics. As public interest in the battle flared, officials in Washington feared that the United States might suffer a humiliating defeat. President Johnson became so preoccupied with the battle that he had a detailed photomural of the Khe Sanh plateau mounted on the walls of the Situation Room in the basement of the White House. Demanding that the Joint Chiefs of Staff assure him that Khe Sanh would not fall, Johnson barked that he did not want "any damned Dien Bien Phu."

Confident that he possessed ample firepower to hold the line at Khe Sanh, Westmoreland hoped that Giap would go all-out in an attempt to take the marine base. American forces stood poised to strike a dramatic blow that would cripple the North Vietnamese army. But Giap never had any intention of having his troops capture the encircled marine base. He simply wanted to direct American resources away from the population centers located in the lowlands of South Vietnam. So while American eyes were riveted upon Khe Sanh, Vietcong units moved into position around the principal cities and towns in preparation for the second phase of the offensive. And they succeeded in taking the Americans and their South Vietnamese allies by complete surprise. In fact, when the Vietcong attack on the urban areas commenced, Westmoreland thought it was a trick to distract him from the battle at Khe Sanh. He had fallen for Giap's ruse. Noting that the siege of Khe Sanh was only a feint, a military textbook used at West Point teaches the cadets that the American failure to anticipate the urban attacks was an "intelligence failure ranking with Pearl Harbor."

The general offensive erupted on the eve of the Tet holidays in 1968 just as the Vietnamese people were preparing to celebrate the beginning of the lunar new year. Shortly after midnight on January 30, Vietcong assailants stormed the American embassy in Saigon, and during the next few days their comrades surged into more than 100 different cities and towns scattered across South Vietnam. The carefully coordinated series of attacks exploded throughout the country like a string of firecrackers announcing the arrival of the Year of the Monkey. The Vietcong expected that the townspeople would hail them as liberators and that the South Vietnamese army units patrolling the cities would flee rather than fight. But the ARVN defenders did not run. Nor did the urban dwellers take to the streets to support the Vietcong. Contrary to the high hopes of the insurgents, the general offensive failed to precipitate a general uprising.

The Tet offensive, rather than resulting in a communist victory, turned into a military disaster for the Vietcong and the North Vietnamese.

Although caught by surprise, ARVN units succeeded in holding their positions in a sequence of intense firefights while American troops were airlifted into critical areas to help them reestablish control of the besieged cities and towns. The Vietcong attacks were quickly repulsed in every major South Vietnamese city except in Hué, where savage fighting continued for nearly three weeks. During the bloody battles of Tet, the Vietcong and North Vietnamese may have lost as many as 40,000 men, compared with only 1,100 American and 2,300 ARVN soldiers killed in action. The Tet campaigns left the Vietcong in a permanently weakened condition. Their regular units were so thinned that they would never regain their full strength, and their political cadres were so exposed that they could never completely rebuild their underground network.

But if the Tet offensive was a serious military setback for the Vietcong and North Vietnamese, it was at the same time a great psychological and political defeat for the United States. The suddenness and magnitude of the attacks upon supposedly secure urban areas stunned the American people. Having been led to believe by recent statements from General Westmoreland that the enemy was on the run, they were shocked by vivid television accounts of the assault on the American embassy in Saigon and the bitter street fighting in Hué. People in every part of the United States wanted to know how a foe who was on the ropes could have carried out attacks against so many cities and towns in South Vietnam. "What the hell is going on?" CBS newscaster Walter Cronkite asked in disbelief. "I thought we were winning the war!" Convinced that their country was bogged down in a bloody stalemate, Americans became even more disenchanted with the military struggle in Vietnam.

Yet in the aftermath of the Tet offensive, General Westmoreland decided to ask for a significant expansion in the size of his ground forces. He wanted to take advantage of the enemy losses and seize the initiative in an effort to achieve a military victory. Concerned about their global military responsibilities, the Joint Chiefs of Staff hoped to grasp the opportunity to induce President Johnson to call up the Reserves. General Wheeler, the chairman of the JCS, flew to Saigon in late February 1968 to confer with Westmoreland. The two generals agreed to recommend that an additional 206,000 American combat troops should be deployed in Vietnam. When Wheeler formally presented Westmoreland's request for a large number of reinforcements on February 27, he described the Tet offensive as a "very near thing." Wheeler and the Joint Chiefs not only wanted to strengthen the American military position in Vietnam, but they also hoped to rebuild their strategic reserve to enable the United States to meet any contingencies that might arise elsewhere.

Many civilian leaders, however, were worried about the economic position of the United States in the liberal capitalist world system. Wall Street spokesmen complained that the huge military expenditures in Vietnam were creating an inflationary spiral that was not only decreasing the purchasing power of the dollar at home but also making American goods less competitive in foreign markets. The United States had come full circle. Concerned about the dollar shortage of their Japanese and European trading partners, American policymakers in the aftermath of World War II sought to reintegrate underdeveloped areas into the evolving international commercial network. Influential members of the business community initially applauded the American military campaign in Vietnam. But it became clear by the early months of 1968 that the mounting costs of the conflict were sowing the seeds for a balance of payment problem that would increasingly plague the United States. And as their anxiety about the impending foreign trade deficit grew, more and more top corporate managers and their associates in government concluded that the time had come for the United States to negotiate a peace settlement.

President Johnson promptly turned the problem over to Clark Clifford, who had just replaced McNamara as secretary of defense. Doubtful that Westmoreland could win the war even if his troop requests were met, Clifford and his civilian aides in the Pentagon believed that the South Vietnamese would have to assume a greater responsibility for their own fate. They thought that the United States should not only help the South Vietnamese army become an effective fighting force but also pressure the Saigon government to make essential political reforms. Concluding that Westmoreland must not receive more than a token increase in troops, Clifford wrote Johnson on March 4, 1968 that the United States should dispatch only 22,000 additional soldiers to South Vietnam. His recommendation was accepted without serious debate. The president and his top civilian advisers agreed that American military forces in South Vietnam should not be significantly enlarged and that ARVN would have to shoulder a greater burden of the fighting in the future. Encouraged by the performance of ARVN during the Tet attacks, Johnson decided to inform Thieu and Ky that the United States would send only limited troop reinforcements to South Vietnam.

But even before Johnson announced his decision against a major troop increase, he was besieged by mounting evidence that the American people had grown tired of the war. Opinion polls taken in the wake of the Tet offensive indicated that an overwhelming majority of Americans believed that their country was hopelessly mired in an increasingly costly military stalemate. As war-weariness engulfed the United States, Senator Eugene McCarthy embarked upon a campaign for president, and on March 12 the outspoken peace candidate from Minnesota made a surprisingly strong showing in the Democratic primary in New Hampshire. Johnson was even more concerned when Senator Robert Kennedy of New York announced on March 16 that he would seek the Democratic nomination and run for president on an antiwar platform. Then the elite Senior Advisory Group on Vietnam, sometimes known as the Wise Men, delivered the final blow. After a series of private briefings on March 26, this distinguished group of former government officials told Johnson that time had run out for the American war effort in Vietnam. Former Secretary of State Dean Acheson summarized the majority view when he said that "we can no longer do the job we set out to do in the time we have left and we must begin to take steps to disengage."

President Johnson kept silent until the evening of March 31 when he made a dramatic television address to the American people. Johnson announced that henceforth the bombardment of North Vietnam would be limited to the enemy staging area just above the Demilitarized Zone. Noting that the United States had recently sent approximately 11,000 combat troops to help counter the Tet offensive, Johnson explained that he would dispatch only about 13,500 additional soldiers to South Vietnam. He emphasized that the United States was ready to send representatives to any place at any time to discuss peace. In a strong appeal for national unity, Johnson said that he had decided not to devote any of his time to partisan causes. "Accordingly," he declared, "I shall not seek, and I will not accept, the nomination of my party for another term as your President."

Despite his conciliatory language, however, Johnson was not about to abandon his effort to assure the survival of an independent noncommunist South Vietnam. Johnson believed that the prospects for a satisfactory peace settlement remained bleak, but he hoped that the partial bombing halt would convince domestic critics that he was doing everything possible to bring about negotiations. "It is hoped," General Wheeler cabled American military commanders in the Pacific, "that this unilateral initiative to seek peace will reverse the growing dissent and opposition within our society to the war." In a message to American ambassadors in Southeast Asia, the State Department noted that the peace gesture would cost the United States nothing since weather conditions over the northern portion of North Vietnam would continue to be unsuitable for air operations for at least the next four weeks. The State Department further explained that Hanoi would be "most likely to denounce the project and thus free our hand after a short period."

President Johnson was therefore caught by surprise when the North Vietnamese responded positively to his plea for peace. Although he had no choice but to accept their proposal for direct negotiations, Johnson still hoped to blame Hanoi if the peace discussions proved fruitless. Secretary of State Rusk reasoned that if the North Vietnamese refused to make concessions they would have to take "responsibility for breaking off the talks." When formal negotiations opened in Paris in May 1968, neither side showed any willingness to compromise on fundamental issues. The American delegation said that the United States would call a complete halt to the bombing of North Vietnam if Hanoi would take reciprocal steps of deescalation in South Vietnam. But the representatives from Hanoi insisted upon the unconditional cessation of American bombing raids and all other acts of war against North Vietnam. With each side repeating past arguments, the dialogue quickly reached an impasse.

While maintaining a firm stand in Paris, the Johnson administration began the process that came to be called Vietnamization. General Creighton Abrams was sent to Saigon in July 1968 to replace General Westmoreland who had been recalled to Washington to serve as the army chief of staff. Upon assuming command of MACV, General Abrams began scaling down American military operations and preparing the South Vietnamese army to take primary responsibility for the ground war. The United States provided ARVN units with modern weapons and urged the Saigon government to make political reforms to win popular support. At the same time, Abrams shifted military tactics in the direction of small-unit patrols in an attempt to keep pressure on the enemy while avoiding the heavy casualties that often resulted from big-unit search and destroy sweeps. Abrams also committed a major share of his military resources to an accelerated pacification campaign to extend American and ARVN control over a greater portion of the South Vietnamese countryside.

Neither the government nor the army of South Vietnam, however, appeared ready to live up to American expectations. Although its force level was rapidly expanded from 685,000 to 850,000 men, ARVN continued to suffer from incompetent leadership and low morale. Desertions from the South Vietnamese army reached an all-time high after the bitter fighting during the Tet offensive. The performance of the Thieu regime was equally disappointing. In response to American pressure, Thieu launched an anticorruption campaign and promised to give civilians a larger voice in his government. But Thieu did little to promote land reform in the countryside or to improve living conditions for the throngs of refugees who had flocked into the cities. Nor did he try to satisfy the widespread desire for peace in South Vietnam. As the fighting continued and draft calls rose, the Buddhist militants openly demanded the formation of a peace cabinet in Saigon and urged ARVN soldiers to lay down their arms. Thus it became apparent that Thieu could not create unity within South Vietnam by promising cosmetic changes.

While causing deep political divisions in South Vietnam, the war also produced growing discord among Americans as they prepared to elect a new president. The Democratic convention was held in August 1968 amid great turbulence in Chicago. While antiwar protesters clashed with local policemen and national guardsmen on the streets outside the convention hall, the delegates nominated Vice President Hubert H. Humphrey as their candidate to succeed Johnson in the White House. Humphrey wanted to run on a compromise platform that would satisfy Johnson loyalists and yet appeal to those who had supported Robert Kennedy before his assassination two months earlier. But Humphrey capitulated when Johnson insisted on a Vietnam plank that endorsed his policies. As Richard M. Nixon launched a vigorous campaign after accepting the Republican nomination, some Democratic party leaders urged Johnson to make a dramatic peace move to assist Humphrey at the polls. Johnson finally complied. On October 31, he announced a complete halt to the bombing of North Vietnam. But Nixon won the election five days later by a very close margin, and now he would have the chance to make good on his campaign pledge to "end the war and win the peace."

SEVEN

Withdrawal Without Victory

The bastards have never been bombed like they're going to be bombed this time.

President Richard M. Nixon, 1972

The Madman Theory

When he took the oath of office in January 1969, Richard M. Nixon was determined to extricate the United States from the military stalemate in Indochina before the rapidly growing antiwar movement wrecked his administration. But the new president was not about to abandon the long-standing American policy of integrating Southeast Asia into the liberal capitalist world system. Convinced that the strategy of attrition was doomed to fail, Nixon sought a diplomatic solution that would end the protracted conflict without undermining the prestige and credibility of the United States. Thus he aimed to negotiate a peace settlement that would enable South Vietnam to survive as an independent noncommunist nation. By engineering an American disengagement from the bloody struggle while avoiding even the slightest appearance of a defeat for the United States, Nixon hoped to go down in history as a great president who had succeeded in achieving "peace with honor."

Even before he assumed the reins of power in Washington, Nixon had devised a plan to end the Vietnam War during his first year in the White House. Nixon figured that he could scare the North Vietnamese into accepting American peace terms by employing a tactic that President Eisenhower had used to bring the Korean War to a satisfactory conclusion. When Nixon was serving as vice president under Eisenhower in 1953, the Chinese and North Koreans were stalling at the conference table while fighting to improve their position on the battlefield. But negotiations moved swiftly toward an armistice after Eisenhower hinted that the United States might use atomic weapons if the communists continued to drag their feet. It was a lesson that Nixon would never forget. With peace discussions now languishing in Paris, he intended to emulate his former boss. Nixon reckoned that he could intimidate the communist leaders in Hanoi by implying that the United States might bomb North Vietnam into the Stone Age.

Nixon intended to portray himself as a rabid anticommunist who might lose all sense of proportion and order the annihilation of North Vietnam. By appearing irrational and unpredictable, Nixon thought that he could frighten Ho Chi Minh into accepting a political settlement that would leave Nguyen Van Thieu firmly in control of South Vietnam. "I call it the Madman Theory," he confidently told one of his aides. "I want the North Vietnamese to believe I've reached the point where I might do *anything* to stop the war. We'll just slip the word to them that 'for God's sake, you know Nixon is obsessed about Communism. We can't restrain him when he's angry—and he has his hand on the nuclear button—and Ho Chi Minh himself will be in Paris in two days begging for peace." Nixon decided to test his reputation as an anticommunist fanatic shortly after he became president. Using a French intermediary, he proposed the mutual withdrawal of North Vietnamese and American troops from South Vietnam as a first step toward an enduring peace.

To supplement his overture to Hanoi, Nixon made a parallel approach to Moscow. He hoped to persuade Soviet leaders to put pressure on Ho Chi Minh to come to terms with the United States. In exchange for Russian diplomatic support, Nixon was prepared to offer the Soviet Union such things as wheat, modern technology, and an agreement to limit strategic armaments. Nixon called upon National Security Adviser Henry A. Kissinger to put his concept of "linkage" into practice. In March 1969, Kissinger sent Cyrus Vance to Moscow to open preliminary discussions on the control of nuclear weapons. He instructed Vance, a member of the American negotiating team in Paris, to tell the Russians that their cooperation in Vietnam would facilitate an arms deal with the

United States. Complementing Vance's positive message with a negative one of his own, Kissinger personally warned the Soviet ambassador in Washington that the United States would intensify the war unless a peace settlement could be reached in the near future.

To convince both Hanoi and Moscow that the United States meant business, President Nixon ordered massive air strikes against North Vietnamese bases inside Cambodia. General Wheeler and General Abrams had been urging the bombardment of the North Vietnamese sanctuaries in Cambodia to make it harder for General Giap to direct attacks against South Vietnam. But Nixon was primarily interested in implementing his Madman Theory. On March 16, the president told his top foreign policy aides that the only way to get the communists to negotiate was to do something on the military front that they would understand. The Cambodian bombing began a day later. During the next fourteen months, B-52's would make 3,630 raids, dropping more than 100,000 tons of bombs on Cambodia. Complying with White House demands that the bombing remain secret, the air force devised a deceptive reporting system to make it appear that the B-52s were dropping their payloads in South Vietnam. Nixon wanted to conceal the Cambodian bombing from the American people because he feared a national uproar if they knew that he was widening the war.

While secretly bombing Cambodia to get Hanoi to comply with his desire for a cease-fire, President Nixon decided to advertise his efforts to achieve an "honorable" settlement in Vietnam. Nixon hoped to counter the spread of antiwar sentiment in the United States by going public with the proposal that he had made in private to the North Vietnamese. During a nationally televised address delivered on May 14, the president issued a call for "the withdrawal of all non-South Vietnamese forces from South Vietnam." Nixon assumed that the Vietcong, after having suffered such terrible losses during the Tet offensive, would never again be able to stand alone against the armed forces of the Saigon government. He therefore concluded that, if the North Vietnamese troops discontinued their operations below the seventeenth parallel, the Thieu regime would be able to regain control of the South Vietnamese countryside.

But the communist leaders in Hanoi were not about to recognize the Demilitarized Zone as a permanent boundary separating the northern and southern halves of Vietnam. Acting upon instructions from home, the North Vietnamese delegates at the Paris discussions publicly denounced the American proposal as a "farce." And they continued to insist upon the unconditional withdrawal of all United States forces from South Vietnam and the establishment of a new coalition government in

Saigon. While maintaining a rigid negotiating posture in Paris, the North Vietnamese reverted to a protracted war strategy so that they could rebuild their military strength to the level reached prior to the Tet attacks. The North Vietnamese believed that time was on their side. Adopting a familiar ploy, they continued fighting in South Vietnam and talking in Paris in an effort to exhaust the patience of the American people.

Hoping to outmaneuver the North Vietnamese, President Nixon tried to convince domestic opponents of the war that he was winding down American military operations in Southeast Asia. Nixon met with Thieu on Midway Island in early June 1969 and announced that he would immediately repatriate 25,000 American troops from South Vietnam. A month later, during a talk with journalists in Guam, he proclaimed a principle widely publicized as the Nixon Doctrine. The president told the reporters that in the past the United States had committed men as well as money to protect Asian countries against the threat of communism. Although the United States would continue to provide Asian nations with economic and military assistance, he explained, henceforth they would have to rely upon their own troops. Thus Nixon hoped to shore up the home front by making a token disengagement of American forces from South Vietnam and by promising to shift the burden of ground combat throughout Asia to Oriental soldiers.

While indicating to the American people that he would pursue a policy of deescalation, however, Nixon was threatening the North Vietnamese with total devastation. First, to strengthen his hand, he ordered the chief of naval operations to prepare a top secret study for a massive bombing campaign against North Vietnam. Then, through a French intermediary on July 15, Nixon delivered an ultimatum to Ho Chi Minh. The president warned that unless some progress toward a peace settlement was made by November 1, he would resort to "measures of great consequence and force." But the North Vietnamese leader refused to be intimidated. In a personal letter to Nixon on August 25, Ho demanded the withdrawal of all American troops from South Vietnam and the dissolution of the Thieu government in Saigon. He insisted that there could be no peace until the United States ended its "war of aggression" and allowed the Vietnamese people the right to resolve their own political differences "without foreign influence." Although Ho died on September 3 at the age of seventy-nine, his comrades in Hanoi pledged to carry on their struggle for national reunification.

President Nixon was infuriated when the "cold rebuff," as he termed it, arrived from Hanoi. Acting under White House orders, Kissinger promptly assembled a special work group to consider the bombing plan that had been developed by the chief of naval operations. "I refuse to believe that a little fourth-rate power like North Vietnam does not have a breaking point," Kissinger declared at the opening meeting. "It shall be the assignment of this group to examine the option of a savage, decisive blow against North Vietnam." But the study group quickly concluded that the plan to bomb North Vietnam would lead to heavy civilian casualties without seriously diminishing Hanoi's capacity to continue the war in South Vietnam. A savage blow, in other words, would not be decisive. Worse yet, Secretary of Defense Melvin R. Laird warned that the proposed air strikes would provoke strong antiwar protests in the United States. Nixon consequently decided, at least for the moment, to shelve the plan for the massive bombardment of North Vietnam.

The Vietnamization Policy

Having failed to frighten Hanoi into complying with his wishes, Nixon fell back on the Vietnamization policy that he had inherited from Johnson. Like his predecessor in the White House, Nixon believed that the army fighting for the Saigon government should assume primary responsibility for the conduct of ground operations in South Vietnam. But he realized that in the immediate future ARVN would not be able to stand up against both the Vietcong and North Vietnamese forces without American combat support. Despite his desire to stifle the antiwar movement in the United States, therefore, Nixon refused to authorize a rapid withdrawal of American troops from South Vietnam. Instead he decided that the American disengagement should proceed very gradually while ARVN steadily gained strength. If the United States continued to provide the Thieu regime with economic and military assistance, Nixon concluded, American infantry units eventually might not be needed to prevent a communist takeover in Saigon.

Such reasoning prompted the United States to make a concerted effort to alter the balance of forces in South Vietnam before too many American troops were brought home. While the Saigon government increased its force level to over 1 million men, the United States furnished ARVN with a vast array of modern weapons. The South Vietnamese received automatic rifles, machine guns, grenade launchers, heavy mortars, armored vehicles, jet planes, gunboats, and helicopters. The United States also expanded the campaign to pacify the South Vietnamese countryside. Americans repaired bridges and roads, established schools and hospitals, and provided other basic services in an attempt to help Thieu win popular support. Americans also trained South Vietnamese agents to mix with the peasant population to gather information on Vietcong organizers. As a result of this so-called Phoenix program, thousands of Vietcong cadres were arrested and slain.

While endeavoring to cripple the enemy in Vietnam, President Nixon also sought to quiet his critics at home. Hence he announced in September 1969 that 35,000 more American troops would be pulled out of Vietnam by the end of the year. Hoping to quell antiwar protests by students returning to college, Nixon simultaneously noted that he had ordered a reduction in draft calls. But the president could not stop antiwar sentiment from spreading among vocal elements in American society. Press commentators, religious leaders, corporate executives, and other prominent figures increasingly spoke out against the war. On October 15, young liberals staged a peaceful "moratorium" to express their opposition to the war. Huge crowds of sober middle-class citizens assembled in cities across the country to listen to antiwar speakers. In Washington, thousands of protesters marched by candlelight in a solemn procession from Arlington Cemetery to Capitol Hill. Nixon was alarmed. He immediately ordered his staff to draft a speech that would isolate his domestic opponents before they could stage another moratorium a month later.

In a nationally televised address on November 3, Nixon tried to rally the American people behind his long-range Vietnamization program. The president spelled out his plan for the gradual withdrawal of American troops from Vietnam as ARVN units steadily gained strength. Realizing that most of his listeners wanted the United States to disengage from the fields of fire in Vietnam without losing the war, Nixon offered them a policy that promised to reduce American casualties and yet not lead to a defeat for the United States. But he warned that the enemy would be less likely to negotiate if Americans became more divided at home. Thus Nixon appealed to the "great silent majority" in the United States to support his efforts to end the war and win the peace. "Let us be united for peace," he declared. "Let us also be united against defeat. Because let us understand: North Vietnam cannot defeat or humiliate the United States. Only Americans can do that." His plea for national unity initially paid handsome dividends. Although the moratorium on November 15 was even bigger than the one held a month earlier, opinion polls showed that most Americans approved the way the president was handling the war.

After gaining public backing for his Vietnamization policy, Nixon pushed ahead with a phased American disengagement from the war. The number of United States servicemen stationed in Vietnam declined steadily during his first term in the White House. From a peak of 543,300 reached shortly after his inauguration in January 1969, the American force level in Vietnam fell to 475,200 by the end of the year. The pullout proceeded by fits and starts in response to public pressure in the United States. Thus American troop strength decreased from 334,000 in December 1970 to 156,800 in December 1971, and by the end of 1972 there were only 24,000 American soldiers remaining in Vietnam. The number of casualties suffered by the United States also declined in a dramatic fashion. While 222,351 Americans were killed or wounded in Vietnam during the years of escalation under Johnson between 1964 and 1968, the United States casualty count dropped down to 122,709 during the period of deescalation under Nixon between 1969 and 1972.

But with the American involvement in the war slowly winding down, the United States army confronted a crisis of discipline in Vietnam. The gradual withdrawal of American troops led those who were still fighting in Vietnam to conclude that the United States would never achieve a victory. Military morale drastically deteriorated as more and more American grunts decided that they did not want to die for what they regarded as a lost cause. While many American soldiers went on "search and evade" missions, others deserted or went on strike to avoid combat. Some American officers who persisted in giving orders to fight were killed or injured by fragmentation grenades that their own men had lobbed into their bunks. The Defense Department has admitted that as many as 788 such fraggings occurred in Vietnam during the 1969–1972 period. At the same time, racial tension between white and black soldiers in the United States army increased sharply, and the number of American troops using hard drugs became so great that more than a half million were addicted in Vietnam.

The crisis of discipline in Vietnam was compounded by the rampant growth of careerism in the United States army. By the time Nixon entered the White House, many American army officers had become more interested in personal advancement than in military accomplishment. Upwardly mobile officers competed for command assignments in Vietnam to get promotions without risking their lives in combat. The statistics speak for themselves. The ratio of medals distributed to army officers serving in Vietnam was higher than ever before, but the ratio of officer deaths was lower than in any other American war. As a result of its careerist orientation, the United States officer corps was plagued by incompetence. The army usually rotated officers out of Vietnam after only a six-month tour of duty to provide their replacements with an opportunity to get their tickets punched and move up the ranks in the military bureaucracy. Since army officers were transferred before they could learn their job, they frequently made mistakes that endangered the men under their command. And the poor performance of the officer corps contributed to the general demoralization of the American military establishment in Vietnam.

But while the process of disengagement and demoralization undermined American military strength, conditions in Cambodia provided an opening for the United States to weaken the enemy before the South Vietnamese army assumed greater responsibility for the fighting. Cambodian Prime Minister Lon Nol had become disenchanted with the neutralist policy pursued by the Phnom Penh government, and in March 1970 he led a coup against Prince Norodom Sihanouk. After seizing power, Lon Nol immediately insisted on the withdrawal of North Vietnamese troops from Cambodia. The North Vietnamese responded by increasing their support for the Khmer Rouge guerrillas, and before long the communist forces were pushing deep into the interior of Cambodia. On April 14, with the communists closing in around Phnom Penh, Lon Nol asked the United States for military help. President Nixon jumped at the chance to buy time for his Vietnamization program, and on April 30 he appeared on television to announce an incursion into Cambodia. While Nixon was speaking, 20,000 American and ARVN troops began attacking North Vietnamese base areas and logistical networks in Cambodia.

This combined United States and South Vietnamese military operation produced mixed results. During their two-month stay in Cambodia, American and ARVN soldiers captured large stores of rice, weapons, and ammunition abandoned by North Vietnamese troops who temporarily fled from their sanctuaries near the border of South Vietnam. But the Nixon administration paid a heavy political price for these minor military gains. Colleges all across the United States erupted in protest when it became clear that Nixon was actually widening the war in Indochina. Then, on May 4, at Kent State University, four student demonstrators were shot to death by overzealous members of the Ohio National Guard. Coming like thunderbolts on a spring day, the Kent State killings sent shock waves throughout the American academic community. Students and professors at hundreds of colleges went on strike, and many campuses were officially closed to avert further violence. And when more than 100,000 antiwar protestors marched on Washington and encircled the White House, a siege mentality began to pervade the Nixon administration.

The Cambodian adventure also aroused the wrath of political leaders on Capitol Hill. Senators John Cooper of Kentucky and Frank Church of Idaho sponsored an amendment that would cut off all funds for American military operations in Cambodia. Advocating even greater restrictions on executive authority, Senators George McGovern of South Dakota and Mark Hatfield of Oregon sponsored an amendment that would require the president to withdraw all American forces from Vietnam. Neither amendment could secure enough support to be translated into legislation that would immediately limit the power of the president to wage war. But in a symbolic act of defiance, the Senate voted overwhelmingly in June 1970 to terminate the Gulf of Tonkin Resolution. The House, moreover, soon joined with the Senate in reducing appropriations for the defense budget and in lowering quotas for the selective service. And in December 1970, while permitting the president to continue the air campaign in Cambodia, Congress prohibited the use of funds to support the deployment of any American combat forces or military advisers in ground operations outside South Vietnam.

But the conflict in Indochina continued to spread despite the rapid expansion of antiwar sentiment in the United States. As soon as the North Vietnamese troops began their temporary retreat from Cambodia, General Giap reinforced his base camps in Laos and renovated the Ho Chi Minh Trail running down the Laotian panhandle toward South Vietnam. In response, President Nixon immediately ordered the heavy bombardment of North Vietnamese staging areas and supply lines in Laos. He also authorized American air strikes against targets in the Hanoi-Haiphong area and other parts of North Vietnam. Finally, after considerable deliberation, Nixon decided in February 1971 to sponsor an invasion of Laos. The military campaign in Laos, like the earlier one in Cambodia, was designed to buy time for Vietnamization by disrupting enemy logistical facilities. But the congressional prohibition against the deployment of American infantry units or military advisers outside South Vietnam meant that the ground operations in Laos would have to be conducted solely by ARVN soldiers.

Launched amid great optimism on February 8, the Laotian invasion quickly turned into a complete disaster. The original plan called for the South Vietnamese forces to remain in Laos until May when the onset of heavy rains would make further military operations impractical. But after his troops encountered fierce resistance from North Vietnamese army units, President Thieu abruptly decided on March 9 to pull out of Laos. The South Vietnamese took a terrible beating during their hasty twelve-day retreat. Despite extensive American air support, the expeditionary forces of the Saigon government suffered a casualty rate approaching 50 percent before they could complete their disorganized withdrawal from Laos. Television viewers in the United States were disturbed by pictures of ARVN soldiers clinging desperately to the skids of American helicopters departing from Laos. Many American observers worried that the Thieu regime might not be able to carry out the Vietnamization program once the last contingent of United States combat troops returned home.

The poor ARVN performance in Laos during the winter of 1971 raised a fundamental question: why did the Vietcong and North Vietnamese fight so much better than the South Vietnamese? The answer lay partially in the fact that ARVN lacked honest and effective leadership. Like Diem before him, Thieu promoted officers from privileged urban backgrounds to the top positions in the South Vietnamese army as a reward for their personal loyalty rather then their military competence. But the weakest links in the military chain girdling Saigon were the peasant soldiers who saw no reason to risk their lives to protect the social and political system that paid them to fight. "These people don't need advisers; or if they do, then we have already failed," a senior American military adviser explained. "Charlie doesn't need advisers when he conducts a sapper attack. He doesn't need Tac air or gunships or artillery. He's hungry and he's got a cause and he's motivated. Therein lies the difference. On our side, nobody is hungry and few are motivated."

Painfully aware of this contrast, the Nixon administration was further embarrassed by a series of events that came fast on the heels of the Laotian fiasco. After a highly publicized trial ending on March 29, a military court found Lieutenant William Calley guilty of the premeditated murder of at least twenty-two South Vietnamese civilians in the village of My Lai. The Vietnam Veterans Against the War wanted to make the American people realize that the massacre at My Lai was not a unique incident. After arriving in Washington on April 20, a group of 1,000 Vietnam veterans testified to their own war crimes and threw their medals down upon the steps of the Capitol. The American public received additional revelations about the real nature of the Vietnam War on June 13 when the *New York Times* began publishing secret Defense Department documents that had been stolen by Daniel Ellsberg while he was working at the Pentagon. President Nixon secured an injunction to prevent the publication of these so-called *Pentagon Papers*, but the Supreme Court overturned the order. Hoping to prevent future disclosures, Nixon approved the creation of a clandestine group of "plumbers" to plug leaks within the government.

But Nixon could not stop the continuous barrage of shocking stories about American conduct in Vietnam from generating even greater war-weariness in the United States. Public opinion polls taken in the summer of 1971 indicated that disillusionment with the war had reached an all-time high among the American people. While over 70 percent thought that the United States had made a mistake by sending armed forces to Vietnam, nearly 60 percent regarded American military operations in Indochina as immoral. A mere 31 percent of the American population expressed approval for the way that Nixon was handling the war. Disenchantment with the prolonged military ordeal had become so widespread that a substantial majority of those surveyed said that they favored the removal of all American troops from Southeast Asia by the end of 1971 even if the result would be a communist takeover in South Vietnam.

The Paris Peace Treaty

Faced with such overwhelming domestic opposition to the war, President Nixon sent Henry Kissinger to Paris to try to break the deadlock in peace negotiations. During secret meetings beginning in May 1971, Kissinger presented a plan calling for the withdrawal of all United States troops from South Vietnam in exchange for the release of the American prisoners of war (POWs). But Le Duc Tho, the chief delegate from Hanoi, responded that North Vietnam would not agree to an armistice until the Thieu regime was replaced by a coalition government that included Vietcong representatives. When the United States refused to abandon Thieu, the political arm of the Vietcong issued a public statement explaining that the disagreement over the eventual status of the Saigon government remained the major obstacle to a peace settlement: "The U.S. Government must really respect the South Viet Nam people's right to self-determinism, put an end to its interference in the internal affairs of South Viet Nam, cease backing the bellicose group headed by Nguyen Van Thieu at present in office in Saigon, and stop all maneuvers, including tricks on elections, aimed at maintaining the puppet Nguyen Van Thieu."

As the diplomatic deadlock in Paris continued, the North Vietnamese decided that they would have to improve their position on the battlefield in order to achieve their political objectives in South Vietnam. General Giap immediately drew up plans for a military offensive to be launched in the spring of 1972 in an effort to topple the Thieu regime and to force the United States to leave South Vietnam. While Soviet ships carried hundreds of battle tanks and other heavy equipment into Haiphong

Harbor, Giap recruited tens of thousands of fresh troops. The balance of forces shifted rapidly in favor of the North Vietnamese as American combat units continued to withdraw from South Vietnam. Aware of the strong antiwar feelings in the United States, the communist leaders in Hanoi assumed that Nixon would not risk creating an uproar at home by sending American reinforcements to South Vietnam in an endeavor to save the Saigon government.

General Giap struck with massed forces during the last days of March 1972 as the American troops that still remained in South Vietnam were observing the start of the Easter weekend. Although the Central Intelligence Agency had gathered information about the North Vietnamese military buildup, the American and ARVN field commanders were stunned by both the magnitude and the method of the communist offensive. They expected that the North Vietnamese would employ traditional guerrilla tactics, but Giap launched a conventional three-pronged attack against ARVN units in an attempt to prove that the Vietnamization policy was a failure. The first group of North Vietnamese soldiers raced across the seventeenth parallel and penetrated deep into the northern provinces of South Vietnam; the second group swept through the Central Highlands; the third group rushed into the area above Saigon. Despite suffering heavy losses, the North Vietnamese attackers steamrolled over the ARVN defenders. Nixon was alarmed. "The real problem," he noted in his diary, "is that the enemy is willing to sacrifice in order to win, while the South Vietnamese simply aren't willing to pay that much of a price in order to avoid losing."

President Nixon responded quickly and vigorously to the Easter offensive. On April 6, he ordered the resumption of full-scale bombing attacks against North Vietnam. The American air campaign, codenamed Operation Linebacker, was designed to prevent Giap from resupplying his advancing forces in South Vietnam. During the intensive raids, B-52s dropped new "smart" bombs, guided by small computers receiving signals from laser beams, on fuel depots and ammunition dumps in North Vietnam. Nixon wanted to punish the North Vietnamese. "The bastards," he bellowed, "have never been bombed like they're going to be bombed this time." On May 8, the president announced that he had ordered the mining of Haiphong and the imposition of a naval blockade against North Vietnam. Nixon also declared that American planes would continue plastering targets above the seventeenth parallel. During the next month, B-52s dropped more than 100,000 tons of bombs on North Vietnam in an effort to blunt the communist offensive.

Besides conducting strategic bombing missions against North Vietnamese base areas and supply lines, American planes provided tactical air support for the beleaguered ARVN forces in South Vietnam. The United States used massive aerial assaults and heavy naval gunfire to hammer the aggressive armored units charging down from North Vietnam. American tactical air strikes alone were responsible for approximately half of the tank losses and personnel casualties suffered by the enemy. The struggling South Vietnamese defenders finally managed to hold the line against the ferocious North Vietnamese attackers, but only after receiving crucial aid from American air crews along with strong encouragement from American ground advisers. Since American air power ultimately saved the day for the Thieu regime by enabling ARVN to cope with the communist onslaught, the bloody fighting during the spring and summer of 1972 did not constitute a real test of the Vietnamization policy.

Neither side emerged from the Easter offensive stronger than before. Still hoping to obtain a negotiated settlement favorable to the United States, President Nixon was relieved when the American people remained relatively passive as he renewed the bombardment of North Vietnam. Nixon continued to withdraw American ground forces from South Vietnam in order to minimize public criticism of his administration in the United States. But while the last contingent of actual American combat troops was returning home in August 1972, the United States was making a strenuous effort to strengthen the South Vietnamese army. Nixon eagerly authorized Operation Enhance to provide Thieu with large numbers of aircraft and other military equipment to replace what his forces had lost during the recent fighting. As the United States continued shipping supplies to South Vietnam, the North Vietnamese realized that their energetic offensive had merely escalated the military stalemate to a higher level of violence.

After their campaign to crush the South Vietnamese army had failed, the communist leaders in Hanoi decided in the autumn of 1972 to make a major concession in an attempt to break the diplomatic deadlock with the United States. The North Vietnamese dropped their persistent demand that Thieu must be removed from his position of authority in Saigon before the fighting could stop. During a secret meeting in Paris on October 8, Le Duc Tho handed Kissinger a new peace proposal calling for an immediate cease-fire and the opening of negotiations for a future political settlement. There would be an exchange of all prisoners and a total withdrawal from South Vietnam of American and other foreign troops supporting the Saigon government. The United States would

be allowed to provide ARVN with replacements for weapons and supplies worn out or damaged after the cease-fire. Following the truce, the
contending parties in South Vietnam would establish a Council of
National Reconciliation and Concord and arrange for "genuinely free
and democratic general elections" to be held under international supervision. The United States would contribute to the postwar economic
reconstruction of North Vietnam, and finally both halves of Vietnam
would be reunited "step by step through peaceful means."

The United States government was elated with the North Vietnamese
proposal. Kissinger promptly put forth a schedule for implementing
the accord, and on October 20 Nixon sent Prime Minister Pham Van
Dong a personal message confirming that the text of the agreement could
be considered essentially complete. Nixon also pledged that on October
31 the United States would formally sign the peace treaty. While still
working in Paris on the wording of the pact, Kissinger advised Thieu in
repeated cables that his troops should seize as much territory as possible, especially in the densely populated areas around Saigon, in advance
of the truce. Nixon simultaneously issued orders for the crash delivery to
South Vietnam of new aircraft, tanks, armored personnel carriers,
trucks, and heavy artillery pieces. During the six-week program, code-
named Enhance Plus, the United States airlifted to South Vietnam more
than $1 billion worth of military equipment. The massive American
operation provided Thieu with the fourth largest air force in the world. In
fact, the South Vietnamese received more planes than they could maintain or fly because of a lack of skilled mechanics and trained pilots.

As American weapons began pouring into South Vietnam, Kissinger
hurried to Saigon to obtain approval for the peace plan. But Thieu was in
no mood for compromise. After meeting with Kissinger on October 19,
the South Vietnamese president raised two basic objections to the proposed agreement. Thieu said that, in the first place, he would not accept
a cease-fire that did not require the withdrawal of North Vietnamese
troops from South Vietnam. In the second place, Thieu indicated that he
would not tolerate the implication that Vietnam was one country. He
insisted that North Vietnam must recognize the independence and sovereignty of South Vietnam and acknowledge the DMZ as a permanent
international boundary. Kissinger was upset. On October 22, he handed
Thieu a letter written by Nixon. "Were you to find the agreement to be
unacceptable at this point and the other side were to reveal the extraordi-
nary lengths to which it has gone in meeting demands put upon them,"
Nixon warned, "it is my judgment that your decision would have the

most serious effects upon my ability to continue to provide support for you and for the government of South Vietnam."

But when Thieu remained adamant, President Nixon reneged on his commitment to carry out the peace plan according to the agreed schedule. Nixon wanted to avoid a public confrontation with the South Vietnamese government during the last weeks of his 1972 campaign for reelection. He therefore decided to stall for time. In a message to Hanoi on October 23, Nixon maintained that unexpected difficulties encountered in Saigon made further peace talks necessary. The North Vietnamese responded to the American maneuver on October 26 with a radio broadcast that reviewed the history of the negotiations and outlined the text of the agreement. "The Nixon administration" the Hanoi announcement concluded, "must bear before the people of the United States and the world responsibility for delaying the signing of the agreement, and thus prolonging the war in Vietnam." Kissinger immediately held a press conference at the White House in an attempt to defuse the situation. Claiming that the remaining issues could easily be settled during one more meeting with the North Vietnamese, he dramatically declared that "peace is at hand."

Nixon hoped to bring Thieu aboard before proceeding with peace negotiations. On November 14, just a week after winning a landslide victory over George McGovern in the presidential election, Nixon sent Thieu a personal letter that addressed his anxiety about the status of the North Vietnamese troops deployed in South Vietnam. Nixon said that he intended to deal with this problem in the draft agreement by proposing a clause that would provide for the withdrawal of North Vietnamese and American forces from South Vietnam on a one-for-one basis. "But far more important than what we say in the agreement on this issue is what we do in the event the enemy renews its aggression," he asserted. "You have my absolute assurance that if Hanoi fails to abide by the terms of this agreement it is my intention to take swift and severe retaliatory action." Insisting that the existing agreement was essentially sound, Nixon concluded that it was imperative that the Saigon government "does not emerge as the obstacle to a peace which the American people now universally desires." But Thieu was unmoved. On November 18, the South Vietnamese presented the United States with a list of sixty-nine amendments to the draft treaty.

When secret peace talks resumed in Paris on November 20, Kissinger demanded several substantive changes in the draft agreement including a new clause that would make it illegal for the North Vietnamese to maintain a military presence below the seventeenth parallel. But Le Duc

Tho countered by citing the Geneva Accords, which held that the Demilitarized Zone "should not in any way be interpreted as constituting a political or territorial boundary." And since the Saigon government had been arresting communist suspects and classing them as common criminals, the North Vietnamese delegation proposed that civilian detainees in South Vietnam be made part of an overall prisoner exchange. The two sides were unable to resolve their differences, and on December 13 Kissinger left Paris empty-handed. During a press conference in Washington three days later, he blamed North Vietnam for the diplomatic impasse and announced that the United States "will not make a peace which is a disguised form of victory for the other side."

President Nixon had already decided to authorize a massive dose of bombing designed to inflict maximum damage on North Vietnam. The air force called the operation, carried out during the Christmas holidays of 1972, Linebacker II. During the twelve-day blitz, between December 18 and 30, American planes flew over 1,700 sorties and dropped over 36,000 tons of bombs on Hanoi and Haiphong. "I don't want any more of this crap about the fact that we couldn't hit this target or that one," Nixon lectured the chairman of the Joint Chiefs of Staff. "This is your chance to use military power effectively to win this war, and if you don't, I'll consider you responsible." B-52 crews received new orders to press ahead toward their targets even if they met stiff enemy resistance. As a result, entire neighborhoods were obliterated, and as many as 1,600 civilians were killed. But the United States paid a high price for the pain inflicted upon the two cities. Using surface-to-air missiles, the North Vietnamese shot down fifteen B-52s and eleven other American planes. They also killed or captured nearly 100 American airmen, and the additional prisoners of war strengthened their bargaining position.

The Christmas bombing brought a torrent of denunciation that isolated the United States and weakened the Nixon administration. Bitter criticism rained down upon the United States not only from Russia and China but also from England and France and other friendly countries. While the prime minister of Sweden compared the air raids on North Vietnam with the atrocities committed by the Nazis, a German newspaper called the American action "a crime against humanity." Outrage in the United States was equally intense. Appalled by the bombing, columnists for the *New York Times* charged that Nixon was acting like a "maddened tyrant" and that he was waging "war by tantrum." Members of Congress threatened to cut off funds for the war when they returned to Washington after the Christmas recess. Realizing that time was running out, Nixon indicated that he would stop the bombing if the North Vietnamese agreed to resume peace talks. He managed to avoid stern congressional action when Hanoi consented.

Nixon was determined to get out of the war during the first month of 1973. In a letter to Thieu on January 5, Nixon explained that the United States intended to conclude a settlement even if the North Vietnamese refused to remove their troops from South Vietnam. "The gravest consequences would then ensue," he warned, "if your government chose to reject the agreement and split off from the United States." Nixon then repeated his secret pledge to retaliate with full force should the North Vietnamese violate the settlement. Kissinger and Le Duc Tho began their final round of negotiations in Paris on January 8, and after six days they were able to resolve their differences. In another letter to Thieu on January 16, Nixon warned that the United States would terminate economic and military assistance to South Vietnam in the event that the Saigon government refused to sign the peace treaty. But Thieu continued to balk until Nixon issued a blunt ultimatum. Only when he threatened to have Kissinger initial the agreement without the concurrence of South Vietnam did Thieu at last capitulate.

The peace treaty, formally signed in Paris on January 27, did not fundamentally differ from the agreement that had been made two months before the brutal Christmas bombing. While obtaining a few cosmetic changes to help Thieu save face, the United States accepted the North Vietnamese description of the DMZ as neither a political nor a territorial boundary. On the positive side, the Paris treaty extricated the United States from the war and secured the return of American POWs. But North Vietnamese troops remained in South Vietnam, and the fighting continued despite the truce. Above all, the treaty was flawed at the core because it did not resolve the basic political issue that had led to all the killing: who would rule South Vietnam? Nevertheless, the Nobel Peace Prize was offered to the two diplomats who had labored in Paris to settle the conflict. Always eager to bask in the limelight, Henry Kissinger gladly accepted the award. But Le Duc Tho declined the prize. "Peace," he candidly declared, "has not yet been established in South Vietnam."

The Fall of Saigon

The Paris treaty of January 1973 had merely established a new framework for the continuation of fighting in South Vietnam without direct American participation. Just before the cease-fire went into effect, communist troops seized hundreds of hamlets that they had never controlled. They hoped that their political agents would be able to win popular support in the areas acquired during their eleventh-hour flag-raising campaign. But after the truce, the South Vietnamese army continued fighting to recapture the contested villages. These battles following the cease-fire marked the beginning of a new ARVN offensive to win control of South Vietnam. According to official statistics, more than 6,600 ARVN soldiers were killed during the first three months of the truce. The political provisions of the peace agreement carried no greater weight than the military clauses. While Saigon authorities demanded the withdrawal of all North Vietnamese forces operating below the DMZ, the Vietcong insisted upon the restoration of full democratic freedoms in South Vietnam. Thus a Council of National Reconciliation and Concord was not established, and general elections to decide the future of South Vietnam were never held.

Though hoping that the Vietcong and the Saigon government would settle their differences through peaceful discussions, Nixon and Kissinger were determined to provide Thieu with enough military muscle to fend off any attack from North Vietnam. Therefore the United States did not remove its powerful fleet from the Gulf of Tonkin and the South China Sea or its awesome B-52 squadrons that were stationed in Guam and Thailand. Nor did the United States dismantle its huge military bases and storage facilities in South Vietnam. American military installations and equipment were simply turned over to ARVN before the cease-fire took effect. At the same time, several thousand men were hastily discharged from the United States military service and reemployed by the Saigon government. A small American military assistance group, in other words, continued to operate in South Vietnam as a "civilian" team of advisers and technicians.

But while preparing to employ the club of military retaliation, Nixon and Kissinger simultaneously held out the carrot of economic reconstruction to restrain the North Vietnamese. The United States had promised in Paris to help heal the wounds of war throughout Indochina, and on the first day of February 1973 Nixon wrote Pham Van Dong that the American contribution to the postwar rehabilitation of North Vietnam would fall in the range of $3.25 billion over a five-year period. Details of the financial aid program were to be worked out by a Joint Economic Commission composed of an equal number of members from the United States and North Vietnam. However, although Nixon pledged that the financial assistance would be provided without any political conditions, he planned on making the American aid contingent upon North Vietnamese compliance with the peace agreement. Nixon hoped that he could induce the North Vietnamese to leave their neighbors alone by slowly doling out the dollars for postwar reconstruction. But on February 7, the North Vietnamese announced that they would continue to support the Khmer Rouge struggle to turn Cambodia into a communist country.

The United States resopnded without delay. To buttress the Lon Nol regime in Phnom Penh, Nixon issued orders on February 9 for the resumption of American bombing in Cambodia. Waves of B-52s attacked Khmer Rouge units and North Vietnamese camps in Cambodia with far greater intensity than ever before. During the next six months, the United States dropped more than 250,000 tons of bombs on Cambodia—more than fell on Japan during all of World War II. Many of the American bombs were dropped on densely populated areas west of the Mekong River in an attempt to hit communist troops that were sweeping out from their bases in the sparsely populated mountainous region along the border of South Vietnam. As the American bombing spread across the Cambodian heartland, millions of peasants fled from their villages to seek protection in Phnom Penh. The population of the capital city swelled from around one-half million to about three million, while rice production declined drastically in the countryside. As a result of increasing food shortages, the Cambodian refugees suffered from hunger and malnutrition.

In the meantime, the tenuous relationship between the United States and North Vietnam began to fray. President Nixon told news reporters in the middle of March 1973 that the United States had expressed concern to Hanoi about the movement of North Vietnamese military equipment into South Vietnam. On April 3, almost immediately after the last American prisoners had been released in Hanoi, Nixon warned that continued North Vietnamese violations of the peace agreement "would call for appropriately vigorous reactions." The United States reinstituted reconnaissance flights over North Vietnam two weeks later. Complaining that the North Vietnamese had not withdrawn their troops from Cambodia, the United States recalled the naval task force that had been clearing mines in North Vietnamese waters. The United States also abruptly broke off the Joint Economic Commission talks concerning postwar reconstruction aid for North Vietnam. In response to these moves, authorities in Hanoi began to withhold information about American servicemen listed as missing in action.

Although Kissinger urged Nixon to resume the bombardment of North Vietnam, the imperial powers of the president had already begun to unravel. The process was accelerated by an assortment of odd jobs that the White House plumbers had sought to do for the president. Besides breaking into the office of a psychiatrist to obtain records that might discredit Daniel Ellsberg, the plumbers attempted in June 1972 to wiretap the Democratic Party National Headquarters at the Watergate office complex in Washington. Nixon tried to cover up their effort to help assure his reelection, but in April 1973 one of his key aides resigned amid charges that the president was guilty of obstructing justice. As evidence of White House involvement in the Watergate affair mounted, Nixon found himself fighting for his political life. The president realized that he was in no position to order the renewed bombing of North Vietnam against the wishes of the American people and their representatives in Congress. Despite the militant advice coming from Kissinger, therefore, Nixon permanently shelved all plans for a new series of air strikes against North Vietnam.

During the summer and fall of 1973, as the Watergate scandal eroded the political clout of the president, Congress became bold enough to reassert its legal authority in the field of foreign affairs. Many legislators no longer felt compelled to appropriate money to support military operations in Southeast Asia since American troops had been withdrawn from Vietnam. Antibombing resolutions began to move through the House and Senate, and on June 29 Congress voted to cut off funds for any American military activity in or over Indochina after August 15. Hoping to check the unwarranted extension of executive power, more and more lawmakers drew inspiration from the constitutional principle that prohibits the president from ordering military action in the absence of a congressional declaration of war. Their desire to reestablish a balance between the executive and legislative branches of government manifested itself on November 7 when Congress passed the War Powers Act over a presidential veto. The measure required the president to inform Congress within forty-eight hours about the deployment of American military forces abroad and obligated him to withdraw them within sixty days unless Congress approved the undertaking. Combined with the vote terminating funds for military operations in Indochina, the passage of the War Powers Act signaled the end of direct American involvement in the Vietnam conflict.

South Vietnam soon plunged into the throes of an economic crisis. Poor rice harvests throughout Asia together with the Arab oil embargo imposed in late 1973 forced the South Vietnamese to pay sharply increased prices for their food and fuel. And as American military aid declined from $2.3 billion in 1973 to about $1 billion in 1974, ARVN soldiers suffered from a severe drop in their purchasing power. The

United States troop withdrawal contributed to the economic woes of South Vietnam. When American military bases closed, about 300,000 South Vietnamese civilians lost their jobs. American servicemen were no longer spending large sums in South Vietnam for food, drinks, taxi rides, and other pleasures. Living costs nearly doubled between January 1973 and July 1974 while the jobless rate climbed to almost 20 percent of the urban population. As the dual scourges of unemployment and inflation plagued South Vietnam, growing numbers of beggars, pimps, and whores roved the streets of Saigon and other major cities.

Military morale in South Vietnam plummeted to an all-time low. While the children of the elite purchased exemptions from military service, the sons of the poor were drafted into the army in droves. Graft and corruption pervaded the entire South Vietnamese military establishment. ARVN soldiers frequently stole from civilians because they could not provide for their families on their regular income while South Vietnamese pilots sometimes demanded bribes to fly missions in support of ground troops. Rather than reporting the death or desertion of thousands of their men, ARVN commanders kept their names on the payroll and pocketed their wages. Discipline deteriorated even further as the death toll of the South Vietnamese army rose from around 25,000 in 1973 to nearly 31,000 in 1974. During the latter year, when more than 200,000 soldiers and militiamen deserted, the armed strength of South Vietnam declined by about one-fifth. People in every part of the country sensed that the end was near for the military forces of the Saigon government.

The curtailment of American military assistance heightened the level of anxiety in South Vietnam. Concerned about rising inflation in the United States, congressional leaders began looking for ways to reduce federal expenditures. Few reacted sympathetically, therefore, when Kissinger proposed in the spring of 1974 that the United States provide $1.45 billion to support the South Vietnamese army during the next fiscal year. Critics warned that much of the money would end up in the pockets of corrupt officers and bureaucrats. Viewing the appropriation of vast sums for ARVN as a needless drain on the budget, Congress voted on August 6 to authorize only $700 million in military aid for South Vietnam. The armed forces of the Saigon government had unfortunately acquired expensive habits under American tutelage. During the fighting in 1974, ARVN soldiers used 56 tons of ammunition for every ton used by their enemy. But the cut in American military aid meant that they could no longer afford to employ an endless amount of firepower. Unable to continue fighting a rich man's war, ARVN officers began to doubt their ability to survive a major communist offensive.

At the same time, the movement to impeach President Nixon set the stage for a political crisis in South Vietnam. The House Judiciary Committee charged Nixon with obstructing justice and abusing his power in late July 1974 after the Supreme Court had ordered him to turn over key tapes dealing with the Watergate coverup. Then, on August 9, Nixon resigned in order to avoid the humiliation of impeachment. The departure of his American patron left Thieu vulnerable to his own critics. Tran Huu Thanh, a conservative Catholic priest, led a popular anticorruption campaign against the Saigon government. On September 8, Father Thanh and his associates issued a provocative document that accused Thieu and his family of several specific acts of corruption. Three Saigon newspapers printed the full text of the indictment in defiance of government censors, and many Catholics who had been strong backers of the Thieu regime joined the anticorruption movement. On October 30, in an effort to placate the protesters, Thieu fired three of his four corps commanders. But large anticorruption demonstrations continued to shake the political foundations of the Saigon government.

Amid the growing turmoil in Saigon, the leaders of the Communist Party in Hanoi decided that the time had arrived for a final offensive to achieve a military victory. Preparations had been made during the past year for a major campaign to topple the Thieu regime and reunite the Vietnamese people under communist rule. Soldiers and supplies had been quietly infiltrated into South Vietnam, roads had been built to carry troops and arms to future battlefronts, and a fuel pipeline running down from North Vietnam had been extended to within 100 miles of Saigon. Members of the Politburo held an important meeting in October 1974 to discuss the situation with the Central Military Committee of the Communist Party. After concluding that the possibility of renewed American intervention seemed remote, the conferees unanimously approved a plan for a large-scale offensive that would begin during the next spring. The Politburo members met again to review the situation, and in January 1975 they adopted a two-year plan for winning the war. "Large surprise attacks would be launched in 1975," they agreed, "creating conditions for the general offensive and uprising in 1976."

The North Vietnamese offensive for 1975 opened on March 10 with an attack in the Central Highlands of South Vietnam. When Ban Me Thuot fell to the communist forces within two days, a panicky Thieu ordered his troops to withdraw to the coast. The retreat quickly turned into a rout that resulted in the destruction of two ARVN divisions and the loss of six South Vietnamese provinces. After taking the Central Highlands, the North Vietnamese began advancing down the coast like a hot knife through butter. South Vietnamese army units rapidly disintegrated as soldiers joined civilians in a disorganized flight from the pursuing enemy. Hué capitulated on March 26. Danang was abandoned in anarchy during the next three days. ARVN troops looted the deserted city while frightened refugees crowded aboard departing ships and fishing boats. After capturing Danang without meeting any resistance on March 30, the North Vietnamese forces moved swiftly southward to take Cam Ranh Bay. ARVN soldiers continued to flee rather than fight, and within a few days the communists were in control of the entire northern half of South Vietnam.

Shocked by the avalanche, President Gerald R. Ford asked Congress on April 10 for $722 million in supplemental military aid for South Vietnam. He argued that the South Vietnamese needed a quick infusion of American assistance to replace the equipment that had been lost during the precipitous retreat from the northern portion of South Vietnam and to organize new ARVN units to defend the remainder of the country. Appearing before Congress to rationalize the request on April 15, Kissinger claimed that the United States had a deep moral obligation to aid the Saigon government and the South Vietnamese people. "Our failure to act in accordance with that obligation," he warned, "would inevitably influence other nations' perception of our constancy and our determination." Kissinger concluded that American credibility would consequently be weakened to the detriment of "the peaceful world order we have sought to build." But his argument fell upon deaf ears. Refusing to authorize additional military assistance for South Vietnam, Congress eventually approved $300 million to be used for the evacuation of Americans and to provide relief for hundreds of thousands of homeless refugees.

The aid debate masked the harsh realities in South Vietnam. Kissinger had attributed the collapse of the South Vietnamese army largely to cuts in American military assistance to Saigon after the peace agreement. But intelligence agencies in Washington estimated that North Vietnam had received only $730 million in military aid from Russia and China in 1973 and 1974 compared with the $3.3 billion that South Vietnam had received from the United States in the same years. The hard fact of the matter is that the South Vietnamese army suffered more from a lack of leadership than from a shortage of supplies. ARVN soldiers did not desert to take care of their families until after they had been abandoned by their senior officers. Despite many years of indoctrination and training, American military advisers had failed to build a professional army in South Vietnam. The military forces supporting Thieu remained rotten from top to bottom, and in 1975 the day of reckoning had come. It was apparent that South Vietnam was too sick to be saved by a last-minute injection of American aid.

Surprised by the sudden collapse of the South Vietnamese army, the communist leaders in Hanoi realized that the historic moment to complete their anticolonial revolution was at hand. Only the badly demoralized forces of the Saigon government stood between them and their long-cherished goal of national reunification. On March 31, the Politburo decided to seize the opportunity to achieve a total military victory and to raise the red flag over South Vietnam. The Ho Chi Minh campaign began on April 26 in honor of the great Vietnamese hero, and on May 1 Saigon fell to the communist forces. The Khmer Rouge had captured Phnom Penh two weeks earlier. After Congress had banned the bombing of Cambodia, Nixon rushed shiploads of new military equipment to Lon Nol. But his army was just as incompetent and corrupt as the one supporting Thieu, and the Khmer Rouge gradually took control of the Cambodian countryside before making a final assault on Phnom Penh. When the Pathet Lao assumed power in Laos a few months later, the communist triumph in Indochina was at last complete.

During the spring of 1975, as Americans began celebrating the two hundredth anniversary of their own war for independence, they were already pondering the significance of the debacle in Indochina. *Newsweek* attempted to put the tragedy in a broad historical perspective in an essay published just two days before the last American officials were evacuated by helicopter from the roof of the United States embassy in Saigon: "The high hopes and wishful idealism with which the American nation had been born had not been destroyed, but they had been chastened by the failure of America to work its will in Indochina. In the second century of its independence, the United States gradually—but indisputably—emerged as the most powerful nation in the world. Now, the world and the ability of the United States to influence it have changed. It was still far too soon to tell what the third century of America's independence would bring, but there was no question that it was dawning in a spirit of doubt and contrition."

CONCLUSION

The actions of the United States in the realm of foreign affairs have often run counter to long-cherished American ideals. In line with the revolutionary heritage of the United States, policymakers in Washington have again and again pledged their support for the democratic principle of national self-determination. They have also consistently articulated a strong humanitarian desire to help other countries achieve prosperity and security. But American leaders have never abandoned their fundamental belief in the vital importance of foreign commerce for the successful functioning of free enterprise in the United States. Thus they have frequently attempted to force other countries to participate in the international trading network that the United States helped establish in the aftermath of World War II. Therein lies the tragedy of American diplomacy. For in their determination to buttress the liberal capitalist world system and thereby preserve entrepreneurial freedom in the United States, American leaders have repeatedly acted contrary to their clearly expressed humanitarian values and democratic principles.

The protracted involvement of the United States in Vietnam provides a classic example of the tragedy of American foreign policy. Although the United States intervened in Vietnam in the name of extending the blessings of freedom, American actions in fact curtailed the liberty of the Vietnamese people. In his determination to prevent the Vietminh from transforming Vietnam into a communist nation, President Truman decided in 1950 to subsidize the French military struggle to reimpose colonial rule over Indochina. Yet the French met with defeat in 1954 at Dien Bien Phu. The subsequent Geneva peace settlement, though temporarily partitioning Vietnam along the seventeenth parallel, stipulated that general elections were to be held in 1956 to reunify the country. Realizing that Ho Chi Minh would win an overwhelming victory at the polls if elections were conducted according to schedule, President Eisenhower decided to abort the Geneva Agreement and keep Vietnam permanently divided. The United States then made a concerted effort to help Ngo Dinh Diem build the southern half of Vietnam into an independent nation that would stand as a bastion against the spread of communism in Southeast Asia. But neither Diem nor his successors in Saigon were able to win the allegiance of the majority of the South Vietnamese population. Despite their devotion to democratic institutions, therefore, Americans found themselves supporting a series of dictatorial governments in South Vietnam.

The tragedy in Vietnam unfolded because American leaders placed economic considerations above their own political ideals. Following the fall of China to communist forces in 1949, President Truman and his advisers sought to make Japan a junior partner in the evolving Pax Americana. But they feared that Japan, if denied access to noncommunist markets in Southeast Asia, would quickly become dependent upon trade with China and ultimately be pulled out of the capitalist orbit. State Department officials acknowledged that Ho Chi Minh, should he gain control of Vietnam, might well behave like an Asian Tito and remain free from either Russian or Chinese domination. Yet they thought that Ho and his Vietminh colleagues would adopt a Soviet model for economic development and thus restrict the flow of trade between Vietnam and the rest of the world. Though they understood that Vietnam by itself possessed little value as a market for Japanese goods, American diplomats believed that a Vietminh victory in Indochina would encourage radicals to challenge the status quo elsewhere in Southeast Asia.

By the beginning of the 1960s, the domino theory had assumed global dimensions. United States policymakers worried that a successful communist revolution in Vietnam would have a ripple effect not only in the rest of Southeast Asia but also in Latin America and Africa. Besides possessing direct commercial and financial interests in underdeveloped areas around the world, the United States was shipping large quantities of goods to industrial nations, which in turn depended upon trade with underdeveloped regions. President Kennedy and his successors in the White House remained convinced that unless American producers could continue to export their surplus commodities to industrial and nonindustrial countries alike the United States would eventually have to resort to centralized economic planning to create an internal balance between supply and demand. The stakes were high. By maintaining the prestige and credibility of the United States in Indochina, American leaders hoped to dampen the zeal of radical groups throughout the Third World. Thus they were determined to stay the course in Vietnam.

The ensuing American military operations in Vietnam had disastrous consequences. Although those responsible for shaping American foreign policy were not evil men, their decision to dispatch growing numbers of bomber squadrons and combat troops from the United States led to widespread death and destruction in Indochina. Millions of inhabitants of Vietnam, Laos, and Cambodia lost their lives, and those who survived had to eke out an existence on land that had been seared by napalm, defoliated by chemicals, and pulverized by explosives. Americans also suffered during the bloody ordeal. Nearly 60,000 United States soldiers died in the distant jungles and rice paddies of Vietnam, and a great many more received wounds that left them with permanent disabilities. Nor did those who remained in the United States escape from the ravages of the war. The huge military expenditures in Vietnam placed an added burden upon American taxpayers and forced cuts in social welfare programs in the United States. They also helped generate an inflationary spiral that decreased the purchasing power of the dollar at home and made American goods less competitive in foreign markets.

The mounting cost of the conflict in Vietnam produced a massive antiwar movement in the United States. Reports that American bombs were killing thousands upon thousands of Vietnamese civilians pricked the conscience of people across the country. And as draft quotas sharply increased, more and more college students participated in antiwar demonstrations. Grass roots support for the antiwar crusade grew apace as it became clear that American troops were fighting to protect a corrupt dictatorship in Saigon. Pointing to the mushrooming expenditures on the war, critics charged that American military operations in Vietnam were irrational as well as immoral.

Prominent members of the American Establishment also began to question the wisdom of the war. They had supported the American military campaign in Vietnam as part of their commitment to help maintain the liberal capitalist international order. But the American war effort was contributing to a balance of payment problem that threatened the position of the United States in the world trading system. Convinced that the military means were undermining the economic ends of American diplomacy, many distinguished Estalishment figures concluded after the Tet offensive in 1968 that the time had come for the United States to negotiate a peace settlement.

But instead of abandoning their objectives in Southeast Asia, American leaders sought to take the steam out of the antiwar movement. President Johnson initiated the Vietnamization policy in an attempt to shift the burden of fighting in Indochina away from American ground forces and back to ARVN soldiers. Continuing that program, President Nixon began reducing draft quotas and withdrawing American combat troops from Vietnam. He also unveiled the Nixon Doctrine, which served notice that the United States would henceforth supply money and arms, but not men, to help Asian countries fight communism. Despite these maneuvers, however, antiwar sentiment continued to spread across the United States.

An angry Nixon lashed back against his critics. He portrayed antiwar protesters as traitors who were giving aid and comfort to the enemy during the heat of battle. He also sought a court order to block the publication of the *Pentagon Papers* to prevent American citizens from learning the truth about Vietnam. As his endeavor to stifle domestic dissent became an obsession, Nixon approved a number of illegal wiretaps and burglaries that culminated in the Watergate scandal. The irony was bitter. In the name of making Southeast Asia safe for democracy, American officials were destroying liberty in the United States.

But perhaps the greatest tragedy lies in the lesson that decision makers in Washington learned from the American experience in Vietnam. Realizing that few participants in the antiwar movement ever made a sophisticated analysis of American foreign policy, they concluded that in the future the United States could engage in covert rather than overt operations to combat revolutions in the Third World. As a result, the United States became increasingly inclined to fight wars by proxy. President Reagan, for example, employed a variety of clandestine measures in an effort to destabilize the Sandinista government in Nicaragua. Besides ordering the navy to mine the Managua harbor, he sent military advisers to train Nicaraguan counterrevolutionaries. And after Congress cut funds for the antigovernment forces in Nicaragua, White House aides surreptitiously sold arms to Iran in order to obtain money to buy weapons for the Contras.

The message seems clear. Unless the people of the United States gain a better understanding of the nature of American diplomacy, the tragedy that occurred in Vietnam might be repeated with equally dire consequences in other parts of the world and with perhaps even worse results for democratic institutions in the United States.

SELECTED BIBLIOGRAPHY

Documents

The best place to begin is the *Pentagon Papers*, a collection of primary sources prepared by the Department of Defense and eventually published in several editions. U.S. Congress, Senate, Subcommittee on Building and Grounds, *The Pentagon Papers (The Senator Gravel Edition)*, 4 vols. (Boston, 1971) is an orderly and easy-to-use set. The *Foreign Relations of the United States*, a series of official documents prepared by the Department of State, contains valuable material dealing with Vietnam. William Appleman Williams et al., *America in Vietnam: A Documentary History* (New York, 1985) is a superb collection. Gareth Porter, *Vietnam: The Definitive Documentation of Human Decisions*, 2 vols. (Stanfordville, N.Y., 1979) is also excellent.

General Works

The most comprehensive standard accounts are Stanley Karnow, *Vietnam: A History* (New York, 1983) and George C. Herring, *America's Longest War: The U.S. and Vietnam, 1950–1975* (New York, 1985). On the Vietnamese side, see the excellent works of Joseph Buttinger: *The Smaller Dragon, A Political History of Vietnam* (New York, 1958); *Vietnam: A Dragon Embattled*, 2 vols. (New York, 1967); and *A Dragon Defiant, A Short History of Vietnam* (New York, 1972). George M. Kahin, *Intervention: How America Became Involved in Vietnam* (New York, 1986), is especially good in analyzing the American response to the Buddhist movement and the subsequent political turmoil in South Vietnam. For accounts by two insiders, see Chester A. Cooper, *The Last Crusade: America in Vietnam* (New York, 1970); and Paul Kattenburg, *The Vietnam Trauma in American Foreign Policy, 1945–1975* (New Brunswick, N.J., 1980). Gabriel Kolko, *Anatomy of a War: Vietnam, the United States, and the Modern Historical Experience* (New York, 1985), examines the political and social structures underlying the Vietnam War. For a provocative interpretation of the relationship between American culture and the Vietnam War, see Loren Baritz, *Backfire: A History of How American Culture Led Us into Vietnam and Made Us Fight the Way We Did* (New York, 1985).

Origins—1941

In addition to the general works by Karnow and Buttinger listed above, see John Cady, *The Roots of French Imperialism in Asia* (Ithaca, N.Y., 1954). Martin J. Murray, *The Development of Capitalism in Colonial Indochina, 1870–1940*

(Berkeley, Calif., 1980), analyzes the French economic exploitation of Indochina prior to World War II. On the rise of Vietnamese nationalism, see John T. McAlister, Jr., *Vietnam: The Origins of Revolution* (New York, 1971); William J. Duiker, *The Rise of Nationalism in Vietnam, 1900–1941* (Ithaca, N.Y., 1976); and David G. Marr, *Vietnamese Anti-Colonialism, 1885–1925* (Berkeley, Calif., 1971), and *Vietnamese Tradition on Trial, 1920–1945* (Berkeley, Calif., 1982). Jean Lacouture, *Ho Chi Minh: A Political Biography* (New York, 1968) portrays Ho as Vietnamese nationalist with a charismatic personality. On the roots of communism in Vietnam, see Douglas Pike, *History of Vietnamese Communism* (Stanford, Calif., 1978).

1941–1954

For American attitudes toward the colonial question and the trusteeship scheme embraced by Franklin D. Roosevelt, see Christopher Thorne, *Allies of a Kind: The United States, Britain, and the War against Japan, 1941–1945* (New York, 1978); and William Roger Louis, *Imperialism at Bay: The United States and the Decolonization of the British Empire* (New York, 1978). Archimedes L. Patti, *Why Vietnam? Prelude to America's Albatross* (Berkeley, Calif., 1980), is a firsthand account by an Office of Strategic Services agent who dealt with the Vietminh during World War II. For the American decision to support the French war effort in Indochina, see Andrew J. Rotter, *The Path to Vietnam: Origins of the American Commitment to Southeast Asia* (Ithaca, N.Y., 1987); and William S. Borden, *The Pacific Alliance: United States Foreign Economic Policy and Japanese Trade Recovery, 1947–1955* (Madison, Wis., 1984). Ronald H. Spector, *Advice and Support: The Early Years of the U.S. Army in Vietnam, 1941–1960* (New York, 1985), analyzes the American military assistance program in Vietnam. Lloyd C. Gardner, *Approaching Vietnam: From World War II through Dienbienphu, 1941–1954* (New York, 1988), places American involvement in Southeast Asia in a broad global perspective. Also see Robert M. Blum, *Drawing the Line: The Origin of the American Containment Policy in East Asia* (New York, 1982). Graham Greene's *The Quiet American* (London, 1955) is a classic novel that provides added insight into the covert operations of the CIA in Vietnam. The standard account of the First Indochina War is Ellen Hammer, *The Struggle for Indochina, 1945–1955* (Stanford, Calif., 1966). For additional analysis of the French side, see Ronald E. Irving, *The First Indochina War: French and American Policy, 1945–1954* (London, 1975). Bernard B. Fall, *Street without Joy* (New York, 1972), describes the French military operations in Vietnam. For detailed discussions of the French defeat at Dien Bien Phu, see Jules Roy, *The Battle of Dienbienphu* (New York, 1965); and Bernard B. Fall, *Hell Is a Very Small Place* (Philadelphia, 1966). Robert F. Randle, *Geneva 1954: The Settlement of the Indochina War* (Princeton, N.J., 1969), analyzes the peace conference that marked the end of the French empire in Indochina.

1954–1963

In addition to the excellent study by Spector listed above, a good work to begin
with is Robert Scigliano, *South Vietnam: Nation under Stress* (Boston, 1964).
On the origins of the insurgency against the Ngo Dinh Diem regime, see Jeffery
Race, *War Comes to Long An* (Berkeley, Calif., 1972); and William J. Duiker,
The Communist Road to Power in Vietnam (Boulder, Colo., 1981). Truong Nhu
Tang, *A Vietcong Memoir* (New York, 1985), is a brilliant firsthand account of a
Vietnamese participant in the National Liberation Front. Roger Hilsman, *To
Move a Nation* (New York, 1967), a memoir by an American diplomat, sheds
light on the development of the counterinsurgency program. David Halberstam,
The Making of a Quagmire (New York, 1964), is an account by a dissident
American journalist whose reports from Saigon challenged the official line dur-
ing the Kennedy administration. On the overthrow of Diem, see Ellen Hammer,
A Death in November: America in Vietnam, 1963 (New York, 1987). Neil Sheehan, *A Bright Shining Lie: John Paul Vann and America in Vietnam* (New York,
1988), illustrates the difficulties encountered by American military advisers in
their effort to help the South Vietnamese army.

1964–1968

In addition to the penetrating study by Kahin listed above, the memoir by Lyn-
don B. Johnson, *The Vantage Point* (New York, 1971), is a good place to start.
For a different viewpoint from an insider, see George W. Ball, *The Past Has
Another Pattern: Memoirs* (New York, 1982). Larry Berman, *Planning a
Tragedy: The Americanization of the War in Vietnam* (New York, 1982), is an
excellent study of the decision-making process that led to the deployment of
American combat troops in Vietnam. For a detailed account of American
ground operations in Vietnam, see Shelby L. Stanton, *The Rise and Fall of an
American Army: U.S. Ground Forces in Vietnam, 1965–1973* (New York, 1985).
The American air war in Vietnam is described in James C. Thompson, *Rolling
Thunder: Understanding Policy and Program Failure* (Chapel Hill, N.C.,
1980). William C. Westmoreland, *A Soldier Reports* (Garden City, N.Y., 1976),
is a defensive memoir that explains the American strategy of attrition in Viet-
nam. For critical studies of American military policy in Vietnam, see Dave
Richard Palmer, *Summons of the Trumpet: A History of the Vietnam War from a
Military Man's Viewpoint* (San Rafael, Calif., 1978); Guenter Lewy, *America in
Vietnam* (New York, 1978); Harry G. Summers, Jr., *On Strategy: A Critical
Analysis of the Vietnam War* (San Rafael, Calif., 1982); and Bruce Palmer, Jr.,
The 25-Year War: America's Military Role in Vietnam (Lexington, Ky., 1984).
Robert Pisor, *The End of the Line: The Siege of Khe Sanh* (New York, 1982),
places the battle of Khe Sanh in the context of the 1968 Tet offensive. Townsend
Hoopes, *The Limits of Intervention* (New York, 1970), discusses the reappraisal
of the strategy of attrition during the Johnson years. Among the many excellent

accounts depicting the combat experience of American infantrymen in Vietnam, see especially Philip Caputo, *A Rumor of War* (New York, 1977); Michael Herr, *Dispatches* (New York, 1977); James Webb, *Fields of Fire* (New York, 1978); Frederick Downs, *The Killing Zone* (New York, 1978); Al Santoli, *Everything We Had* (New York, 1981); and Wallace Terry, *Bloods: An Oral History of the Vietnam War by Black Veterans* (New York, 1984).

1968–1975

For standard defenses of the Vietnam policies of the Nixon administrations, see Richard M. Nixon, *RN: The Memoirs of Richard Nixon* (New York, 1978); and Henry Kissinger, *White House Years* (Boston, 1979), and *Years of Upheaval* (Boston, 1983). For highly critical accounts of Nixon and Kissinger, see William Shawcross, *Sideshow: Kissinger, Nixon and the Destruction of Cambodia* (New York, 1979); and Seymour M. Hersh, *The Price of Power: Kissinger in the Nixon White House* (New York, 1983). Gareth Porter, *A Peace Denied: The United States, Vietnam, and the Paris Agreements* (Bloomington, Ind., 1975), is an excellent analysis of the 1973 peace treaty. The best overall interpretation of the situation in Indochina during the two years following the Paris pact is Arnold R. Isaacs, *Without Honor: Defeat in Vietnam and Cambodia* (Baltimore, 1983). Frank Snepp, *Decent Interval: An Insider's Account of Saigon's Indecent End Told by the CIA's Chief Strategy Analyst in Vietnam* (New York, 1977), describes the disintegration of the South Vietnamese army prior to the fall of Saigon.

INDEX